Capitalising on constraint

MANCHESTER 1824

Manchester University Press

European Politics

Series Editors: Professor Dimitris Papadimitriou (University of Manchester), Dr Kathryn Simpson (Manchester Metropolitan University) and Dr Paul Tobin (University of Manchester).

The *European Politics* series seeks to tackle the biggest issues facing Europe in the twenty-first century.

Previously published under the *European Policy Research Unit (EPRU)* name, this long-established and highly respected series combines an important scholarly legacy with an ambitious outlook on European Studies at a time of rapid change for the discipline. Its geographical coverage encompasses the European Union, its existing and aspiring members, and 'wider Europe', including Russia and Turkey, and the series actively promotes disciplinary, theoretical and methodological diversity.

The editors particularly welcome critical scholarship on the politics and policy making of the European Union, on comparative European politics, and on contemporary issues and debates affecting the future of Europe's socio-political and security outlook. Key areas of interest include Brexit, the environment, migration, identity politics and the ever-changing face of European integration.

Previously published:

Regulating lobbying: A global comparison, 2nd edition
Raj Chari, John Hogan, Gary Murphy and Michele Crepaz

Towards a just Europe: A theory of distributive justice for the European Union
João Labareda

Made in France: Societal structures and political work
Andy Smith

Capitalising on constraint

Bailout politics in Eurozone countries

Catherine Moury, Stella Ladi,
Daniel Cardoso and Angie Gago

Manchester University Press

Published by Manchester University Press
Altrincham Street, Manchester M1 7JA

www.manchesteruniversitypress.co.uk

British Library Cataloguing-in-Publication Data
A catalogue record for this book is available from the British Library

ISBN 978 1 5261 4988 6 hardback

First published 2021

Typeset
by New Best-set Typesetters Ltd

Contents

Figures

Tables

Contributors

Catherine Moury is Associate Professor of Political Science at the NOVA University, Portugal. Her research focuses on comparative politics and institutional change in the European Union. She has published in the *American Journal of Political Science*, *European Journal of Political Research*, *Comparative Political Studies*, *Journal of European Public Policy*, and elsewhere. She is the author of *Coalition Government and Party Mandate: How Coalition Agreements Constrain Ministerial Action* (Routledge, 2013), co-author of *Changing Rules of Delegation: A Contest for Power in Comitology* (Oxford University Press, 2013) and co-author of *Parliamentary Ascendant: Strategies of Parliamentary Self-Empowerment in the EU* (Palgrave, 2019), among other books.

Stella Ladi is Senior Lecturer at Queen Mary University of London and Assistant Professor at Panteion University in Athens. She previously worked as a lecturer at the University of Sheffield and University of Exeter. She has also been a Research Fellow at the Barcelona Institute of International Studies and has acted as a public policy expert at the Ministry of the Interior and the Ministry of the Aegean, Greece. In July 2002, Stella completed her PhD thesis at the University of York. Her research interests include the Eurozone crisis, public policy and public administration reforms, Europeanisation, global public policy and transnational administration, and the role of experts in public policy. She has published in journals such as the *Journal of European Integration*, *JCMS*, *Policy and Society*, *Regulation and Governance*, *Public Administration*, *West European Politics*, *New Political Economy*, *Comparative European Politics* and *Political Studies Review*. She is co-convenor of the Greek Politics Specialist Group of the Political Studies Association.

Daniel Cardoso is an Assistant Professor at the Autonomous University of Lisbon and a researcher at Observare – Observatory of Foreign Relations, Portugal. He was awarded his PhD by the Free University of Berlin, Germany. His research interests include the Eurozone crisis, public policy, foreign policy, and the intersection of national and international politics. He has published in the *South European Society and Politics*, *European Journal of Social Security* and *Third World Quarterly*.

Angie Gago is a Senior Researcher at the Centre of Comparative, European and International Law of the University of Lausanne and a post-doctoral Fellow of the National Center of Competence in Research (NCCR – On the Move) for migration and mobility studies. She obtained her PhD in Political Studies at the University of Milan in 2018. Her research interests are multi-level politics, institutions and public policy. More specifically, she is interested in the interplay between European Union politics and national political dynamics and policy-making. Her research has been published in the *Journal of European Integration*, *Irish Political Studies* and *South European Society and Politics*, among others.

Acknowledgements

For this research, over a hundred people who participated closely in the negotiations and/or in the implementation of the adjustment programmes were interviewed by the authors of this book. These people kindly took time out of their busy schedules to talk to us, speaking with enthusiasm and sincerity and opening the normally closed door of real politics to us. Without them, the book would have been impossible, and we are extremely grateful to them.

We are greatly in debt to the research assistants who worked on the Irish case (Adam Standring, who is also a co-author of chapter 3, and Prokop Kolinsky) and on the Greek and Cypriot cases (Vivian Spyropoulou and Aggeliki Petridou); to Rachel Evans for the English proofreading and to Antonio Dias for the editing.

We also extend our thanks to our colleagues from Lisbon, Athens, London and Lausanne, and elsewhere, namely to Dima Mohammed, Enrico Borghetto, Rui Branco, Alexandre Afonso, Stefano Sacchi, Jonathan Hopkin and Adonis Pegasiou, among others. This book benefited so much from their very useful suggestions and feedback.

Our thanks also go to participants in the Barcelona Institute of International Studies Workshop 'IO Conditionality: One Size Fits All', for their very useful comments, notably the discussant Ben Cormier and the organisers Yannis Karagiannis and Nikitas Konstantinidis.

Finally, we are also grateful to the anonymous reviewers for their astute comments, and the Manchester University Press editors Jonathan de Peyer and Robert Byron. Thanks also go to Dimitris Papadimitriou, co-editor of the European Politics series of MUP, who encouraged us to submit our manuscript to MUP.

This research was supported primarily by the Grant 'Democracy in Times of Crisis: Power and Discourse in a Three-Level Game', funded by the Portuguese Foundation for Science and Technology, FCT (Grant nr PTDC/IVC-CPO/2247/2014). Part of the English proofreading was funded by the

Swiss National Science Foundation (SNSF) [51NF40-182897]. Aggeliki Petridou's grant was funded by the Erasmus + Programme.

What made this endeavour so special for us was the opportunity to exchange information with each other, allowing us to shed light on aspects of our case studies which had not been obvious to us before the comparison. It permitted a more holistic analysis of this important period of European history than would otherwise have been possible.

Abbreviations

AKEL	Progressive Party of the Working People (Cyprus)
ANEL	Independent Greeks
BE	Left Bloc (Portugal)
CDS–PP	Social Democratic Centre–Popular Party (Portugal)
CGTP	General Confederation of Portuguese Workers
COLA	Cost of Living Adjustment
CYTA	Cyprus Telecommunications Authority
DIKO	Democratic Party (Cyprus)
DISY	Democratic Rally (Cyprus)
DoF	Department of Finance
EC	European Commission
ECB	European Central Bank
ECOFIN	European Economic and Financial Affairs Council
EDP	Excessive Deficit Procedure
EFSF	European Financial Stability Facility
ELA	Emergency Liquidity Assistance
EMU	Economic and Monetary Union
ERC	Republican Left of Catalonia
ERT	Hellenic Broadcasting Corporation
ESM	European Stability Mechanism
EU	European Union
FF	Fianna Fáil (Ireland)
FG	Fine Gael (Ireland)
GESY	National Health System (Cyprus)
IMF	International Monetary Fund
LAOS	Popular Orthodox Rally (Greece)
MONA	Monitoring Fund Arrangements
MoU	Memorandum of Understanding
ND	New Democracy (Greece)
NRP	National Recovery Plan
OECD	Organisation for Economic Co-operation and Development

PASOK	Panhellenic Socialist Movement
PCP	Portuguese Communist Party
PP	People's Party (Spain)
PRSI	Pay Related Social Insurance
PS	Socialist Party (Portugal)
PSD	Social Democratic Party (Portugal)
PSI	private sector involvement
PSOE	Spanish Socialist Workers' Party
SGP	Stability and Growth Pact
SYRIZA	Coalition of the Radical Left – Progressive Alliance (Greece)
UGT	General Union of Workers (Portugal)

Introduction

Since 2010, five Eurozone governments have received financial assistance from the International Monetary Fund (IMF) and the European Union (EU), on the condition that a long list of policies were implemented. This is often described as a period in which powerless bailed out governments had no choice but to follow the lenders' prescriptions; and it was contested whether these were in the former's best interest (see for example Capelos and Exadaktylos, 2015 on media representation). The effectiveness and fairness of conditionality have also been called into question.

Despite the widespread media coverage, leaks and memoirs, there is actually very little empirical research about how domestic governments have dealt with conditionality. While the crisis has attracted a lot of academic attention, most of the studies have examined the content and effects of the reforms passed during the crisis (Perez and Matsaganis, 2018, 2019; see for example Taylor-Gooby *et al.*, 2017). Many have also stressed and highlighted the shift in power at the European level to the benefit of richer member states like Germany (Finke and Bailer, 2019; Offe, 2017; see Schimmelfennig, 2015; Tsebelis, 2016) and of the European institutions (Afonso, 2019; Bauer and Becker, 2014; Schmidt, 2016). Other studies have focused on the reasons why European leaders chose to include the IMF (Henning, 2017) and the subsequent divergence of views between the lenders (Clift, 2018; Lütz and Kranke, 2014). Finally, others have looked at the crisis from an international political economy perspective, stressing the centrality of domestic interests and interstate bargaining in shaping the European decisions (see for example the special issue from Copelovitch *et al.*, 2016).

This large bulk of research, however, often assumes that Eurozone bailed out countries were forced to implement very specific reforms against their will. We believe that this assumption is incorrect. Together with a handful of others (e.g. Hick, 2018 for Eurozone bailouts; Vreeland, 2004 and Pop-Eleches, 2008 for IMF lendings), we claim that bailed out governments had room for manoeuvre and, under certain circumstances, were able to exploit the constraint of conditionality to their own advantage.

Our understanding is even more restricted in relation to what happened when conditionality finished, and to the policy-makers' leeway and motivations to revert (or alternatively maintain) changes introduced under conditionality. Indeed, with the exception of studies on compliance after Eastern enlargement (e.g. Epstein and Sedelmeier, 2008; Levitz and Pop-Eleches, 2010) and on the long-term economic effects of IMF programmes (i.e. Remmer, 1986; Vreeland, 2004), scholars have made surprisingly few systematic attempts to measure the resilience of reforms adopted under conditionality. As an exception, Rickard and Caraway (2019) observe that the public sector wage cuts induced by IMF conditionality do not persist in the longer term; and the special issue edited by Moury and Afonso (2019) looks at the (relatively few) policy reversals in Spain and Portugal after the Eurozone bailouts. In this book, we argue that after a bailout programme governments could use their discretion to reverse measures in order to attain the greatest benefits at a lower cost.

In this introduction, we will start by briefly recalling the context and the main events of the period covered in our work. As individual countries will be analysed in depth in the following chapters, this section focuses mainly on the European level. We then briefly present our arguments and methodology choices before describing the remaining chapters.

A brief chronology of the Eurozone crisis and its aftermath (2007–2020)

To understand the crisis, one must recall that a common currency was introduced in countries with different types of capitalist economies ('varieties of capitalism'; Hall and Soskice, 2001). On the one hand, the Eurozone included 'coordinated market economies', which are productive economies where firms typically make long-term investments, finance their workers' training and where industrial bargaining allows for coordinated wage restraint. The growth of those countries (typically Germany, but also the Netherlands, Austria, Denmark, Finland, etc.) is driven by their exports. On the other hand, mixed-market countries of the periphery (and for some time Ireland, see chapter 3) had pursued a demand-led growth, which consists of economic stimuli, jobs creation in non-trade sectors and, before Economic and Monetary Union (EMU), frequent devaluations of their currency (Hall, 2012; Johnston and Regan, 2016; Parker and Tsarouhas, 2018).

Those different types of growth model, combined with the lack of labour mobility and of fiscal transfers, signify that the Eurozone is not an 'optimal currency area' (Hall, 2012; Krugman, 1993). In other words, economic models predicted that introducing a single currency in the EU would not create higher economic benefits than the status quo. Those warnings were dismissed by the EMU architects on the ground that the need to attract capital would 'discipline' states into making supply-side reforms such as wage containment (Parker and Tsarouhas, 2018). Also, EMU was more a political than an economic political project, initiated by President François Mitterand in order to bind a newly unified Germany to Europe (Dyson, 1994).

Another potential problem with the design of EMU was the prohibition of the European Central Bank (ECB) acting as a 'lender of last resort' (i.e. to loan money to states when they have exhausted all other options). As de Grauwe (2012) explains in his 'fragility hypothesis', without such a possibility member states are vulnerable to a self-fulfilling market sentiment. This hypothesis goes as follows: when a member state cannot turn to its central bank to borrow money, investors will stop buying its bonds if they fear that it will default – pushing interest rates up and creating a liquidity crisis, and, possibly, the feared default. This prohibition is one of the reasons that decisions were delayed when the crisis hit Greece (see chapter 2).

Despite these flaws, entry into EMU was mostly beneficial to its members at the beginning, but to a different extent for core and periphery. Given that their trading partners could not devalue their currencies anymore, the coordinated market economies increased their relative competitiveness and thus their exports within and outside EMU (Parker and Tsarouhas, 2018). By contrast, member states of the periphery, deprived of the possibility to devalue their currency, could not compensate for the inflationary effects of their growth model (Hall, 2012). The fact that those countries specialised in low- or especially medium-quality products implied that their economies were more vulnerable to price variation and to competition from emerging economies, China (Nölke, 2016). This asymmetry gave rise to large current account (imports/exports) imbalances between some core countries like Germany and large Southern countries like Spain and Italy (Dooley, 2019).

However, the common currency implied cheaper loans for the periphery, as financial markets – notably the sovereign debt market – assumed that within EMU all sovereign bonds were safe bets (Barkbu *et al.*, 2016). This cheap capital allowed public and private consumption and fuelled demand-driven growth, which thus became 'debt-driven growth' (Stockhammer, 2016, p. 365). In other words, in the periphery growth was driven 'by a growing dependence of firms, households, and governments on cheap credit' (Dooley, 2019, p. 79).

Capital to sustain demand thus flew from the core countries (and UK) to the periphery, but also between peripheral countries (notably from Spain to Portugal; Dooley, 2019). Such flows were facilitated by the deregulation of financial markets that had started in the 1980s but had been deepened with the creation of EMU (Stockhammer, 2016). In that context, inadequate regulation and supervision encouraged the growth of a banking sector which became increasingly unmanageable and leveraged (Barkbu *et al.*, 2016). Moreover, capital was channelled in the South into consumption, 'quick win' financial assets or housing bubbles at the expense of longer-term, productive investments (Parker and Tsarouhas, 2018, pp. 5–7).

In 2007, a housing bubble burst in the United States, a process fuelled by 'low interest rates, easy and available credit, scant regulation, and toxic mortgages' (Financial Crisis Inquiry Commission, 2011, p. xvi). This did not just shake the United States, as these mortgages had been 'repackaged' as mortgage-related securities (collateralised debt obligations) that were sold to investors around the world. The crisis reached seismic proportions in September 2008, when the global financial firm Lehman Brothers failed. Fearful that more institutions would follow suit, banks stopped lending to each other, investors sold their bonds and the stock market plummeted. With their economies lacking liquidity, the United States and Europe plunged into a deep recession.

At this point, EU actors were mostly concerned about the slowdown of the economy; and the early phase of the crisis proved to be a Keynesian moment. In October 2008, the European Commission (EC) eased the EU's State Aid Rules (European Commission, 2008a). This allowed European governments to take counter-fiscal policies and to refinance their domestic banking systems. One month later, a €200 billion European Economic Recovery Plan was adopted to boost demand and stimulate confidence across the EU.[1]

At this time, governments of many countries stepped in to nationalise or capitalise financial institutions (i.e. France, Ireland, Spain, Portugal, UK) and/or unleash rescue plans (i.e. France, Germany; Caporaso and Rhodes, 2016; Degryse, 2012; Ladi and Tsarouhas, 2014). This resulted in huge increases in public debt everywhere: in the Eurozone, for example, it grew from around 65 per cent in 2007 to 85 per cent in 2010 (De Grauwe, 2010; see Figure 0.1).

The sudden stop in the flow of liquidity, however, caused greater damage to the countries that were running current account deficits, and hence were dependent on cash flows from abroad (Greece, Ireland, Italy, Portugal and Spain, or the 'GIIPS' countries; plus, later, Cyprus). Here it is important to note that neither Spain nor Ireland had a public deficit or high debt before the crisis. As a matter of fact, the first countries to violate the Stability and Growth Pact's (SGP's) limits, in 2003, were Germany itself together with France. This illustrates that excessive government borrowing was not solely to blame for the crisis (Blyth, 2013; Caporaso and Rhodes, 2016; Ladi and Tsarouhas, 2014). As mentioned above, the economies of the GIIPS countries

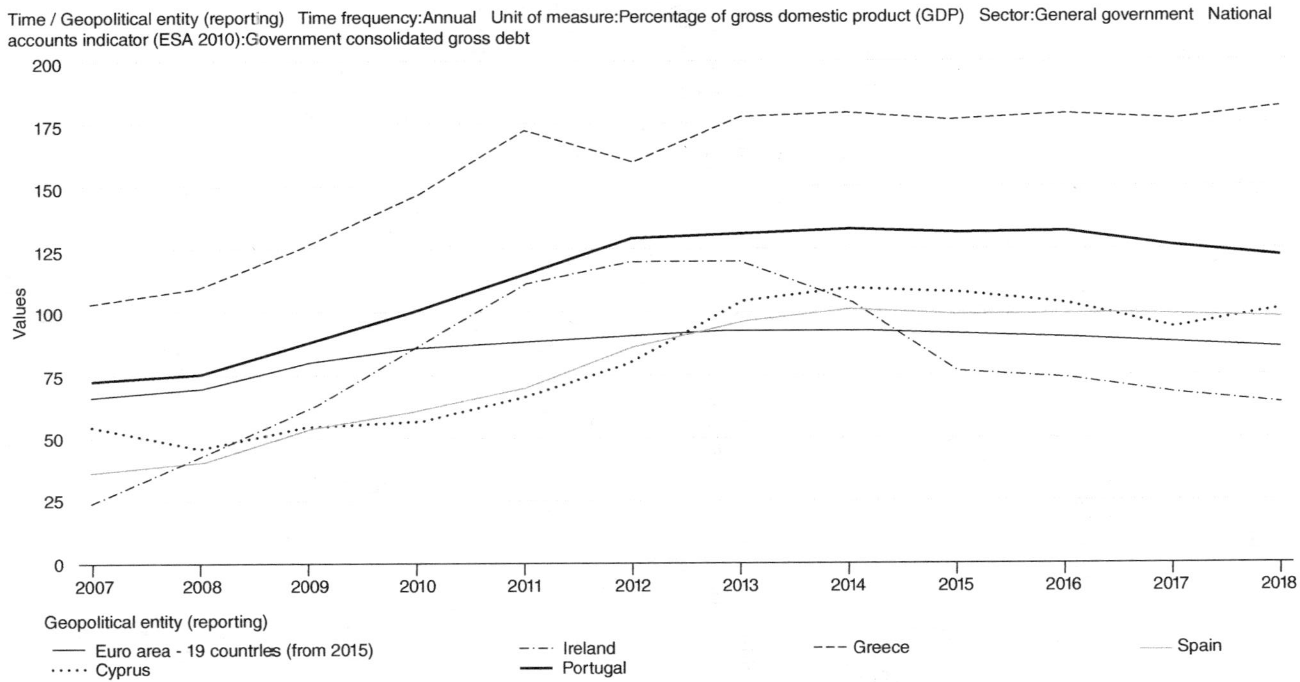

Source: Eurostat.

Figure 0.1 General government gross debt – annual data

were weakened by a combination of low use of technology (Dooley, 2019), high private debt, bursting housing bubbles and bank crises. In Cyprus, the public debt was a little higher, but the origin of the crisis was mostly banking. In Italy, Greece and, to a lesser extent, Portugal, the public debt was already very high before the crisis but grew exponentially with the recession and bank bailouts (Henning, 2017).

In March 2009, the EC started to worry about the sustainability of the public debt. It made a U-turn in its neo-Keynesian stance and activated the Excessive Deficit Procedure (EDP) for Greece, Ireland, Spain and France (Ladi and Tsarouhas, 2014). Things took a dramatic turn when, in October 2009, the Greek government revealed a big deviation from the estimated fiscal deficit, from 5.1 to 12.7 per cent of GDP (see Figure 0.2). Investors stopped giving credence to the capacity of governments to serve their debts, and interest on government bonds in many indebted countries skyrocketed (see Figure 0.2).

At this juncture, EU actors asked governments of periphery countries to implement fiscal consolidation measures and deregulatory structural reforms, to reduce their debt and thus reassure investors (Degryse, 2012, p. 20). Despite compliance (to varying degrees), both the debt and the yields of these governments kept growing and it became uncertain that they could finance themselves on the market.

The Maastricht Treaty's (Article 125) 'no bailout' provision prevented countries being given financial assistance, and some countries, including Germany, were firmly against stretching the rules (Ladi and Tsarouhas, 2014). Greece, the country in greatest difficulty, started discussing the possibility of financial help with Russia, the IMF and primarily the EU. After much hesitation and negotiation, the last two finally agreed to give assistance (see chapter 2). At the European Council of 24–25 March 2010, member states announced a rescue mechanism for Greece consisting of coordinated bilateral loans provided by the EU (two-thirds) and the IMF (one-third). This mechanism would be available only as a last resort if a country lost access to markets (chapter 2), and would be subject to conditionality with the oversight of a 'Troika' composed of the EC, the IMF and the ECB (Henning, 2017). In May 2010, Greece received a bailout of €110 billion.

In the week after the announcement of the Greek rescue package, the market situation deteriorated for Greece, Spain and Portugal, forcing European leaders to take action to stop the contagion (Gocaj and Meunier, 2013). The core question was who would bear the costs of the adjustment. Countries in financial difficulty plus the EC initially, later known as the 'debtors', advocated common European solutions based on mutualising the debt, such as the creation of European financial assistance mechanisms. In contrast, another group of countries, the 'creditors', led by Germany, instead put the

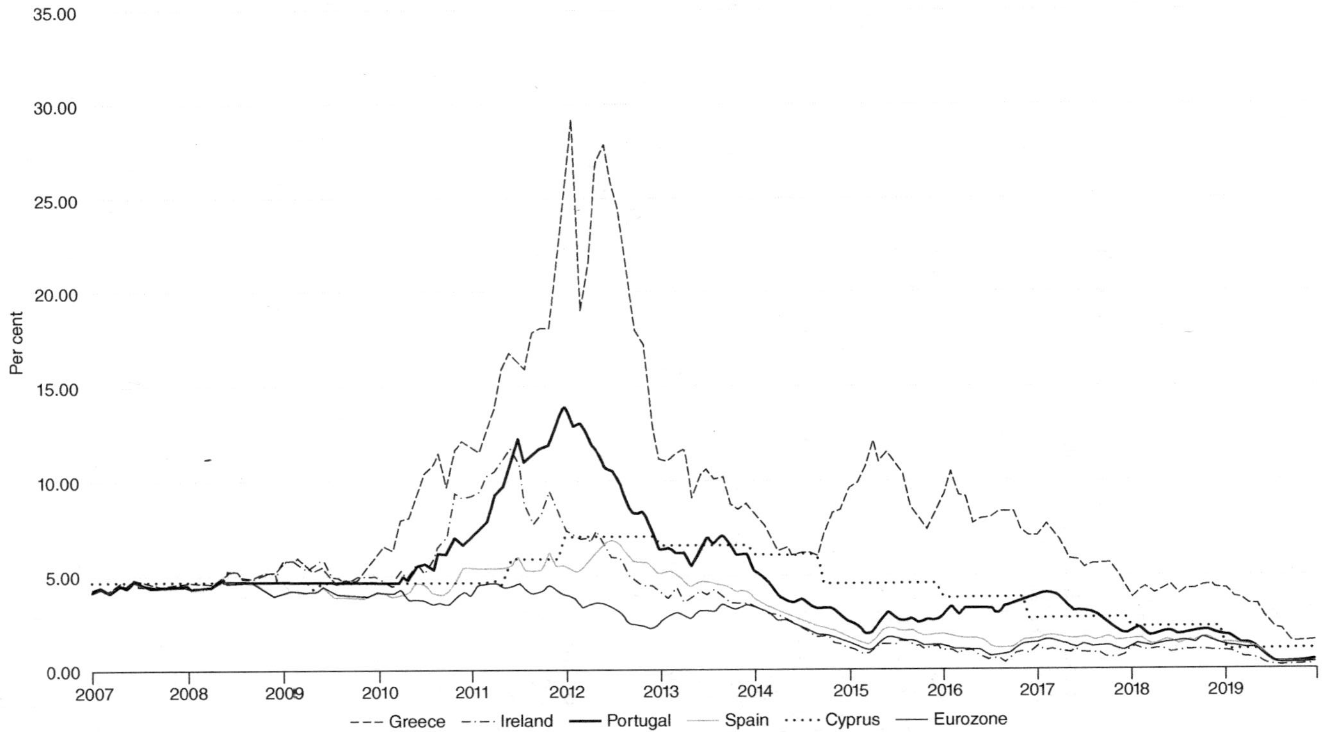

Note: Monthly rate for the Eurozone, Greece, Portugal, Spain and Ireland, yearly rates for Cyprus.
Source: FED economic data and Investing.com, interpretation by the authors.

Figure 0.2 Ten-year government bond yields

emphasis on loans and the need to implement austerity policies and structural reforms, as well as to reinforce the rules of the SGP (Gocaj and Meunier, 2013; Schimmelfennig, 2015, p. 183). Discussion also concentrated on the conditions for bailing in private creditors, but no concrete decision was taken at this point on Greek debt restructuring (Cline and Wolf, 2012, p. v).

During a summit of 9–10 May, the creditors' camp won and the European leaders announced a €750 billion bailout package, including an unprecedented bailout institution, the European Financial Stability Facility (EFSF), comprising €60 billion of EU-backed funds (European Financial Stability Mechanism), €440 billion of guarantees by Euro area countries and €250 billion of IMF money.

One important mistake made in this period (Henning, 2017, p. 131) occurred in October 2010, when the leaders of France and Germany met in Deauville and publicly discussed the possibility of restructuring sovereign debt and of private sector involvement (PSI). This declaration backfired immediately, giving potential investors the message that 'Euro area sovereign debt should no longer be considered a safe asset' (Orphanides, 2013, p. 55). The interest rates on the bonds of the governments rose dangerously (Laffan, 2012). Ireland was the first casualty of this misguided declaration (Henning, 2017, p. 110) and, in December 2010, it became the second country to enter an adjustment programme (of €85 billion).

The very same month, the European Council agreed to create a permanent mechanism for the provision of financial assistance to countries, and thus the European Stability Mechanism (ESM) took over the tasks of the EFSF. In March 2011, the Portuguese government asked for financial assistance after seeing its austerity packages defeated in Parliament, and it received a €78 billion loan.

Meanwhile, all countries pursued fiscal consolidation but despite (or because of) this the deficit and debt kept rising (see Figure 0.1). Fiscal tensions were intensified by the July 2011 decision to accept a modest 'private sector involvement' in the reduction of the debt, that was superseded by the much deeper (50 per cent) 'haircuts'[2] for private creditors in late October (Hodson, 2012).

Economic activity in the Euro area then contracted again in what is referred to as the 'double-dip recession' (Heimberger, 2017). At this time, too, the EU's institutional framework was strengthened, notably through the 'six pack' which reinforced the SGP (in December 2011), and a 'fiscal compact' requiring its Eurozone members to observe prudent fiscal behaviour (in March 2012). In March, Greece requested a second bailout of €130 billion including, as planned, a significant haircut for private creditors. At this time, France and Belgium began to experience the contagion effects when a Franco-Belgian bank, Dexia, was nationalised by the Belgian authorities

(Parker and Tsarouhas, 2018, p. 10). In June 2012, Eurozone leaders endorsed the idea of a banking union, in which Eurozone banks would operate under a set of common rules, with a single supervisory authority and a single resolution mechanism for bank failures – a project that would be left incomplete.

Spain, too, was in trouble and, in the same month, it became the fourth and largest Eurozone economy to seek an international bailout. The Prime Minister at the time, Mr Rajoy, had been resisting EU assistance since his centre-right government was voted in office in December. Eventually, the agreed loan (of up to €100 billion) was solely to recapitalise banks and the Memoranda of Understanding (MoUs) applied to the financial sector only. A few days later, on 29 June 2012, the European Council agreed to create a European banking supervision mechanism and a resolution mechanism.

A benchmark event came on 26 July 2012 in London, when ECB President Mario Draghi gave the assurance that: 'Within our mandate, the ECB is ready to do whatever it takes to save the Euro.' This declaration – together with the subsequent decision of the ECB to buy public bonds in the secondary market – was considered the real 'watershed' for the euro area (Alcaraz *et al.*, 2019, p. 2), a crucial move that calmed the markets and prevented the failure of the euro (Van Der Heijden *et al.*, 2018, p. 1169).

With yields decreasing everywhere, this was not enough for Cyprus, which sought external financial assistance in May 2013. It received a loan of €10 billion, but also agreed to an estimated €7 billion bail-in solution involving the recapitalisation of the banking system (Michaelides, 2014). Later the same year, in December 2013, Draghi's 'Whatever It Takes' enabled Ireland to exit its adjustment programmes without the safety (and conditions) of a supplementary credit line. One month later, in January 2014, Spain followed suit.

The recession continued in the periphery in 2013, with GDP contracting everywhere except Ireland. Things started to change in 2014. In Spain and Portugal (plus Ireland), growth finally kicked in and yields fell below 3 per cent by the end of the year. In May 2014, Portugal exited the programme even though its bond yields remained higher than for other peripheral Eurozone members (Hodson, 2015, see Figure 0.2). A few months later, in January 2015, the ECB Governing Council introduced a programme of quantitative easing that lowered the yields even more in eligible countries (which did not include Greece).

In July 2015, after many twists and turns – including a referendum against the MoU – Greece asked for a third bailout and borrowed a further €86 billion. The following year, things finally started to improve everywhere including Greece. All (previously) bailed out countries recorded GDP growth and the deficit was below 3 per cent in Portugal, Cyprus and Greece. In

Table 0.1 A chronology of the EU responses to the Eurozone crisis

2 May 2010	First Economic Adjustment Programme to Greece (€80 billion)
9–11 May 2010	Creation of the European Financial Stability Mechanism and the European Financial Stability Facility
21 November 2010	Economic Adjustment Programme to Ireland (€85 billion)
7 April 2011	Economic Adjustment Programme to Portugal (€78 billion)
11 July 2011	Treaty establishing the European Stability Mechanism
12 December 2011	'Six pack' adopted
30 January 2012	The Fiscal Compact signed
12 February 2012	Second Economic Adjustment Programme to Greece (€130 billion)
4 July 2012	Economic Adjustment Programme to Spain (€100 billion)
2 August 2012	Creation of Outright Monetary Transactions
8 October 2012	Setting up of the European Stability Mechanism
14 May 2013	Economic Adjustment Programme to Cyprus (€10 billion)
15 December 2013	Exit of programme in Ireland
23 January 2014	Exit of programme in Spain
12 June 2014	Exit of programme in Portugal
19 August 2015	Third Economic Adjustment Programme to Greece (€86 billion)
31 March 2016	Exit of programme in Cyprus
21 August 2018	Exit of programme in Greece

Source: Own compilation.

March 2016, Cyprus exited the bailout. This episode of the Eurozone crisis officially ended in July 2018 when Greece exited its third bailout programme, eleven years after the American bubble burst. The main chronology of those events is summarised in Table 0.1.

Our argument in a nutshell

How did bailout countries deal with the challenges of the Eurozone crisis over those thirteen years? The main idea of this book is that domestic actors are also capable of extracting policy benefits from a bailout both *during* and *after* the adjustment programme. We start by arguing that, contrary to how it might appear, a bailout is not a diktat but rather a two-sided process in which executives negotiate with international lenders. Bailed out governments keep leverage, we claim, because the lenders value 'ownership' and 'insider knowledge'. Indeed, the IMF recognises that governments often do not implement unilaterally imposed deals. Moreover, lenders are generally not experts of a particular country so need insider knowledge to understand the causes of the crisis and design efficient solutions.

Considering this domestic leverage, we expect elections to make a difference during a bailout, as governments of different political persuasion are sometimes able to renegotiate or resist the implementation of the deals agreed by their predecessors. We further argue that conditionality is to some extent useful to executives. This is because the negotiations of the bailout take place behind closed doors and the costs of its rejection are very high. This sometimes allows executives to pass reforms that they deem necessary but could not have passed in the past because they were very unpopular or were blocked by powerful interest groups.

The leverage of governments – and their capacity to pass reforms corresponding to their preferences – inevitably varies from case to case and is dependent on the bargaining context. In this book, we argue that the degree of external credibility of domestic actors is a crucial variable and, in itself, a variable of the willingness and capacity of the government to implement the agreed deals. When the lenders think that the government shares the lenders' main assumptions and is in a position to fulfil what has been agreed, its leverage will be higher. We claim that this holds true not only when the MoU is drafted but during the entire term of the programme, when progress is reviewed.

We finally posit that, after a bailout, executives are both able and willing to reverse what was done under conditionality. They are able to do so because the lenders do not have the same 'sticks' and 'carrots' as during the programme (Drazen, 2002; Vreeland, 2004). Given this ability, we expect governments to selectively pick reversals that bring them more electoral benefits at a lower cost.

Methodology

This book covers the period during and beyond the crisis (2007–2019). The case selection includes the Eurozone's five bailed out countries (Greece, Ireland, Portugal, Spain and Cyprus). Even though in Spain the conditions of the MoU only concerned the financial sector, the Commission (mandated by the Council) started a programme of strict monitoring of fiscal consolidation measures and structural reforms in 2011. It explicitly linked its recommendations for change to the disbursement of the loan instalments. Spain's bailout, and in particular its negotiation and implementation, is therefore more similar to the other Eurozone bailouts than might appear at first glance.

To demonstrate our arguments, we opt for a mixed-methods approach. We rely on the congruence method to explore the constraints of conditionality, the use of these constraints by different governments, and the motivation and willingness to reverse what was done during the programme. In this method, the researcher examines whether or not the predictions of the theory are consistent with the outcomes (George and Bennett, 2005, p. 200). We combine the congruence method with a process-tracing methodology, that is, a tool that involves 'the systematic examination of diagnostic evidence selected and analysed in the light of research questions and hypotheses posed by the investigator' (Collier, 2011, p. 1). This combination increases confidence in the findings (George and Bennett, 2005, p. 201; Héritier *et al.*, 2019).

Regarding our empirical sources, validity was ensured by triangulating different types of data. First, we drew on the primary and secondary sources that reported the policy-making processes in the period under study (academic research, press reports, investigative books by journalists, memoirs). Secondly, we relied on a qualitative analysis of official documents from the government, the IMF, the EC and trade unions. Thirdly, we conducted face-to-face interviews (between 2014 and 2018) with major actors in policy-making during the period. We contacted all Ministers and Secretaries of State in key sectors (finance, economy, etc.), officials from the Troika, key members of trade unions and journalists. In total, we interviewed 130 individuals,[3] after which saturation was reached (Buthe *et al.*, 2015, p. 10). The average duration of interviews was forty-five minutes. They were recorded with the authorisation of the respondent and transcribed verbatim. Anonymity was guaranteed. This allowed us to obtain a full understanding of what happened behind the closed doors of international meetings.

In addition, we develop an original, independent and detailed data set on conditionality policies. For each country, every testable policy objective included in the summaries of the IMF and the EC MoUs are coded as a 'condition' as well as subsequent monitoring reports (this means that objectives for policy *outcome* are not coded, as their fulfilment is not solely dependent on governmental actions). We code every implemented policy mentioned in these documents as a 'reform'.

We then measure congruence between conditions and reforms. On the one hand, we track whether the conditions had been fully, partially or not implemented by the end of the bailout. This entailed looking for an action by the government implementing it for each of the conditions. Although the reports by the EC and the IMF were very useful, we sometimes had to consult government official websites as well as other documents, interviews, legislation and the media to double-check. In line with previous investigation on pledge fulfilment (Thomson *et al.*, 2017), the categories of fully and partially fulfilled are merged to increase inter-coder reliability.

On the other hand, we confirm whether or not the reforms adopted during the crisis were included in the MoU. This allows us to examine the reforms made in the period from the crisis to the signing of the MoU and to differentiate between the countries that passed many reforms before the bailout (like Ireland) and other countries.

We decided not to use the data made available by the IMF for Monitoring Fund Arrangements (MONA) for two reasons. First, we are interested in political willingness to pursue reforms, and hence we disregard the economic objectives (which are not totally dependent on states' willingness to reform). Secondly, researchers and the IMF's own Independent Evaluation Office (for a review see Stubbs *et al.*, 2017) have drawn attention to several problems with the MONA database, including ubiquitous underreporting and misclassification.

In a final step, we investigated whether the reforms were partially or fully reversed during or after the programme or maintained until the end of 2019. We coded the factors that can explain the presence or absence of reversals as follows:

- *Structural*: we assigned number 1 to structural reforms. These are defined as reforms that are designed to boost productivity and improve the supply-side functioning of the economy in the medium and long term; they include labour code reforms, reduction of business and trade union monopolies, decreased regulation and red tape, privatisation, removal of licensing, improvements to the functioning of the court, public administration reforms, enforcement of property rights, and so on. We assigned 0 to reforms aimed primarily at cutting spending in the short or medium term.
- *Concentrated benefits*: we assigned 1 when the benefits of the (possible) reversal were concentrated in a specific group of the population and/or specific actors and costs were diffused.
- *Concentrated costs*: we assigned 1 when the benefits of the (possible) reversal were concentrated in a specific group of the population and/or specific actors and costs were diffused.
- *Inter-reliability tests* for this coding ranged between 0.85 and 1.

The organisation of the book

Chapter 1 presents the theoretical framework underlying the book. Cross-cutting the literature on policy change, bargaining, Europeanisation, enlargement and political economy, this chapter outlines the different constraints and incentives faced by governments during and beyond conditionality. It also specifies our theoretical expectations regarding variation within and across countries.

Chapter 2 focuses on the Greek case, from the start of the crisis in 2008, during the three successive bailout programmes (2010–2018), and in the period after the end of the bailout until September 2019. As Greece was the first country to ask for a bailout, this chapter allows us to analyse the negotiations for the creation of the EU rescue mechanism, which were closely related to the first bailout. Given the succession of programmes, the Greek case also permits a comparison between the negotiations and implementation of different memoranda led by different parties in the same country.

Chapter 3 analyses the financial crisis and its aftermath in Ireland. Given its growth model and the fact that it was already very liberalised when the crisis began, Ireland is interesting and quite different from most of the other countries. However, it bears similarities with Cyprus in that the crisis was largely the result of an oversized and overexposed financial/banking sector and, as said above, the economy was already very liberalised when the crisis began.

Chapter 4 looks at Portugal, another interesting case as the MoU was negotiated by the Socialist caretaker government and implemented by its successor from the centre-right – whose preferences were strongly aligned with those of the lenders. After the bailout, a Socialist government was installed with the support of radical left parties, all of which had promised large-scale reversals during the electoral campaign.

Chapter 5 analyses the margin of manoeuvre of Spanish governments during and after the Eurozone crisis. The Spanish case is theoretically interesting because Spain is the fourth biggest European economy, thus allowing us to consider the importance of the size of the country in the negotiations with external actors. It is also a special case in that the Spanish MoU only addressed the financial sector.

Chapter 6 focuses on Cyprus, a case which has warranted much less discussion in the literature. This therefore constitutes an important contribution to the understanding of the contagious nature of the Eurozone crisis. Among other things, it sheds light on the conditions that forced the Cypriot government to accept the haircut of uninsured deposits in Cypriot banks.

Chapter 7 concludes. We compare countries and their policy fields, and show that our argument 'travels' well: even in least likely cases, governments had some leeway to shape the policies adopted under conditionality and to reverse some of these after a bailout. Additionally, we present the comparative results of our database on conditionality and policy reversals during and after conditionality. Finally, we address the theoretical and policy implications of our findings and discuss their implications for the current economic crisis resulting from the spread of COVID-19.

Notes

1 Communication from the Commission to the European Council – A European Economic Recovery Plan /* COM/2008/0800 final */https://eur-lex.europa.eu/legal-content/EN/ALL/?uri=CELEX:52008DC0800 (accessed 5 March 2020).
2 The difference between the current market value of an asset and the value ascribed to it.
3 Of these, 30 were in Portugal, 17 in Ireland, 26 in Spain, 14 in Cyprus, 34 in Greece and 9 in Brussels. In the period between January 2014 and November 2018.

1

The politics of conditionality: a theoretical framework

In this chapter, we present our arguments at length, situating them in the broader literature. We start by briefly describing the constraints faced by European governments. We then explain why we believe that governments try to keep room for manoeuvre during a bailout. We detail the implications of this leverage, and the variables influencing it. Finally, we explain what we think happens when the bailout terminates.

On the constraints faced by European governments

As several authors have noted, parties in government are torn between two increasingly conflicting goals: *responsibility* (i.e. the respect of the international commitments taken by their predecessors and the promotion of their external credibility) and *responsiveness* (i.e. the response, of political leaders or governments, to the demands of their citizens) (Laffan, 2012; Mair, 2009).

It is difficult to address these two objectives simultaneously due to the growing internationalisation of trade and finance. Governments that increase their deficit and debt excessively, or deviate too far from supply-side policies in this context, risk damaging their currency's credibility and their firms' competitiveness (Clift and Ryner, 2014; Hallerberg and Basinger, 1998; Rodrik, 1998; Schmidt, 2002, pp. 22–23).

Governments in the EU are also bound by the European treaties (and the rules thereof) which, unlike other constitutions, are not only extensive but difficult to amend (De Witte, 2009). As many scholars have noted, these EU rules are increasingly shaped by ordoliberalism – a German school of thought that posits that the principles of neo-monetarism and supply-side economics should be imposed by constitutional rules, sanctions and through independent institutions (Feld *et al.*, 2015; Ferrera, 2020; Warlouzet, 2019; Young, 2014). The SGP is a paradigmatic example of the constitutionalisation of ordoliberalism as it calls for sound public finances, institutionalises monitoring devices and sanctions, and delegates monetary policy to the

ECB. Moreover, global and European constraints are interrelated, as Eurozone members lost the power to print money and hence to guarantee bondholders that they will be paid back whatever the circumstances (De Grauwe, 2012).

The shrinking discretion of European governments became crystal clear during the sovereign debt crisis (Ferrera, 2017; Ladi and Graziano, 2014; Streeck, 2014), a period of 'coercive Europeanisation' (Ladi and Graziano, 2014). As described in the introductory chapter, European economic governance rules were modified over this period, and the new instruments increased the EU's surveillance and enforcement capacity regarding the implementation of structural reforms (Heins and de la Porte, 2015, p. 3).

A fundamental constraint on European governments during the crisis also came from the dramatic divergence between the costs of Eurozone countries' sovereign bonds. Periphery countries became increasingly concerned about their credibility and therefore engaged in spending cuts and reforms (Moury and Standring, 2017). However, these efforts were not very successful (Afflatet, 2016; Rommerskirchen, 2015), and financial speculation only declined when the ECB put the Outright Monetary Transactions in place in September 2012 (Van Der Heijden *et al.*, 2018 see Introduction).

These circumstances forced some EU countries to respond to implicit and explicit conditionality. *Implicit conditionality*, which is 'based on an implicit understanding of the stakes and sanctions involved, underlain by some measure of power asymmetry' (Sacchi, 2018, p. 1) was exercised, for example, by the European Central Bank when it warned Italy and Spain to stop buying government bonds unless they pursued reforms (Bosco and Verney, 2012, p. 138; Lütz *et al.*, 2020; Sacchi, 2018). Implicit conditionality was also enforced by EU actors and/or powerful member states in '"backroom" diplomacy' (De la Porte and Natali, 2014, p. 735) – their influence deriving from the liquidity they could eventually provide to weaker countries and/or from the knock-on effect their declarations would have on investors (Moury *et al.*, 2021). Countries that asked for a bailout – such as Greece, Ireland, Portugal, Spain and Cyprus – were additionally subject to *explicit conditionality* as the progressive payments of the loans granted to them were conditional upon a series of reforms detailed in MoUs.

The MoUs negotiated with the Troika (ECB, EC and IMF) on behalf of international lenders were based on common assumptions. First, the belief that investors' confidence and growth depended on reducing public and private debt as quickly as possible. Hence, all MoUs include measures to cut state expenditure and incentivise banks, companies and individuals to deleverage (Greer, 2014). Secondly, the idea that 'internal devaluation' through lower wages and the deregulation of labour wage provisions was necessary to make economies more competitive given that external devaluation was not possible (Afonso, 2019; Clauwaert and Schömann, 2012). Thirdly, that consumers would be better served if competition was increased everywhere, and public ownership dwarfed. Hence, the privatisation of public enterprises, the liberalisation of protected professions and the reduction of firms' excessive profit ('rents') were present in all MoUs.

On the leverage of executives during a bailout

Despite these commonalities, however, we observe some important differences across bailed out countries. To start with, as the chapters of this book show, there was never an unequivocal need to call in international lenders: the decision to ask for a loan rather than to explore alternatives was ultimately political. Moreover, the MoUs differ in their size, content and emphasis in ways that cannot be explained solely by prior macroeconomic conditions (Hardiman *et al.*, 2016). Elections in the middle of a programme often led to renegotiations of the MoUs (Hick, 2018; Moury and Standring, 2017) and the success of implementation seems to have varied across governments and countries (Afonso *et al.*, 2015; Hardiman *et al.*, 2016; Walter, 2016).

This evidence suggests that executives had some leeway in the timing, design and implementation of the MoU, a leverage that could be explained by two principal factors. First, that 'ownership', that is, a country's interest 'in pursuing reforms independently of any incentives provided by multilateral lenders' (Drazen, 2002, p. 37), is highly valued by international lenders. This is because programme ownership raises the probability of the programme's success and hence avoids a waste of resources (Drazen, 2002). It is thus in the lenders' interest to leave governments some leeway in the negotiations, and – as two IMF officials claim – to let them have 'an active role ... in the formulation of the programme' and be open to discuss 'alternative policy options' (Khan and Sharma, 2001, p. 28).

Secondly, domestic leverage emerges from the fact that international lenders need insider knowledge to design efficient plans. As one IMF official explained: 'It's up to the government to come up with a plan ... It's not like the troika comes with a list of things and says that they have to do these things and then get the money. It doesn't make sense partly because only the government knows how things work' (quoted by Moury and Freire, 2013, p. 46).

Of course, it is not only the success of the programme that international lenders value when negotiating the MoU. More specifically, as politicians, members of the European Council and ECOFIN are also concerned about their own re-election (Bulmer, 2014; Henning, 2017) and hence act with a view to protecting their constituency first and foremost (Bastasin, 2009). Even members of technically 'technocratic' institutions, such as the IMF or the EC, are entangled in diverse political games (e.g. Dominique Strauss

Kahn was campaigning in 2011 to become the Socialist Party candidate for the 2012 French presidential election). Nevertheless, both lenders and bailed out executives are obviously concerned about the success of the programme, and the domestic origin of reform is therefore valued during negotiations.

On the basis of this reasoning, we posit, as a theoretical premise, that governments of all bailed out countries enjoyed room for manoeuvre – which means that they had the capacity to influence the policies implemented during conditionality according to their own preferences. We should stress that this influence is not limited simply to the drafting phase of the MoU; it also extends to the entire bailout period, when concrete policies need to be formulated and/or new ones inserted to address changing political and economic circumstances. The periodical reviews of the programmes provide opportunities for such changes to take place.

On the crisis as a window of opportunity for reformist ministers

Ownership, however, is not without ambiguity, since conditionality would not be necessary if the country was willing to undertake the policies in the programme even in the absence of a bailout. Our argument here is that the bailout is sometimes useful for executives to pass measures that they favour but could not have passed in the past.

It is useful to distinguish between three scenarios here (Bird and Willett, 2004). One is that the government radically disagrees with the principles and assumptions of the lenders detailed above. In this case, the bailout seeks to coerce the government to make fundamental changes to its policies but the programme's success is not guaranteed because of this lack of ownership. A second scenario is that the executive agrees entirely with the lenders about the diagnostics and the remedies to be adopted and are willing and able to pass them whatever the costs. In this case, little is changed by conditionality.

In the third scenario, which we assume to be the norm, the government neither radically disagrees nor agrees with the lenders' principles. First, the executive might concur with some postulates and disagree with others. It could be the case, for example, that a government agrees that rents enjoyed by some firms should be decreased but not with the proposal to cut civil servants' wages.

Also, the executives might be divided between reformist and pro-reformist ministers, possibly from different parties, party factions or professional backgrounds (think for example of the likely conflict between a Labour minister from a trade union and a finance minister from the Central Bank). In this case, the arrangement with the Troika may 'tip the balance' in favour of those supporting economic reforms (Bird and Willett, 2004, p. 429).

Finally, in such a third scenario, the executive might consider the reforms required by the Troika desirable but, outside of the programme, would not be willing or able to pay the costs associated with them. During a bailout, these costs might be lower as opponents to policy changes take into consideration the risk of losing the loan when choosing their strategies (Vreeland, 2004). Also, international negotiations usually take place behind closed doors. This grants executives privileged information about the constraints they face (Moravcsik, 1994) and hence the possibility of using 'false dilemmas' (Gago and Moury, 2018) – that is, a choice between two options (e.g. the policy change or bankruptcy) despite there being other solutions available.

Additionally, when a country is bailed out, pro-reform ministers might shield themselves, at least partially, from the electoral costs of unpopular measures. We know that most incumbents are quite reluctant to publicly blame the Troika and accuse their predecessors instead; this is either because they do not want to be seen to be externally controlled (Moury and Standring, 2017) or as opposing the EU (Ladi and Tsagkroni, 2019). Yet it is also true that a crisis decreases the electoral costs of unpopular measures. For example, Giger and Nelson (2011) analyse eighteen advanced industrialised countries during the period 1970–2002 and observe that, when controlling for growth and unemployment, religious and liberal parties actually gain votes when they reduce social spending during a crisis, and that Social Democrats are not affected by retrenchment. Along a similar line, Lobo and Lewis-Beck (2012) demonstrate that voters' attribution of blame is affected by global economic and European political interdependence.

Assuming that this third scenario is the most likely, our second argument is that as ministers have some leeway in the design of adjustment programmes, they are able to use conditionality, at least to some extent, to pass measures that they had been favouring but could not previously have passed. In other words, and to quote Putnam, bailout sometimes allows executives 'to do what they privately wish to do, but are powerless to do domestically' (Putnam, 1988, p. 457; see also Schelling, 1980, p. 22).

Hence, we expect to find evidence in all bailout countries, during the entire duration of the programme, *of the capacity of government to define policies, to insert new measures, to avoid the insertion (or implementation) of specific measures*; and that some of these *policies had been on the government's agenda for some time but could not have been passed until that time (Proposal One).*

This domestic empowerment of executives due to the conditionality imposed by the EU or the IMF has been demonstrated empirically. Dyson and Featherstone (1996), for example, demonstrate how a small technocratic elite in Italy chose to submit their country to the constraints associated with EMU in order to 'bind themselves to the mast' (Elster, 1979, p. 90) and impose policy changes they would not otherwise have been able to pass and maintain. Featherstone (2003) notes how the Greek government, also during EMU negotiations, supported the inclusion of a requirement that the government could only borrow for investment purposes, not consumption. Similarly, Pochet (1999) illustrates how Belgium used EMU to pursue reforms desired at the national level. De la Porte and Natali (2014) demonstrate that the Danish government used the Excessive Deficit Procedure in the aftermath of the financial crisis to pass sensitive pension reforms that would not otherwise have been possible politically. Rogers (2009) shows that even when a loan is not necessary, some governments enter into IMF arrangements because they want particular conditions to be imposed on them. Vreeland (1999) recalls the story of President Cardoso of Brazil, who entered into an IMF arrangement in 1998 to be able to cut federal expenditures and infrastructure projects and to reform the social security system – measures that he had been unsuccessfully trying to get approved within his governing coalition. In a subsequent article, the same author demonstrates that executives facing more veto players are more likely to turn to the IMF (Vreeland, 2004).

In relation to the specific cases of the bailed out Eurozone countries, there is also some evidence of the leverage of executives. Hick (2018) examines the Troika's influence on the retrenchment and reform of social security in Ireland and concludes that a large part of the decisions had domestic origins (see also Dukelow, 2015). Moury and Standring (2017) show that executives in Portugal were to a great extent convinced of the need to introduce spending cuts and deregulate structural reforms, and passed reforms that went beyond the lenders' original demands. Lütz *et al.* (2019) made the same argument, again for Portugal, but also for Cyprus. MacCarthaigh and Hardiman (2020) argued that the Troika allowed the Irish government and the administrative elite to invoke the Troika's *force majeure* to strengthen their own hand vis-à-vis the public sector workforce and to engage in a profound reform of the Irish public administration. Asensio and Popic (2019) demonstrate how the health reforms in the MoU corresponded to the Portuguese government's working documents of previous years. Finally, Cioffi and Dubin (2016) show that Spain's conservative government pursued radical neoliberal labour law reforms that were not requested by external actors. While interesting, these studies focus on most likely cases such as the (centre)-right governments of Ireland, Spain and Portugal, and often cover single-policy areas. In this book, we cover all policy areas and all bailed out governments of the Eurozone.

On the importance of partisanship

If we are right that bailed out governments have leverage and can use external constraint to introduce measures they favour politically, then the partisan composition of government should make a difference even during a bailout. This expectation is coherent with the partisan-effect theory that posits that political partisanship has an impact on socio-economic reforms during a recession or an adjustment programme. More precisely, the hypothesis holds that left-wing political parties are more favourable towards the expansion/limited retrenchment of the welfare state, the redistribution of wealth, and more protective of the labour condition. In contrast, right-wing parties are expected to strive to reduce government intervention, increase the disciplining effects of market mechanisms, and limit the breadth and depth of the welfare safety net (Pop-Eleches, 2008; Starke *et al.*, 2013).

This hypothesis has been challenged, as many authors have argued that the pursuit of the (increasingly affluent) median voter, the loss of low-income households as the core constituency of social democrats, and European and global pressures have led to cross-national party convergence along neoliberal lines (Rodrik, 1998; Ross, 2000). In that vein, Armingeon (2012) does not find robust partisan effects of the impact of political parties on fiscal stimulus programmes in the aftermath of the 2008 financial crisis.

Yet the balance is weighted in favour of scholars who claim that, when faced with similar external pressure, ministers from the left are less likely to embrace neoliberal reforms than ministers from the right. If partisanship can have a diminishing impact during downturns (see Jensen, 2012 for labour market; Lipsmeyer, 2011 for social expenditure), it still seems to matter who is in government. Allan and Scruggs (2004), for example, look at the retrenchment of the welfare state since the 1980s and conclude that governments from the right retrench more than those from the left. Tavares (2004) shows that the left tends to reduce the deficit by raising tax revenues, while the right relies mostly on spending cuts. Starke *et al.* (2013) analyse government responses to four major economic shocks and show that, in less generous welfare states, parties from the right are more likely to retrench the welfare state (see also Cusack *et al.*, 2006; Ha and Kang, 2015; McManus, 2018). Galasso (2014) points out that right parties are more likely to pass pro-market reforms during an economic crisis.

Similarly, a large body of research has shown that the EU or IMF effect is mediated by the government ideology. For example, Mulas-Granados (2003) demonstrates that the ideology of the party in government is the most powerful predictor of fiscal policies in response to the Maastricht Criteria (see also Graziano, 2011 for the European Employment Strategy). Pop-Eleches (2008) and Doyle (2012) find that right-wing governments eagerly apply the IMF's policy prescriptions, whereas leftist governments are much more reluctant to do so. Picot and Tassinari (2017) compared labour market reforms in Spain and Italy and showed that the influence of the centre-left explains the improved protection of workers that was introduced alongside the flexibilisation measures. Finally, Walter (2016) shows how partisan considerations influence the specific policy design of bailouts in Eastern Europe, as all governments try to protect their own constituencies from the consequences of the crisis.

Our proposition is therefore that partisanship matters and governments with different persuasions will implement different policies during a bailout. *Evidence of this should be observed when a new government is elected during a bailout: in this case, we expect the terms of conditionality to change and/or some of the measures passed by its predecessor to be reversed (Proposal Two).*

Before concluding this section, we must note that we do not imply that governments' preferences are independent of the political context. As a matter of fact, we believe that they are strongly influenced by external factors, for three reasons. First, and as observed by Chwieroth (2015) and Alexiadou and Gunaydin (2019), Ministers and advisors who are 'sympathetic' to the IMF and/or the EC are increasingly appointed during times of crisis. The appointment of technical governments, like Monti in Italy or Papademos in Greece, is a paradigmatic example of this. Secondly, research shows that strong external constraints shift the preferences of both left and right parties, so that both centre-right and centre-left governments support pro-competitiveness reforms and retrenchment to some extent. For example, Bremer (2018) provides evidence that while social democratic parties during the crisis still defended the welfare state and became more sceptical of economic liberalism, they simultaneously (and ambiguously) also accepted the need for fiscal consolidation. Finally, we claim it is possible that the preferences of these executives are in turn influenced by their interaction with international actors – through a process of persuasion – as claimed by constructivist scholars (Börzel and Risse, 2009).

On the importance of credibility

Our third argument is that credibility – which we define as the perceived intention to negotiate honestly and the appraised ability to respect one's commitments – is a crucial factor for domestic leverage (Leach and Sabatier, 2005; Moury, 2013). The credibility of governments depends on a variety of factors. First, trust (in this context, the perceived intention to negotiate honestly) is a prerequisite for credibility. As Nelson discusses and empirically demonstrates for the IMF, if the international lenders think that the executive can be trusted 'to do the right thing', then they will behave more freely (Nelson, 2014, pp. 307–308). As the trustworthiness of a given policy-maker emanates from previous interaction, political instability (governmental resignation, new elections, reshuffles, etc.) is detrimental to it (Tallberg, 2008). Moreover, the partisan composition of government is also important for trust and leverage. This is based on the contention that success is more likely in negotiations when actors share the same preferences and values as thenegotiators on the 'other side' (Zahariadis, 2016) and have less extreme positions (Garrett and Tsebelis, 1996).

The government's credibility also depends on the institutional capacity of the state to implement the deals and respect the rules (Exadaktylos and Zahariadis, 2014; Hennessy, 2017; Sacchi, 2018).[1] The institutional capacity and willingness are linked, in turn, to the competency of the public administration (Featherstone, 2015), to the 'goodness of fit' (i.e. the correspondence of the European policies with national policy legacies, Börzel and Risse, 2003) and finally the intensity of costs linked to the necessary adjustments (Walter, 2016 on internal devaluation; Afonso *et al.*, 2015 on patronage). Related to this, when there is consensus on the implementation of the bailout among political (in government, in Parliament) and economic (in social concertation, with firms, etc.) actors, the government's capacity to reform will be greater (Lindvall, 2017), as will its credibility.

Hence, the relationship between ownership, credibility and leverage is circular and self-reinforcing rather than unilateral. While, as discussed earlier, lenders might find it advantageous to give the government leverage ('ex-post ownership'), shared understanding of the problems and solutions ('ex-ante ownership') also increases government leverage.

In short, we propose *that the more the government seems to be/had been willing and able to implement the policies agreed upon, the greater is its credibility, and the greater its capacity to insert its own preferences in the definition of the deals (Proposal Three).*

On the bargaining context

Of course, not all states in international negotiations have equal weight; that is why we should bear in mind that the leverage of governments – and their related capacity to pass their preferred policies during the bailout – is mediated by their material bargaining power.

Bargaining power varies primarily in line with one's material resources (i.e. size, GDP). In the case of the recent bailouts, scholars have shown that the debtors' leverage varies as a function of their GDP and corresponding share of ECB capital and their level of debts (Offe, 2017). Among the borrower countries, Greece is therefore clearly in a weaker position than the others. For example, when it requested its first and second bailouts, Greek debt was around 150 per cent of GDP, and for the third bailout in 2015 it was as high as 175 per cent; in contrast, it was around 100 per cent for Ireland and Portugal, and 80 per cent for Cyprus and Spain.[2]

But other factors also impact states' material bargaining power. First, the attractiveness of fall-back options where bargaining fails also matters, as the lower the cost of the failure of bargaining for a given actor, the greater is its bargaining power (Dür and Mateo, 2010; Moravcsik, 1994). As applied to our cases, research shows that the debtor countries' power in negotiations was mainly dependent on their vulnerability to market pressures, which gave member states different levels of necessity and urgency to strike a collective agreement (De la Porte and Natali, 2014; Finke and Bailer, 2019; Schimmelfennig, 2015).

Related to this, it has been proved that the credibility of the lenders' threats not to grant assistance decreases the borrowers' leverage. This credibility itself also depends on the level of exposure of the creditors' banks in the countries at risk (Howarth and Quaglia, 2016). This, for example, explains – among other things – why the leverage of Greece was higher in the early phase of the crisis than in 2012 and 2015 when the second and third bailouts were drafted (Hennessy, 2017). Similarly, when a country – such as Spain – is 'too big to fail' (Wildasin, 1999), it is in a stronger bargaining position than smaller countries.

Fourthly, many international scholars and bargaining theorists have stressed that saliency is an important factor in negotiations. Saliency refers to the importance which actors attribute to a specific issue, and, hence, to their willingness to invest political resources in it (Beyers *et al.*, 2017; Meissner and McKenzie, 2019). Hence, we could expect that when an issue is salient for the lenders, the government will have less room for manoeuvre. Alternatively, governments that invest a lot of political capital in an issue might eventually win the negotiations on this particular point. The counterpart of this is that the more salient an issue for an actor, the bigger the concessions it is willing to make in other areas (Keohane and Nye, 1977; Moravcsik, 1994).

A fifth factor impacting negotiating power is the credible constraints on agreements (Putnam, 1988; Schelling, 1980). On the lenders' side, the need for the German Parliament to give a positive vote (Moschella, 2017) on any deal further strengthened the German hand. Also, the unity of the creditors impacts negotiations, as negotiators might exploit division in the other camp. Lütz *et al.* (2020) have shown how the three institutions, which have different bureaucratic cultures, goals and legal frameworks, were very often conflicted on the policy conditionalities related to financial stability, and fiscal and structural adjustment. However, they note that this was not exploited by the borrower governments due to the power asymmetries between them and the Troika.

On the debtors' side, their leverage should theoretically be increased by the need to obtain the agreement of veto players such as constitutional courts or regions, or of several parties in the case of minority or coalition agreements. However, Lütz *et al.* again noted that this strategy was not very effective for the debtor countries, which had to find a way to 'work around the veto player', principally by substituting measures (Lütz *et al.*, 2019, p. 1448). Additionally, in cases of a minority or coalition government, or more generally in the case of division within the government, a lack of unity can be prejudicial to bargaining power (Meunier, 2000). Hence, the literature does not lead us to any clear expectations regarding credible constraints.

Testing the weight of each of these variables individually would require an exact assessment of each actor's preferences, which should be compared with the outcome – something that goes beyond our analysis and has been done already by some of the scholars cited above. However, in our process-tracing analysis we will keep an eye on these variables to identify what might explain across- and within-country variation in the borrower's country leverage during and after the bailout.

After conditionality

After 2013, Eurozone bailout programmes started to come to an end and the economic situation has since improved (to some varying extent). This has obviously made executives freer than before. To start with, the available evidence suggests that IMF surveillance activities (in force during the reimbursement period) are not very effective (Lombardi and Woods, 2008). In the European Union, monitoring agents such as the Commission have been hesitant to apply sanctions to governments that fail to comply with EU rules, out of fear of the political consequences of the strict application of the rules (Schmidt, 2016). Investors might not scrutinise policy developments in a given country so closely, and declining yields make governments less dependent on the ECB's conditionality. In that context, the conditions that allowed reformist ministers to push for their favourite policies are no longer met; and the current executive, even if there is continuity in office, might be tempted in this new context to please its constituency or surrender to interest groups' pressure.

Yet external constraints do not disappear after a bailout. As described above, EU rules within the SGP have been tightened so that the EU now monitors a large spectrum of indicators (including wages, house prices, private debts, etc.) and sanctions for noncompliance are easier to pass (Bauer and Becker, 2014). Countries benefiting from the ECB's quantitative easing are still vulnerable to the bank's conditionality. A third, more informal source of pressure is that recently bailed out countries want to avoid being seen as going back to the same risky behaviours. Such an image might diminish their bargaining power when dealing with their peers and EU institutions (Sacchi, 2018) and weaken investors' trust in their sovereign bonds (Matthijs and McNamara, 2015; Tavares, 2004).

The dominant narrative is another contradictory movement. As time goes by and uncertainty decreases, the efficiency of austerity and – to a lesser extent – of various structural reforms has been questioned (including by the IMF itself), challenging the discourse of necessity that had prevailed at the peak of the crisis (Blanchard and Leigh, 2013). On the other hand, the economic growth that most of the countries had witnessed after a bailout was interpreted by many as proof that the reforms were working.

To sum up, governments have been pulled and can go in two contradictory directions, towards reversals or the maintenance of what had been done under conditionality. The question that remains is which policies they would reverse. Our answer to this is that governments will selectively pick the reversals that bring more benefits than costs to them.

First, we predict that policy-makers would reverse policies when it is most electorally beneficial to do so, that is, when changes concentrate benefits but imply diffuse costs to the population at large (Wilson, 1980). For example, we expect governments to reverse civil servants' tax rises or salary cuts rather than VAT increases (which imply diffuse benefits). In that vein, Rickard and Caraway (2019) show that the public sector wage cuts made under IMF conditionality do not persist in the longer term. They note that 'Once the knife of conditionality is no longer at a government's throat, governments will increase public sector spending to appease powerful domestic constituents' (Rickard and Caraway, 2019, p. 18). Similarly, Afonso and Bulfone (2019) show that political parties' proposals for reversals are linked to the interests of their constituencies.

Secondly, we argue that reversals are more frequent when transactional costs (i.e. the costs associated with reaching a decision) are lower. It could be argued that transactional costs vary from one type of policy to another. This argument is based on the famous works of Lowi (1964) and Wilson (1980) according to which the type of policy affects which actors mobilise and along which lines (and hence the costs of passing a decision). Lowi identifies three categories of policy: i) distributive policies, that involve the non-zero-sum transfer of resources and are generally passed without conflict; ii) redistributive policies that bring in zero-sum distribution of resources and lead to conflict between social classes; and iii) regulatory policies that aim to control economic activity and hence pit the losers and winners of the policy against each other. The latter are the most costly to pass, as they often involve diffuse benefits and concentrated costs (Freeman, 2006) – the combination that leads to most protest (Martin and Gabay, 2018). Hence, we expect that structural reforms – rather than spending cuts – are most costly to reverse (and hence least likely).

Related to this, Patashnik (2014) also shows that general-interest reforms that hurt firms' interest are often dismantled afterwards, as firms use their resources (e.g. economic weight and capacity to create employment) and instrumental power (lobbying) to regain their rents. However, his research also showed that this is less the case when the reform created influential actors who benefited from the change and would mobilise against a reversal (see also Mandelkern and Koreh, 2018).

To conclude, *when the bailout terminates, we expect governments to reverse what was done during the crisis, but to do so only partially and selectively (Proposal Four).*

These partial reversals offer governments the possibility to claim credit for policies with limited costs (a different kind of 'affordable credit claiming' from that identified by Bonoli and Natali, 2012). For example, if governments end the freezing of the minimum wage, or partially increase pensions and salaries that had been cut, the incomes of those affected are still lower than they would have been without the bailout and governments can claim credit even though welfare states had been retrenched. Similarly, governments that reverse only limited aspects of structural reforms after a bailout but keep their core can reap the benefits of those reforms and claim credit for the reversals. Reversals of policies that were never implemented also afford 'cheap' credit-claiming.

Finally, it must be noted that who is governing after conditionality also makes a difference – especially considering our argument that governments have some leverage during a bailout. If there is continuity in office, ministers will be less keen to reverse the reforms that they had themselves passed. By contrast, if a new government is elected it might be more likely to (campaign to) undo its predecessor's reforms. Along that line, Pop-Echeles (2008) argues that, in Latin America and Eastern Europe, reversals during or after conditionality occur when a left-wing government follows a right-wing one (see also Campos and Horváth, 2012). Sedelmeier (2012) shows that, in the absence of lock-in, reversals of gender equality institutions are explained by a change in government orientation. Research by Branco *et al.* (2019) and Moury *et al.* (2019) also testifies to the crucial importance of partisanship turnover in explaining reversals in Spain, Portugal and Italy. Nevertheless, we believe that every government will be torn between these contradictory forces and that partial reversals will occur in all cases.

Conclusion

To sum up, the main idea of this book is that domestic politics still matters, even in the era of Europeanisation and globalisation and under the harshest circumstances. We claim that governments are capable of extracting policy benefits from the bailout, during and after the process. During a bailout, the executives are not powerless and have some leverage although the degree of constraint depends on their bargaining position. In fact, the bailout not only strengthens them domestically but also – our argument goes on – provides pro-reformist ministers with an opportunity to pass reforms that they personally favour but could not previously have passed (Proposal One). Another implication of the bailed out governments' room for manoeuvre is that it makes a difference who is governing, and when a new government is appointed, policies are renegotiated or reversed (Proposal Two). Governmental room for manoeuvre, however, is dependent on the government's credibility (Proposal Three) – itself a variable of its capacity and willingness to implement the agreed policies.

After a bailout, we further argue, all executives will select the measures that are worth reversing (enabling 'affordable credit-claiming'). Given these incentives, we expect partial reversals in all cases (Proposal Four).

In a nutshell, our argument is that bailouts not only offer ministers the possibility to pass reforms that they could not have previously passed, but also to gain credit by partially reversing them.

Notes

1 The risk here is one of 'inertia' – a situation in which domestic actors refuse to replace norms, rules and practices with new ones (Radaelli, 2003).

2 Source: Eurostat, available at: https://ec.europa.eu/eurostat/en/web/government-finance-statistics/statistics-illustrated (accessed 1 March 2021).

2

Greece

Introduction

Greece is a central case study since this is where the Eurozone crisis broke out and where the European rescue mechanism was developed. It also offers significant variation in terms of partisanship and levels of trust between the government and the lenders. Finally, it is a case that allows a comparison to be made between the negotiation and implementation of three programmes within the same country. Indeed, the period of Economic Adjustment Programmes for Greece lasted ten full years with four governments alternating in power. Moreover, Greece was seen as the weakest link in the Eurozone because of its poor economic performance and structural problems, the roots of which preceded the crisis. However, the much discussed Grexit never occurred and the country rose from its ashes in August 2018.

The Greek case allows us to demonstrate that governments have at least some room for manoeuvre during a bailout, even in the least likely case in which executives had very little bargaining power due to the country's economic vulnerability and very low levels of trust (Proposal One). We also show in this chapter that, despite these constraints, reversals did take place during and after the end of the programme, but only when the benefits of those reversals were concentrated and the costs were diffused. Together with these partial reversals, partial implementation can also be observed during the whole period of the crisis; this signals governments' power to evade undesirable measures even when they are under international scrutiny (Proposal Four). Interestingly, partisanship does not seem to play an important role in Greece as far as the content of the MoUs is concerned. In fact, the three MoUs are a continuation of each other and the measures did not change dramatically during the entire period (Proposal Two). However, each new government brought renewed levels of trust that lasted from a few weeks to some months but certainly not for very long (Proposal Three).

This chapter is organised chronologically in eight sections.

September 2008–April 2010: before the First Economic Adjustment Programme: from a ND government to a PASOK government

The 2008 global financial crisis found Greece in a state of post-Olympics euphoria. Greece entered the EMU in 2001 and successfully organised the 2004 Olympic Games in Athens. Both events created a positive economic and political environment and the Greek economy presented fast economic growth rates. However, subsequent Greek governments led either by the Panhellenic Socialist Movement (PASOK, socialist party) or by New Democracy (ND, conservative party) failed to seize the opportunity to reduce the public debt or to perform structural reforms that would increase Greece's competitiveness (Bank of Greece, 2014).

In 2008, K. Karamanlis was in his second term of office as Prime Minister, leading a one-party ND government. At the onset of the global financial crisis, Karamanlis' position was weakening due to domestic politics. Initially, the government did not want to admit the severity of the situation or the likelihood of the global financial crisis being translated into a debt crisis for countries with the macroeconomic characteristics of Greece. Data from the time show that the general government deficit exceeded 4 per cent of GDP and the public deficit stood at almost 97 per cent of GDP (Bank of Greece, 2014). The economic and political elites were publicly stating that this was a foreign crisis which would not immediately affect Greece (Ignatiou, 2015). However, in early October 2008 Greece was the second Eurozone country to pass legislation to guarantee bank deposits even before the European Council decision 'to act in a concerted and comprehensive manner to protect the European financial system and depositors' (Council of the European Union, 2008, p. 1).

The second measure of the Karamanlis government came in November 2008, when it passed legislation to enhance the liquidity of the economy by pumping money into financial institutions that had started showing signs of instability. The government recapitalised the banks with €28 billion. The liquidity provided to the banks together with other spending initiatives came during the EU's Keynesian phase of reacting to the global financial crisis, which served the ND government well as it did not want to push for austerity measures (Kazakos, 2019). The single most important event in this last phase of the Karamanlis government was the violent youth protests that broke out after a policeman killed a young student in the centre of Athens on 6 December. Although the killing had nothing to do with the upcoming crisis, the protests soon turned into riots that lasted for over ten days and spread all over the country. They were described by some as an 'uprising' (Karamichas, 2009, p. 289) that unleashed anger at the socio-political decline that had taken place over the previous few years (Gerodimos, 2015).

In January 2009, Karamanlis announced a government reshuffle in response to the general political disaffection. One of the key changes was the replacement of the Minister of Finance and the Economy, G. Alogoskoufis, with his Deputy Minister, Y. Papathanasiou, in an attempt to show the government's commitment to tackling the worrying economic situation. Papathanasiou was a political appointment and did not have the characteristics of a technocrat, demonstrating that the government was not yet thinking of appealing to the international markets. Papathanasiou remained in the post for just nine months as early elections were announced in September 2009 due to the government's inability to respond to the domestic and external constraints. These nine months were marked by growing demands from the EU and IMF to take decisive measures that would reduce the deficit from 3.7 per cent (the Greek government's forecast) to 3.0 per cent in line with Maastricht Treaty requirements. At the same time, Greece was under increasing pressure to boost its competitiveness and productivity by taking austerity measures and reforming the labour market (Council of the European Union, 2009; ECOFIN, 2009; International Monetary Fund, 2009).

As the global financial crisis spread and the forecasts for the European economy worsened, the European Commission made a U-turn from its Keynesianism approach in March 2009, and activated the EDP for Greece and three other countries (Ireland, France and Spain). Subsequently, Karamanlis passed four austerity measures packages in his last year in office, including the long due privatisation of Olympic Airlines (Featherstone and Papadimitriou, 2008). Despite the European pressure, Finance Minister Papathanasiou (2017, p. 156) insisted in his memoirs that 'our targeting was not the result of EU pressures but a government decision in light of the interests of the Greek people and the national economy. Our decision was to put public economics in order.' The weakening government had little room for manoeuvre but it wanted to appear to be in control of the situation.

However, the EU and the IMF did not consider any of the measures to be fully satisfactory (International Monetary Fund, 2009). This was all taking place in a worsening political environment in which the opposition and the trade unions spoke out against the measures, claiming they were unnecessary (Papathanasiou, 2017). The June 2009 European elections registered the lowest ever turnout (52.61 per cent); PASOK became the first party with 36.65 per cent of the vote, with ND falling from 43.02 per cent to 32.30 per cent.[1] The October 2009 parliamentary elections were catastrophic for ND, which lost to PASOK with a 10 per cent margin. A PASOK government was swiftly formed with G. Papandreou as the Prime Minister.

The new government's celebrations were short lived as the new Prime Minister, G. Papandreou and notably his Minister of Finance, G.

Papakonstantinou quickly realised that the economy was in a worse situation than they had thought before the elections.[2] The first blow came when the government announced within its first month in office that the statistical data produced by the Greek Statistical Office were not accurate and that the deficit was much larger than previously expected. The new forecast in October 2009 was for a deficit of 12.7 per cent of GDP, well above the EC's April forecast of 5.1 per cent (Papakonstantinou, 2016). According to the memoirs of former PASOK Finance Minister Papakonstantinou (2016), all previous governments (ND and PASOK) shared the responsibility for this inaccuracy, which was a reflection not only of bad reporting but also of the mismanagement of the public sector and public finance. As a result of this announcement, Greece was the central topic of the next Eurogroup meeting on 20 October 2009 in Luxembourg. They decided that an asterisk would be put in the Greek data until they could be confirmed and Jean Claude Juncker famously said: 'The Game is over. We need serious statistics' (Barber, 2009). Realising the gravity of the situation, the EC published a report accusing Greece of misreporting its figures (European Commission, 2010a). The credit worthiness of Greek government bonds was immediately downgraded by Fitch Ratings and Moody's. The creation of an independent Hellenic Statistical Authority in February 2010 did not alleviate the situation (Law 3832/2010). The downward spiral for Greece had started.

The Greek government announced four packages of austerity measures and structural reforms (Papakonstantinou, 2016) between November 2009 and May 2010 as it endeavoured to improve its position in the markets and the EU and avoid asking for financial assistance. In December 2009, Greece was put in an 'enhanced surveillance' procedure, which a few months later became part of the 'six pack' of five Regulations and one Directive put together to intensify macroeconomic surveillance of Eurozone member states (Ladi and Tsarouhas, 2014). The purpose was to exert pressure on Greece by keeping an even closer eye on its public finances. The Prime Minister and Finance Minister visited Berlin, Paris, London and Frankfurt to convince European governments of the adequacy of their economic programme.

The reaction from investors, however, was not positive (Papakonstantinou, 2016). By the end of 2009, the deficit had reached 15.7 per cent of GDP, the public debt was 129.7 per cent of GDP and the yield for government bonds was around 5.5 per cent (Bank of Greece, 2014). Measures aimed at reducing the deficit to below 10 per cent, such as fostering private sector development and creating a more efficient public sector, were included in the 2010 budget (European Commission, 2010b; Ministry of Finance, 2010).

The 'open.gov' website was one of the first structural reforms introduced by the Papandreou government. It sought to enhance citizens' trust in the state by introducing a transparent system for the recruitment of personnel to high-level positions in government and by publishing all public bodies' decisions as a precondition for their enactment (Gouskos and Staiou, 2010; Rigou, 2010). In February 2010, the Prime Minister announced further austerity measures; these included the broadening of the tax base (mainly increases for the higher incomes), cuts in public expenditure (e.g. freezing public sector recruitment and cutting salaries), the freezing of pensions and an increase in the retirement age. A final package of austerity measures announced in March again targeted the salaries of public sector employees and both public and private sector pensions. The public sector investment programme was further reduced and tax rises increased. A special solidarity contribution of 1 per cent was announced for incomes over €100,000 (Papakonstantinou, 2016). All these austerity measures came in response to Greece's increasing difficulty in borrowing from the international markets and to the slow progress of negotiations between the Greek government and EU partners for an alternative solution that would allow them to avoid default.

Simultaneously, the Greek Prime Minister and Minister of Finance were engaged in constant talks with the EU in search of positive feedback or the announcement of support that would ease the markets.[3] The government by now realised that a rescue mechanism would be necessary as there had not been the hoped-for response from the markets to its unilateral measures.

Unfortunately, support was slow to come because there were no mechanisms in place. The EU governments had to negotiate with each other and choose the institutional mix and modalities of the rescue plan for a crisis that looked like it was going to affect the whole Eurozone. The Maastricht Treaty's (Article 125) 'no bailout' provision prevented financial assistance to countries in Greece's situation and the European counterparts with especially Germany firmly in support of sticking with the rules did not allow for much flexibility. The key message from the German Finance Minister, Schäuble, EC President Juncker and European Commissioner Almunia, among others, was that there was no 'Plan B' and no possibility of a Greek default or of Greece leaving the euro area (Grexit) (Henning, 2017). This was in reaction to the growing media discourse about the possibility of a default and thus Grexit (e.g. Kutter, 2014).

The government's position was that it wanted a European solution since this was Greece's immediate environment and alliance. If this did not prove to be possible the next best solution would be the IMF (Papakonstantinou, 2016). Papandreou's visit to Davos in January 2010 was a turning point as the IMF's involvement in a Financial Assistance Programme was discussed for the first time at a secret meeting with Strauss-Kahn, the IMF's Managing Director (Ignatiou, 2015; Papakonstantinou, 2016). EU pressure for further measures continued in February but without any commitment to financial assistance. This was when Papandreou visited Moscow to discuss the possibility of a Russian loan; however, President Medvedev advised him to turn to the IMF and the World Bank (Papakonstantinou, 2016).

Papandreou's visit to Washington early in March 2010 proved vital for the creation of a rescue mechanism for Greece. The Americans encouraged the EU and especially Chancellor Merkel to agree on a solution (Ignatiou, 2015). Papakonstantinou's negotiations with the IMF for its participation in a rescue programme for Greece started officially during the visit (Roumeliotis, 2012). The announcement of the rescue mechanism was finally made at the European Council of 24–25 March.

Just before the European Council, Merkel declared that the IMF should participate in the rescue programme for Greece and that theoretically it should be possible for a country to exit the Eurozone if it continuously violated its obligations under the Treaties (Henning, 2017). The rescue mechanism that was announced consisted of coordinated bilateral loans that would only be available as a last resort if a country lost access to the markets; they would be subject to conditionality in a programme that would be overseen by the EC, ECB and IMF (Henning, 2017). The fine-tuning of the rescue mechanism took place in April, when the likelihood of a bank run was increasing daily; yields were as high as 7.83 and default was imminent (Wearden, 2010). Prime Minister Papandreou asked for the activation of the rescue mechanism in a communication to the Greek people on 27 April from the remote island of Kastellorizo.

The First Economic Adjustment Programme for Greece was announced on 3 May. It would last three years and amounted to €110 billion: €80 billion through bilateral loans from the Eurozone member states and €30 billion from the IMF. It was voted through the Greek Parliament on 7 May amid violent demonstrations in Athens that led to the death of three people at Marfin Bank following a fire caused by homemade molotovs. The first instalment was disbursed a few days later (Papakonstantinou, 2016). Greek and EU politicians and policy-makers devoted most of their energy and time to working out the exact financial assistance mechanism given the unprecedented challenge of the financial crisis and Eurozone institutions' unreadiness.[4] This left little time for negotiating the precise measures of conditionality.

While negotiations between the Greek government and the IMF on the actual conditionality started on 20 April, negotiations with the Troika were delayed until 23 April due to a volcanic eruption in Iceland. These discussions were conducted between the team from the Greek Ministry of Finance and the Troika under immense time pressure because default was looming; they lasted just one week.[5] Greece's negotiating position was weakened by its dire economic situation. Social partners were invited to join the negotiations but their answer was 'We don't want to know. We disagree with everything.'[6]

Not only was it the first time that such a programme had been negotiated but it was also the first time the EC, the IMF and the ECB had worked together in a new institutional framework. The IMF was the most experienced partner but was contributing less money than the EC, which was representing the member states and the EU's common interest; although the ECB did not contribute any money, it had significant leverage because the survival of the Greek banking system was in its hands. The roles were quickly distributed with the EC taking the lead in the negotiations and focusing on the structural reforms, the IMF on the fiscal adjustment and the ECB on the banking system (Papakonstantinou, 2016).

Similar to previous IMF programmes, the MoU had three objectives: fiscal adjustment, structural reforms and reforms of the financial sector (European Commission, 2010c). The First Programme focused on the implementation of rapid fiscal adjustment because the Greek crisis was initially conceived as a liquidity crisis, not a solvency crisis; in other words, a temporary cash flow problem rather than a real danger of bankruptcy. This lack of understanding of the situation lost them valuable time to make the structural reforms that are so important when tackling a solvency crisis.[7] An additional problem was that the IMF lacked two of its most important tools for fiscal adjustment: currency devaluation (because of Greece's EMU membership) and debt restructuring (which Germany, the Netherlands and Slovakia, among others, strongly opposed). This group of countries wanted the programme to be short, to focus on austerity measures and structural reforms, and to have a high interest rate that would serve as a punitive lesson to other Eurozone member states facing market pressures (Roumeliotis, 2012).

Hence, internal devaluation was the only option available, achieved mainly by reducing Greece's labour costs so as to increase its international competitiveness. Very strict fiscal measures were imposed by the lenders, leaving the Greek government no room for manoeuvre.[8] According to one of the Greek chief negotiators: 'To be honest, the changes that one could negotiate in relation to the fiscal reforms were marginal', or, in other words, the government could not really negotiate for less austerity.[9] These measures included significant cuts in public sector salaries and pensions, a reduction of pensions in the private sector, an increase in the retirement age, and direct and indirect taxes (European Commission, 2010c). However, the Greek government managed to ensure some beneficial treatment for the benefits and pensions of the lowest incomes, the 13th and 14th salary of private sector employees,[10] and to defer the reduction of the public deficit to below 3 per cent of GDP to the end of 2014 (Papakonstantinou, 2016; Roumeliotis, 2012).

The negotiations on the structural reforms were more straightforward as many of the issues raised by the Troika were already in PASOK's electoral programme and the Greek government saw the MoU as an opportunity to ensure their implementation (Ladi, 2014; PASOK, 2009).[11] Papakonstantinou (2016, p. 173) sets out a list of measures he considered positive, including the opening up of regulated professions, improvement of the business environment, liberalisation of public enterprises, public administration reforms and the reduction of the state's role in the economy generally. He states: 'I believed back then and I still believe today that despite the demonisation of the MoU, most of it should have been implemented a long time ago from subsequent Greek governments without any interference from the Troika' (Papakonstantinou, 2016, p. 175). Even Ministers from the left wing of PASOK admit that there was room for manoeuvre in the negotiation of the structural measures in the first MoU, though not the fiscal measures.[12] Another key Minister in the negotiations explains that there was nothing new in the conditionality of the MoU, which had previously been part of the IMF recommendations and the EC and OECD reports for Greece.[13] She/he goes on to describe MoU measures like the public administration reform and the Kallikrates local government reform as 'self-evident and not imposed by the Troika'. Similarly, the IMF representative in the Troika explains that the specific measures in the first MoU were largely chosen by the Greek government, although the fiscal targets were not negotiable. This representative points out that the IMF's key contribution was to quantify the proposed measures[14] (see Proposal One).

Although the relevant parts of the draft MoU were sent to the competent Ministries for comment, hardly any of their recommendations were included.[15] With default looming, the official negotiations with the Troika could only last a few days. On 30 April, the Cabinet met to ratify the MoU. Despite the many objections and questions, the urgency of the situation meant that the MoU was accepted. The government met with the Troika for the last time on 1 May, in the midst of demonstrations and, after discussions on the final details that lasted all night, the first MoU was ready (Papakonstantinou, 2016).

May 2010–November 2011: implementation of the First Programme and negotiations for the Second Programme: the fall of the PASOK government

The first instalment of the loan arrived just in time for Greece to avoid default.[16] The government immediately pushed for some important structural reforms. One of these was the pension reform which sought to create a more sustainable pension system and introduced the same retirement age for men and women. In fact, the pension system in Greece had become unsustainable because of its huge cost, early retirement benefits to special categories and total dependence on state funds. Law 3863/10 started a process of consolidation of the pension system expenses; although it had an immediate fiscal impact, it was not sufficient to tackle the pension system's structural weaknesses (Tinios, 2013). Another reform addressed fiscal responsibility by establishing specific rules and procedures to control spending at all levels of government. An independent Financial Stability Fund was established by the Bank of Greece to support the banking system (Anastasatou and Tsakloglou, 2019). Further reforms were introduced in public administration to combat corruption and increase transparency and accountability (Spanou, 2018). A reform of local government called 'Kallikrates', which was already part of the PASOK programme before the MoU, was implemented early on (Tsekos and Hlepas, 2019).

The government managed to hold the majority in Parliament to pass these reforms, despite the resentment of members of the Cabinet, trade unions and the public (Papakonstantinou, 2016). The creditors were relieved to see that some progress was being made (Papakonstantinou, 2016).[17] Nonetheless, there was no consensus from the opposition parties; indeed, the second biggest party, New Democracy, claimed it had an alternative plan that would enhance growth without pursuing such harsh austerity measures.[18] The opposition on the left supported constant strikes and actions such as the blockade of Piraeus port against the liberalisation of cabotage. Despite these early reforms, the public debt kept growing (according to Eurostat, 126.7 per cent of GDP in 2009 and 146.2 per cent of GDP in 2010); as a result, the markets were not convinced the government would be able to implement such a difficult programme and thus continued to downgrade the Greek economy. The Troika recognised the positive efforts but warned that better coordination was needed within the government as well as more political consensus in the country (European Commission, 2010d). In September 2010, Papandreou reshuffled his government to appease internal criticism by offering ministerial posts to some of the traditional PASOK members.

The situation in Ireland, Portugal and Spain was also deteriorating and EU leaders were exploring new solutions. Merkel and Sarkozy reached a bilateral agreement in Deauville on 18 October 2010 on the participation of the private sector in the losses of future bailouts; this was adopted by the European Council ten days later and is seen by many of our interviewees from the Greek government as the beginning of the end of the First Programme for Greece.[19] The Deauville agreement introduced the idea that private investors, as well as taxpayers, should be liable for risky loans and participate in the rescue of countries in danger of bankruptcy; this proved counterproductive for the Greek programme. The decision was not supposed to directly affect Greece because the Economic Adjustment Programme was already underway, but the markets reacted instantly. There was an immediate increase in Greek sovereign spreads, with yields reaching 11.52 per cent in November (Mody, 2014, ch. 1).

A month later, the First Programme suffered another blow when the Greek public deficit was revised from 13.6 per cent to 15.4 per cent of GDP on 16 November 2010 due to a more accurate calculation of the social security funds and the inclusion of the deficit of seventeen public enterprises. This increase meant Greece had to take further measures if it were to reach the agreed target because the Troika was not willing to renegotiate the target itself (Papakonstantinou, 2016). A Minister of the Greek government at the time said: 'This crushed us ... These two points were the turning point for the Papandreou government. It was the beginning of the fall.'[20] Just a couple of days before the announcement of the public deficit review, PASOK had managed to win the regional and local elections by more or less maintaining its share of the vote despite the austerity measures and the growing resentment (Ministry of Interior, 2010). The Troika thus misjudged the government's political capital to push further reforms, such as the Medium Term Fiscal Strategy Framework which was a long-term budget and planning framework including measures until 2015 (Ministry of Finance, 2011; Papakonstantinou, 2016). More specifically, it constituted more fiscal measures for the achievement of primary surpluses, an acceleration of privatisations and the development of state assets (Bank of Greece, 2014).

Despite the encouraging second review of the programme and visits by Olli Rhen and Dominique Strauss-Khan to Athens in support of the government's efforts, the climate was deteriorating both internally and externally (European Commission, 2010e). The opposition parties were not only blaming the government for the review of the public deficit but also for the new measures. Tensions were obvious even within the Cabinet, and a civil disobedience movement called 'We Won't Pay' was growing. The 'We Won't Pay' movement was campaigning for non-payment of street tolls, property taxes, public transport fares or any other payment they deemed unfair. Besides the problems in tax revenue collection, this added to an atmosphere of mistrust towards the government and its capacity to deal with the problem (Exadaktylos and Zahariadis, 2014). The deterioration of the Greek economy continued despite the extension of the loan repayment and reduction of the interest rates on its loans agreed in March 2011, mirroring the decisions taken for Ireland (Roumeliotis, 2012). The cost of Greek borrowing continued to rise and rumours about Grexit spread, especially after a 'secret' meeting of EU leaders in Luxembourg in May 2011. The meeting was chaired by

Juncker, attended by the Ministers of Finance of France, Germany, Italy and Spain as well as the EC and the ECB (Papakonstantinou, 2016).

It was already clear in mid-May 2011 that a second programme would be necessary but that this would not be enough to stabilise the Greek economy. Greek officials and experts believed that some type of debt restructuring would also be needed but they had to push for it gently as the ECB was not in favour.[21] The IMF's Dominique Strauss-Khan was the main advocate of a generous debt restructuring until his arrest on 16 May for sexual assault when he had to resign from his position as Managing Director. Although his successor, Christine Lagarde, was initially less keen, she eventually followed the same line (Blustein, 2016). Meanwhile, the fourth review of the First Programme was taking place in a very tense atmosphere with constant interruptions and deadlocks in the discussions since the government was asking for some breathing space which the Troika was not willing to grant.[22]

The government's difficulties in implementing the reforms had diminished its credibility and thus its room for manoeuvre (see Proposal Three). On 3 June, an agreement was finally reached on the disbursement of the fifth instalment of the loan as soon as the Parliament voted for the Medium Term Fiscal Strategy Framework (European Commission, 2011a). A few days later, Papandreou reshuffled his government, replacing his Minister of Finance Papakonstantinou with Evaggelos Venizelos in an attempt to show its renewed effort in implementing the First Programme. Nonetheless, the government continued to struggle, both with pressure from the markets on state bonds and with domestic opposition (within PASOK but also from ND and the Coalition of the Radical Left – Progressive Alliance (SYRIZA)).

The new Minister of Finance, Venizelos, pushed hard domestically to speed up the reforms. He also negotiated in Europe to secure the debt restructuring via PSI – namely the contribution of the private sector to the resolution of the crisis – and an agreement on a Second Economic Adjustment Programme for Greece. However, a general strike was organised. Similarly to the Madrid *Indignados*, the Indignant Citizens movement occupied Syntagma Square for a number of weeks in protest against the austerity measures (Georgiadou *et al.*, 2019). The Greek government showed its determination by pushing for some harsh measures that further infuriated the public. For instance, the infamous labour reserve system was introduced in June 2011 (Law 3896/2011 amended by 4024/2011, Articles 33 and 34) moving 30,000 public sector employees to reserve status by January 2012, withdrawing 60 per cent of their salary for one to two years, and ultimately the possible termination of their employment. This measure was crafted by the government to show immediate results in the cutting of public sector employment costs.

Another controversial tool designed by the government to increase revenue was introduced at the end of August 2011, namely the incorporation of a property tax called EETHDE[23] into energy bills that would be collected by the energy company. Non-payment would lead to power being cut off. The measure caused a 50 per cent drop in the governing party's popularity and, as a result, its punitive elements were watered down with subsequent legislation (Zahariadis, 2013). Labour policy reforms were also high on the agenda but Labour Minister, Louka Katseli, was able to negotiate some of the measures from the First Programme during subsequent reviews (Ladi and Graziano, 2014). For example, she initially managed to renegotiate the reintroduction of the National General Collective Agreement.[24] However, by November 2011 the Troika had changed its mind and decided that the collective agreements and collective bargaining had to be abolished immediately. As a result, Louka Katseli refused to vote in favour of the legislation and was removed from the PASOK parliamentary group.

At a Euro summit on 21 July, agreement was finally reached on a new programme for Greece with voluntary PSI, which was the best possible compromise on debt restructuring. EFSF had been established by then and would be the main financing vehicle rather than the bilateral loans of the First Programme. A Commission Task Force for Greece, composed mainly of European Commission officials, was also announced to provide the Greek government with technical support in its reform efforts (European Court of Auditors, 2017; European Stability Mechanism, 2019). Although this was an encouraging development, the formal negotiations for the Second Programme that started on 29 August proved to be very difficult. Finance Minister Venizelos was trying to push for growth measures to be included in the programme but the Troika took a tough stance, claiming that many of the structural reforms from the First Programme had not been fully implemented, for example the opening up of regulated professions and a reform of tax administration.[25] This is in line with the proposal that partial implementation leads to a lack of credibility and thus limited room for manoeuvre. The tension was such that the Troika representatives walked out of the negotiations on 2 September to put pressure on Greece. Poul Thomsen, the IMF representative, explained that the level of trust had been low since the Troika's summer visits to Athens, when it was made obvious that some Ministries were purposely delaying reforms (Roumeliotis, 2012, p. 166). In order to improve the climate and regain trust, Venizelos and Papandreou got support from the government to pass even more measures, such as the amendment of the labour reserve and a speeding up of privatisations.

Nevertheless, the German Finance Minister proposed a friendly 'Grexit' at a private meeting on 16 September during an informal Eurogroup meeting in Poland, but the proposal was immediately rejected by the Greek team (Papakonstantinou, 2016). In light of the impasse, the Troika representatives returned to the negotiating table a few days later and the fifth review of the programme was completed, taking into account the draft budget for 2012 and the measures introduced; this allowed the sixth tranche of the loan to be disbursed (European Commission, 2011b). On 26 October, the Euro summit approved the new loan of €130 billion for Greece as well as a generous haircut of the Greek debt with PSI (European Stability Mechanism, 2019). This was a great success for Greece given the difficulty of the negotiations and the lack of trust during this particular period of the crisis. The climate back home was tense and there were violent incidents against the President of the Democracy, Karolos Papoulias, the Prime Minister and MPs whenever an opportunity arose, for example at the annual commemoration of the end of the German occupation on 28 October (Mandravelis, 2019, pp. 83–102). In response, George Papandreou announced on 31 October 2011 that he was willing to call a referendum on this last decision reached in Brussels. He stated: 'In these circumstances, the citizen should act first and have the first word. A dominant role without other mediators … For the new agreement, we should hold a referendum. The Greek people and each citizen should decide separately … We believe in citizens, we believe in their judgement, we believe in their decision' (Papakonstantinou, 2016, p. 299).

The call for a referendum caused turbulence both domestically and internationally, and Papandreou was soon forced to cancel it and resign. Domestically, the aim of the referendum was to push the opposition into a compromise, since a vote against the agreement would most probably lead Greece to a default and to exiting the Eurozone (Papandreou, 2015). Internationally, the markets saw the referendum as a sign of instability and uncertainty, so immediately reacted by further downgrading the Greek economy (Smith and Rushe, 2011). The European leaders were also unsupportive. Although no one could openly object to Papandreou's decision, there was a lot of apprehension, and when Sarkozy was informed he suggested that Papandreou should present the people with a clear question: yes or no to the Euro (Papakonstantinou, 2016). This triggered a frenzy about a possible Grexit in the international media, increasing the pressure on the Greek government (Dinas and Rori, 2013). Support for the referendum quickly evaporated, even within PASOK, with the Minister of Finance Venizelos denouncing the idea. This was the last nail in the coffin and Papandreou was forced to resign.

Almost a year after the implementation of the First Economic Adjustment Programme for Greece began, both the markets and creditors considered it insufficient mainly due to the continually growing Greek public debt despite, and to some extent because of, the austerity measures (European Court of Auditors, 2017). Additionally, the fiscal measures taken were probably too ambitious, jeopardising the programme's success from the start, as the IMF's representative Poul Thomsen (2019) later explained in a speech: 'The original programme foresaw fiscal adjustment of more than 12 per cent of GDP over three years. Although not unprecedented, this was ambitious by international comparisons and especially in view of Greece's track-record.'

During the implementation period of the First Economic Adjustment Programme, there are examples of both the Greek government's limited room for manoeuvre and the Troika's lack of flexibility. Although fiscal adjustment or a softening of the austerity measures was not negotiable the government was given some leeway on structural reforms, such as the labour market reform. This was because the issue was not very salient at the time since the cost-cutting measures were the absolute priority and there was a reasonable level of trust between the government and the Troika (see Proposals One and Three). In addition, partial reversals took place even during the implementation phase (e.g. labour reserve and EETHDE) because the cost of implementation was very high for the government and the cost of reversal did not seem so significant. However, these partial reversals, together with the lack of progress in areas such as privatisations and the opening up of regulated professions, created tensions with the Troika and damaged the level of trust. The announcement of the referendum by Papandreou strained the relationship even further (see Proposal Three).

November 2011–June 2012: agreement of the Second Programme – interim government

The situation in Greece in November 2011 was so bad, with a looming default, that there was no time for elections before the signing of the Second Economic Adjustment Programme. The yields soared to 17.92 per cent (see Introduction). An interim government was quickly formed, with Lucas Papademos, ex-Vice-President of the ECB, as the Prime Minister. This government had three specific goals: first, implement PSI; secondly, negotiate the MoU of the Second Economic Programme for Greece; and thirdly, hold elections (Bank of Greece, 2014). The two first goals had to be achieved within its first two months in office. Under the threat of default, ND, PASOK and the right-wing Laikos Orthodoxos Synagermos (Popular Orthodox Rally, LAOS) formed a governing coalition. This was the first time that some type of cooperation between the two biggest political parties had been achieved.

At the Eurogroup meeting of 21 February 2012, the IMF representative pushed for a larger haircut since the forecast for the public debt had deteriorated. After negotiations with the banks, the final percentage of the haircut was set at 53.5 per cent rather than the 50 per cent agreed back in October. The successful implementation of PSI was a precondition for the start of the Second Adjustment Programme for Greece (Eurogroup, 2012a). Two days later, Parliament voted on the necessary legislation outlining the parameters for the exchange of old bonds by the private sector (Law 4050/2012). The total amount of the restructured debt was €206 billion out of a total of €350 billion, and it involved both debt to international investors and to the Greek banks and insurance funds. The repayment of the remaining amount was extended to 2042 and the interest rate was cut to 3.65 per cent (Kazakos, 2019). The debt restructuring was significant although, according to Bank of Greece estimates, the final gain was only €51.2 billion as new debt had to be issued to recapitalise the Greek banks and for other governmental obligations (Bank of Greece, 2014, p. 96).

Negotiations for the MoU of the Second Economic Programme for Greece resumed on 17 January 2012 and needed to be concluded before the Greek government had to repay bonds that were expiring in March. Default was imminent yet again. The Papademos government's main aim in the negotiations was to include more structural and fewer fiscal reforms because Greece had already achieved a significant fiscal adjustment. As Papadimos was a technocrat and a trusted insider in EU institutions, the climate between the government and the Troika was positive. His time at the ECB had assured Papadimos of a strong network of people in Europe with whom he shared a common language (Dijsselbloem, 2018, p. 80). Moreover, a more relaxed approach to debt restructuring and fiscal accommodation was possible following the signing of the ESM treaty (Moschella, 2016). Nevertheless, the Second Programme for Greece would be a continuation of the austerity doctrine and the structural reforms of the First Programme. The key difference was the PSI.

Back home, Papademos was acting as a mediator between the three parties of the interim government (later, two parties following the withdrawal of LAOS) so that a strong, uniform position could be presented to the Troika. This was complicated by the fact that elections would be held in June so the parties were considering the electoral costs of their decisions.[26] A key advisor to the Papademos government explains that, although the negotiations were held at a technocratic level between experts, at the end of the day decisions were made by the parties that had to vote the programme through Parliament.[27] Agreement was reached with the Troika on many of the issues, such as the improvement of public administration and the strengthening of competition in services and goods markets.

However, other issues, such as labour and pension reforms, were more contentious in terms of the time and level of adjustment required.[28] Regarding labour reform a government official explains: 'the final result of the negotiation, which was intense ..., was to abandon the abolishment of the 13th and 14th salary. We agreed on a two-part reduction in the minimum wage: general and for younger workers, like other countries.'[29] The disagreement over pension reform was even stronger because the leader of ND, Antonis Samaras, would not accept a further cut in supplementary pensions (Papakonstantinou, 2016, p. 310). It was difficult to find a compromise with the Troika on this issue but the government managed to postpone the decision to a future negotiation during one of the programme reviews.[30] Interestingly, although the credibility of the Papademos government was higher than that of PASOK at the end of the term, its room for manoeuvre was limited (see Proposal Three). The reluctance of the creditors to allow major changes in the programme may be explained by the fact that it was only an interim government and elections were imminent.

The Second Economic Adjustment Programme for Greece went to the vote in the Greek Parliament on 12 February amid discontent. In light of the forthcoming elections, more than forty MPs from PASOK and ND refused to vote in favour and were removed from their parties. As soon as the PSI was completed and some urgent legislation was passed on prerequisites for the first instalment of the Second Programme, Papademos announced the elections for May 2012, one month earlier than initially agreed. Politicians and especially ND were not willing to wait any longer (Mandravelis, 2019). However, the party landscape had changed significantly, with PASOK and ND in a weakened position. Five new parties covering the whole political spectrum entered the competition.

The elections on 6 May did not result in a government, as ND obtained only 18.85 per cent of the vote and was unable to form a coalition government. Both ND and PASOK were punished for their support of the Memoranda, while anti-Memorandum parties such as SYRIZA, ANEL (Independent Greeks) and Golden Dawn were strengthened (Dinas and Rori, 2013). Panagiotis Pikramenos, a judge, was appointed caretaker Prime Minister until a second election on 7 June 2012. The electoral campaign clearly defined the parties with pro- and anti-Memorandum positions. Although ND won the elections and increased its share to 29.7 per cent, SYRIZA was the biggest winner, going from 4.6 per cent of the vote in 2009 to 26.9 per cent in 2012, thus establishing itself as the key anti-Memorandum opposition party. Soon after the elections, ND formed a coalition government with PASOK (12.3 per cent) and DIMAR (Democratic Left) (6.3 per cent). This was the first elected coalition government in modern Greece since the short-lived coalition in 1989–1990, signifying a change in Greek politics and a new phase in the crisis (Dinas and Rori, 2013).

Negotiations during this period were taking place in a more positive climate as the ESM had at least given a structure at the European level. The PSI can be seen as an important concession on the part of the lenders and an acknowledgement of the significant and quick fiscal adjustment made by Greece. However, the Greek technocratic government's room for manoeuvre during the negotiations of the terms of the Second Programme remained limited as the Troika was still focused on austerity measures. Nevertheless, there were some concessions, including on the 13th and 14th salaries of the private sector and the delay of decisions on further pension cuts. This modest leeway was largely due to the relationship of trust between the Papademos government and the Troika, rather than increased implementation as proposed in Proposal Three. What is also glaring is that fierce competition between the political parties during this period leading up to the forthcoming elections prevented them from uniting behind the interim government and thus limited its capacity to negotiate.

June 2012–January 2015: implementation of the Second Programme – the Samaras government

The main task of the new government was to implement the Second Programme and stabilise the economy in order to return to the markets and to what was perceived as normality. Some reforms were still pending from the First Programme, including the privatisation programme, the opening up of the goods' markets and of the regulated professions, and the deepening of the pension and labour market reforms. There was no let-up in the economic recession, government revenue was low and unemployment was still rising (Bank of Greece, 2014). The first few months were exploratory for both the Troika and the government as attempts were made to improve the climate and rebuild trust.[31] The new Prime Minister, Antonis Samaras, had been a fierce opponent of both the Memorandum and the Troika during his electoral campaign, but now had to prove he would implement what had been signed. Additionally, this type of government was such a novelty for Greece that Samaras had to show both at home and in Europe that his coalition government would last.

A visit to Berlin shortly after he took office sought to reassure the lenders. The choice of Yiannis Stournaras, who was more of a technocrat than a party member, for Minister of Finance served the same purpose (Papakonstantinou,

2016). These notwithstanding, his government's relationship with the Troika never gained momentum and always suffered from a lack of trust and low levels of credibility (see Proposal Three).

Implementation gathered pace in early November when several important measures (the 2013 budget, the updated Medium Term Fiscal Strategy Plan 2013–2016 and the 4093/2012 law introducing a number of the delayed reforms) were all brought into Parliament and marginally approved with 153 votes. Most, if not all, the measures confirmed the austerity path and included pensions cuts, raising the pension age threshold by two years, abolishing bonuses for the public sector, reducing the salaries in special categories of the public sector, agreeing to cut 25,000 public sector jobs over the next two years and reducing the minimum wage for the private sector. The same law also introduced a pilot scheme of the Guaranteed Minimum Income to compensate for some of the cuts (Law 4093/2012 and Kazakos, 2019). This satisfied the Eurogroup (Eurogroup, 2012b, 2012c) and was followed by the release of a €43.7 billion tranche of the loan. At the same time, the Greek banking system went through a major restructuring which led to the merging of smaller banks into four 'systemic' banks. In early 2013, the banks were recapitalised due to the losses caused by the PSI (Papakonstantinou, 2016). The positive climate lasted for the first half of 2013 and was reinforced by the successful privatisation of OPAP, the public gaming company.

Autumn 2012 was one of the most difficult periods for the cooperation between the IMF and the EC, which caused some of the delays at the end of 2012. In the IMF's World Economic Outlook for 2012, two of its chief economists noted that the IMF's fiscal multipliers (namely the negative effect of decreases in fiscal spending on a nation's GDP) were underestimated, which explained why the recession in Greece was worse than expected. The IMF was an advocate of a slower economic adjustment and further debt restructuring. The EC and especially Germany were firm supporters of continuing on the same path of rapid economic adjustment and were not willing to give the wrong signal to other countries in trouble (Blustein, 2016, pp. 349–359).[32] A very close collaborator of the Greek Prime Minister explained: 'The unseen dimension of the story here is the problems in the relationship between Germany, the EC and the IMF because of Greece which ... are now huge.'[33]

In the end, the Eurogroup agreed to lower interest rates further and delay maturities. Greece was promised that the Eurogroup would consider a further debt relief if the country managed to achieve a budget surplus (Eurogroup, 2012d). The tension between the EC and the IMF, however, did not mean that Greece could play one institution against the other. Quite the opposite. A Troika official explains: 'I must say though that it was often the Greeks themselves who pushed for these very ambitious targets and you can say that it was possibly under pressure from the Europeans to do so.'[34] Indeed, the government was trying to gain trust by over-promising. The IMF was not entirely satisfied with Greece's performance and was unconvinced by the ambitious targets of quick adjustment (International Monetary Fund, 2012a, 2013a). Thomsen, the IMF's representative, was very sceptical about Samaras and his circle, and there was often little trust or steady cooperation at the higher level. This negative climate resulted not only from the Greek government's delays but also from the clashes of personality between Thomsen and the Greek team (Blustein, 2016).[35] This probably explains why the government's credibility and room for manoeuvre was not improved by the progress with reforms, contrary to Proposal Three.

In fact, many reforms went forward between 2012 and 2014. One of the government's most controversial decisions was the closure of the National Broadcasting Television Agency (the Hellenic Broadcasting Corporation (ERT)). This was an indirect measure stemming from the Second MoU (European Commission, 2012a) and was implemented in 2013 as part of a series of closures of public sector organisations that were deemed non-essential or no longer necessary (Law 4172/2013). It sparked protests from the opposition and the withdrawal of the Democratic Left party from the governing coalition as DIMAR could not accept the closure on ideological grounds.[36] Although the governing coalition was weakened by the unfortunate decision to close ERT, many reforms were successful and were maintained (at least their key features) and PASOK and ND still held the majority in Parliament. The fiscal and tax administration reform, which was considered fruitful and essential to the economic adjustment, took place with the technical on-site support of the IMF (Law 4270/2014).[37] In contrast, the technical support from the Task Force for public administration did not have such a positive outcome (Kazakos, 2019).[38] Although the public administration reform successfully reduced public sector personnel, it failed to introduce a meaningful evaluation system for public sector employees or fully implement the new organisational charts for all Ministries because of resistance and the impending 2015 elections (Ladi and Katsikas, 2017; Spanou, 2018).

Progress was made in introducing the necessary regulatory framework to open up the product markets but the regulatory reform following the OECD competition assessment toolkit proved difficult to implement. Indeed, the media's dramatisation of the potential effects of opening up the bread, milk, medicine and book markets further undermined the government (Chatzidakis, 2018).[39] There was a gradual opening up of regulated professions, making them easier to access, but vested interests prevented the abolition of internal regulations. Professions requiring higher education degrees and specialised competencies, such as doctors and lawyers, remained more closed

(Kotsi *et al.*, 2016; Stolfi and Papamakariou, 2019). The above examples demonstrate the wide range of the reforms requested and implemented. The government was generally willing to go ahead with reforms, although some could only be partially implemented due to the reactions from the opposition and vested interests. This always lowered the Troika's trust in the government and hence its room for manoeuvre, as discussed in chapter 1.

Despite all these difficulties and tensions, 2014 began with the unexpected news that the Greek economy was showing signs of recovery and, importantly, that a primary surplus was recorded in the 2013 and 2014 budgets. However, neither the Eurogroup nor the IMF would discuss further debt relief despite the 2012 Eurogroup decision. The current account balance dropped significantly to 2 per cent of GDP in 2013 vis-à-vis 151 per cent in 2008. The pace of recession dropped and there was negative inflation in 2013 for the first time in forty-five years (Bank of Greece, 2014, pp. 108–109). To capture the positive climate, the government accessed the market in April 2014 and managed to sell bonds to private investors for the first time in four years.

The excitement about the positive developments in the economy was not shared by the population. Although there were fewer demonstrations, SYRIZA's opposition was hardening. Its appeal was reflected in the June 2014 European elections when SYRIZA came first with 26.52 per cent, four points higher than ND (Papakonstantinou, 2016). The relationship between the government and the Troika also took a turn for the worse in June 2014, probably explaining the IMF's unwillingness to take action on debt relief. The Troika and especially the IMF's Poul Thomsen were unhappy when Harry Theocharis, the General Secretary for Public Revenue, was forced to resign following disagreements with the government. Theocharis was a respected technocrat who had been appointed to this new position in 2013, where he was supposed to stay for five years regardless of government wishes. His remit was to improve tax collection and tackle tax evasion, which were both of paramount significance to the IMF. Additionally, in an attempt to show the public that SYRIZA was not the only party opposing the Troika, Samaras reshuffled the government and replaced some of the Ministers undertaking reforms. Although the newly appointed Minister of Finance, Gikas Hardouvelis, had significant experience and had served as an advisor to Papademos, the Troika remained unconvinced and this marked the start of another period of little trust (Blustein, 2016; Papakonstantinou, 2016).[40]

The deteriorating relationship with the Troika meant the last six months of 2014 were very difficult for the Samaras government. One of the government's policy advisors describes the atmosphere during the last semester of 2014: 'Basically, the Ministers were sending emails and not only did the Troika not visit but they didn't even respond. They didn't want to have anything to do with us. This means that after June 14, they had turned their back to us.'[41] Instead of Greece following Portugal and Ireland in a 'clean' exit from the bailout, it was hit by a new political crisis that led to the January 2015 elections. Following the slight improvement in the economy and fearing SYRIZA's mounting strength, Samaras wanted to claim victory and announce Greece's exit from the bailout. The debate was between a 'clean' exit, that is, both the EU and IMF parts of the programme would terminate at the end of the year, a precautionary credit line with light surveillance or a shorter Third Programme for Greece (Papakonstantinou, 2016). However, the Troika tightened its stance and refused to close the Second Programme and release its last tranche. They insisted that Athens should not have missed any of the programme benchmarks on structural reforms and demanded more cuts in pensions and a further increase in taxes (Henning, 2017).[42]

By September, the negotiations had been moved to Paris to avoid the publicity attracted by the visits to Athens. Poul Thomsen, who had been promoted by then, played a decisive role and supported the German line of zero tolerance for any unfinished measures or lightening of the programme's conditionality (Blustein, 2016; Henning, 2017). The Troika would not even travel to Athens for negotiations, saying they would not return to the negotiating table until all the reforms were completed. The government seemed unable to change its position and pass new measures despite an email from the Finance Minister in November promising to take more austerity actions (Papakonstantinou, 2016). The end came with the Eurogroup's decision to grant Greece a two-month extension to the programme since agreement was not in reach and there was a danger of the last tranche being lost (Eurogroup, 2014). The Troika's insistence was due to their complete lack of trust in the Samaras government; they probably felt better results and more reforms would be achieved with a fresh government in power. Shortly after, Samaras announced the election of a new President of the Republic, despite knowing this would entail parliamentary elections as he did not have the necessary majority in Parliament to ensure the election of a new President. The ensuing elections on 25 January 2015 saw SYRIZA triumph with 36.34 per cent of the vote, an increase of 9.5 per cent on the 2012 elections (Ministry of Interior, 2015).

The period between June 2012 and January 2015 was all about implementation and clinging to power. The coalition government did not have the political capital or the luxury of time to make substantial changes to the measures already agreed by Papademos's interim government. After the PSI, which was seen as a major concession, the Troika was not willing to grant the government much leeway by allowing partial implementation of some of the reforms. This was particularly true after the increase in tensions in June 2014. Many reforms were indeed implemented, or at least put on track, during this period. However, in contrast to Proposal Three, implementation of reforms did not increase the government's credibility and thus its room for manoeuvre in this period. Personal relationships and lack of trust at a personal level could not be overcome that easily. Interestingly, what continued to play an important role in the development of the programme was the relationship between Germany, the IMF and the EC.

January 2015–September 2015: first SYRIZA government – negotiations for the Third Programme – referendum

As SYRIZA's electoral success was not enough for a majority government, the first task was to find a partner to form a coalition government. The choice of the far-right ANEL was unexpected but what brought these two incongruous partners together was their mutual rejection of the bailout and their populist appeal. Additionally, ANEL's power was just enough for SYRIZA to maintain autonomy in the Cabinet (Rori, 2016). Alexis Tsipras became Prime Minister and he appointed a heterogeneous Cabinet that not only represented the different components of his party, but also gave the new coalition partner six Ministers including its leader, Panos Kammenos, as Defence Minister. However, the new Finance Minister, Yianis Varoufakis, proved the most controversial figure. The negotiations with the Troika were difficult from the outset as one of the government's first decisions was to halt the Troika's access to the Ministries and only allow low-level technical visits to Athens.[43] Jeroen Dijsselbloem's visit to Athens in his capacity as President of the Eurogroup, just a few days after the new government took office, was the first of a number of Varoufakis's futile encounters with EU leaders and officials. He remembers, for example, that 'Varoufakis seemed to have a huge talent in provoking hostility. This is what happened in our joint press conference in Athens' (Dijsselbloem, 2018, p. 160).

One of Varoufakis's first threats was that Greece would not pay the ECB a debt instalment due in the summer. This, together with the rejection of the programme, led to the ECB's suspension of Greece's waiver on 4 February. The ECB waiver allowed Greek government bonds to be accepted as collateral for regular auctions of ECB cash despite their junk rating (European Central Bank, 2015). The economy was fast deteriorating with yields reaching 9.72 per cent, and trust was quickly evaporating especially after Varoufakis' first Eurogroup meeting on 11 February (Dendrinou and Varvitsioti, 2019).

The imminent danger of default forced the Greek government to reverse a previous decision by requesting another four-month extension to the Second Economic Adjustment Programme, which was due to finish at the end of

February. The extension granted on 20 February required the government to come up with a list of measures that it was willing to implement. An agreement would have to be reached with the lenders by the end of April before the release of the last instalment of the Second Programme. This would give the Greek government and its lenders two months to negotiate a new agreement (European Commission, undated a).

This first compromise made by the government created a heavy climate in Athens and the party. By then, the Troika had been renamed 'Institutions'[44] and the negotiations, when they resumed, were moved to the Hilton Hotel in Athens since access to the Ministries was still denied. A government official explains: 'This period was full of symbolisms.'[45] However, as no progress was made, the technical negotiations were moved to Brussels and became known as the 'Brussels group' negotiations. These discussions were very general and ideologically loaded given that SYRIZA was not willing to discuss specific alternative measures but was concerned primarily about showing what made the previous programmes socially unfair and ineffective (Dendrinou and Varvitsioti, 2019). One of the members of the Greek delegation at the Brussels group explains: 'We really did not have a very concrete plan. Our tactic was mainly to criticise the MoU, trying to remove some of the measures or improve them to some extent ... But we really did not have the level of analysis or the specification of a policy and detailed plan like an MoU.'[46]

What is interesting during this period and until the July referendum is that, apart from the technical Brussels group negotiations, two more levels of negotiations – Varoufakis's negotiations at the Eurogroup and Tsipras's high-level negotiations with European leaders – were running simultaneously and without much coordination, and this often led to conflicting results.[47] The results of Varoufakis's continued attempts to negotiate with his counterparts at the Eurogroup and the IMF were disappointing; indeed, the Eurogroup meeting in Riga on 24 April will be remembered for the Greek Minister's complete isolation (Dendrinou and Varvitsioti, 2019; Varoufakis, 2017). As a result, Tsipras was forced to replace Varoufakis with Tsakalotos as the key negotiator, although Varoufakis continued to represent Greece at the Eurogroup. Meanwhile, Tsipras spent most of March trying to politicise the negotiations in order to negotiate his proposals outlined in a five-page letter sent to President Hollande and Chancellor Merkel on 15 March. He asked for the reinstatement of the ECB waiver so as to regain liquidity, and for the start of negotiations for a third, more socially just, programme including debt relief. He refused to allow the return of the Institutions and explained that the government had no liquidity so its only option would be to stop paying its creditors, including the IMF, which would mean defaulting (Spiegel, 2015). An informal summit attended by Tsipras, Hollande,

Merkel and EU officials took place on 19 March, followed by a quite successful but long overdue visit to Berlin on 23 March. However, nothing came of these high-level discussions as the European counterparts insisted the proposals had to be quantified and discussed at the Eurogroup (Henning, 2017). In contrast to Proposal Two, Tsipras had miniscule room for manoeuvre and the change in government and partisanship did not lead to changes in the MoU. In accordance with our argument (Proposal Three), the government's refusal to implement the MoU meant low credibility and thus a lack of capacity to change the programme.

While the negotiations with the creditors were ongoing and liquidity was diminishing, legislation was passed in mid-March to provide measures for what had been labelled the ongoing 'humanitarian crisis' (Law 4320/2015). These measures included free electricity for households that had been disconnected during the crisis and rent and food subsidies for people living in extreme poverty. The cleaners and school guards that had lost their jobs under previous government measures were also rehired (Kazakos, 2019). The government reopened the ERT and re-recruited the dismissed personnel (Law 4324/2015). The fiscal cost of these measures and reversals was not high, but they were symbolically important for Tsipras who wanted to show the Greek people that he was true to his pre-electoral promises.

The lenders were taken aback by these reversals and the government's credibility was damaged even further (European Stability Mechanism, 2019). Tsipras's fruitless visit to Moscow at the height of the liquidity crisis in search of alternative loans was also controversial (Dendrinou and Varvitsioti, 2019); one day later, the Greek government repaid a loan instalment to the IMF just in time – a move it repeated several times. A few weeks later the government was even forced to use the reserves of municipalities and other public organisations since its treasury was literally empty. Grexit was back on the table, with Schäuble and other leaders openly suggesting a time-out from the Eurozone. A plan B scenario for Greece leaving the Eurozone had been revived, and a team of EU and IMF officials were already working on details (Dendrinou and Varvitsioti, 2019).[48]

Despite the changes in the Greek negotiating team, the negotiations had stalled by June 2015, aggravated by the differences between the IMF and the EC on the viability of the debt and proposed austerity measures. A Greek government representative at the Brussels group explains:

> What they always wanted was to bring something in common as Institutions, let's say as the opponent but there were delays because there were objections from the IMF… there were times at the Brussels group when we were waiting for a document to come from their side and days passed without the document arriving. We would go to meetings and nobody would come and this was because they couldn't agree among themselves.[49]

On 1 June, Merkel personally took the initiative to breach the deadlock and convened a meeting with Hollande, Juncker, Draghi and Lagarde. Based on a proposal prepared by the Commission, they managed to come up with a common position which Juncker presented to Tsipras on 3 June with a 'take it or leave it' message (Henning, 2017). The only real concessions that the creditors had made were to lower the surplus for 2015 and 2016 to 3.5 rather than 4.5 per cent and to grant a further reduction of interest rates on the loans. In addition, they were requesting further pension cuts and reforms, a continuation of austerity and an increase in VAT (*Reforms for the Completion of the Current Programme and Beyond*, undated). This was followed by several weeks of intense but fruitless negotiations with Tsipras at the highest level and with Chouliarakis, a moderate member of the Brussels group, leading the technical negotiations. By this time, Varoufakis had been excluded from the negotiations (Varoufakis, 2017). The level of trust in the Greek government was at its lowest. Indeed, the government was split, with some believing it would be better to have a complete rupture even if it led to Grexit[50] and others trying to reach a compromise (Dendrinou and Varvitsioti, 2019).[51] The lenders and the Greek government were still trying to come to an agreement during the EU summit of 24–25 June when Tsipras surprised everyone on 27 June with the announcement of a referendum.

The referendum took place one week later on 5 July 2015, which gave little time for any meaningful debate or information campaign. The credibility of the referendum was weakened by a number of institutional flaws, for example the 'no' answer was placed first and the ballot referred to technical documents in English that were not the Institutions' final offer (Crespy and Ladi, 2019). However, the single most important event was the closure of the banks just two days after the announcement of the referendum. It was followed by capital controls imposed by the government in response to the ECB's decision not to raise the ceiling of the Emergency Liquidity Assistance – a mechanism that allows central banks in the Euro area to receive emergency credit.[52] The imminent expiration of the current bailout agreement on 30 June, the refusal of the lenders to give the extension requested by the government because of the referendum, and the €1.5 billion payment to the IMF that was due immediately, meant that default was closer than ever. The one-week campaign was tense and polarised. The 'No' campaign was saying that the referendum was a powerful negotiation weapon that would empower the Prime Minister; it was national pride and dignity that were at stake and not the currency or Eurozone membership. In contrast, the 'Yes' supporters in agreement with Greece's lenders framed the referendum as a vote for Greece's membership in the Eurozone and potentially the EU, describing the referendum as an existential threat and the 'No' vote as a suicide. The result of the vote was 61.31 per cent 'No' and 38.69 per cent 'Yes'. Void and blank votes were 5.80 per cent (Crespy and Ladi, 2019).

This clear victory for Alexis Tsipras and the government had unexpected consequences. Free from his provocative Minister of Finance, Yianis Varoufakis, and with the people on his side, rather than acting upon the 'No' vote in a dramatic way that could lead to the country's exit from the Eurozone, Tsipras returned to the negotiating table. Crespy and Ladi (2019) argue that the referendum was primarily about internal party politics and it allowed Tsipras to clear his government and party of the most radical voices as the people were still in favour of staying in the Euro. Just one day after the referendum Alexis Tsipras asked the opposition to agree to the continuation of the negotiations rather than leading the country to rupture. A few days later the Parliament passed legislation with preliminary austerity measures so that the negotiations for a Third Economic Adjustment Programme could continue (Law 4334/2015).

The Euro summit of 12 July was the last act in the drama. The negotiations lasted seventeen hours when the European partners took a very tough line with Tsipras. The German Finance Minister, Schäuble brought a five-year exit plan from the Eurozone to the table and a Luxembourg-based trust fund authorised the selling off of Greek state assets. Greece found itself marginalised without many allies and the French delegation acted as the main mediator between the Greeks and the rest of Europe.[53]

The agreement for a third bailout programme of €86 billion for the next three years came as a relief to everyone. Even before reaching an agreement on the details of the programme, the Eurogroup approved a bridge loan for Greece to pay the IMF and ECB and avoid default. The Third Programme was an ESM programme to which the IMF was not contributing due to the ongoing disagreement with the European Commission on debt sustainability and a possible haircut. However, the IMF's participation in the missions to Greece would continue and it could enter the programme if agreement on debt sustainability was reached after the first review (Henning, 2017). The fiscal adjustment and structural reforms supervised by the Institutions remained in place and the underlying reasoning of the programme was the same as previously. The Greek government agreed to continue with austerity, increase VAT, implement a pension reform, labour and product market reforms, and a privatisation programme (European Commission, 2015a): basically, everything that had been rejected during the previous six months. Additionally, the levels of trust were so low that the programme required the implementation of actions before any loan tranche disbursement. An attempt was made to add a parallel programme mainly with the social policies the government wanted to pursue but it had to meet the conditionality agreed and most of it was soon abandoned.[54]

As a result, one-third of SYRIZA's MPs, who became known as the left-wing faction, came into direct conflict with the government during the vote on the Third Programme on 14 August and resigned. Tsipras called for an early election to be held on 20 September, when he managed to renew his power with very few losses. Rori (2016) argues that since no austerity measures had been implemented since the party was first elected, there was not much for which to punish SYRIZA. On the contrary, citizens seemed to approve of the hard negotiation strategy although they evaluated the final agreement as worse. To the disappointment of the lenders, SYRIZA renewed its coalition with ANEL rather than including a more pro-European partner in government. The MPs of the left-wing faction split by SYRIZA did not manage to enter Parliament.

The negotiations for the Third Adjustment Programme for Greece took place in such a tense environment and trust levels were so low that the government had very little capacity to alter the previous measures or insert new policies. The lack of implementation of the measures and the rejection of the Second Programme had weakened the Greek government's credibility and gave it no room for manoeuvre in the negotiations. Although some minimal changes could have been achieved as a result of the Brussels group technical negotiations, the referendum stalled the process and worsened the Greek government's negotiating position even further. Contrary to Proposal Two, that change in partisanship would make a difference, the fact that a left-wing government had come into power made little difference to the conditionality of the Third Programme. However, some symbolic reversals, such as the reopening of ERT or the hiring of cleaners, took place as soon as SYRIZA came to power. The benefits of these reversals were concentrated on small groups that had supported SYRIZA in the elections and their fiscal cost was minimal and diffused. But these reversals did have a cost as they damaged the government's credibility and its overall ability to negotiate changes with the lenders during this first period of SYRIZA's governance.

September 2015–August 2018: second SYRIZA government – implementation of the Third Programme

On taking office, the new government was obliged to start implementing a programme that it claimed had been imposed on them. A government Minister from that time explains: 'The logic of necessary evil … for me personally there is no recognition of the paternity and ownership of the programme.'[55]

The combination of the lack of ownership, governing experience and technical expertise led to slow implementation and this meant the first review of the programme was only completed eight months later in June 2016 (European Commission, 2016a). A representative of the Institutions notes that 'a lot of the delay in organising, closing the first review was actually due to the pure inexperience of most of the counterparts in Athens that required hand-holding and, you know ... most of the work we did and I would say still do, is technical assistance."[56] However, the tension between the IMF and the EC over further austerity measures versus a promise for future debt relief was also responsible for the delay (Henning, 2017).

To avoid a further clash with the party and show citizens that a left government did make a difference, Tsipras implemented a 'parallel programme' pushing forward a more social agenda (Law 4368/2016). As discussed in chapter 1, partisanship did signify a preference for a different mix of policies but SYRIZA was unable to implement most of them. The 'parallel programme' was more modest than that which SYRIZA had promised but it was the best it could do given the new MoU. One of SYRIZA's ministers claimed that: 'The reason we agreed [to the Third Programme] is that we believe with a parallel programme you can ease austerity and more importantly because the exercise of governmental authority is a weapon that cannot be surrendered'.[57] However, the situation on the ground was much harsher and the government's room for manoeuvre for introducing new policies was limited. Eight months of unsuccessful negotiations had seriously damaged the economy and the banks needed to be recapitalised again in October 2015 due to losses suffered during the negotiation period (Pagoulatos, 2018). The levels of trust remained very low and a growing immigration crisis was putting greater strain on the Greek government (Mylonas, 2016).

From the start of 2016, the Greek government implemented structural and cost-cutting reforms as well as tax increases. One of the first laws, passed in February 2016, focused on social issues (Law 4368/16). Among the most important of these was the rebranding of the Guaranteed Minimum Income to Social Solidarity Income and its implementation beyond the initial pilot programme. This allowed the government to take ownership of this specific measure and to show it was in line with its left ideology. Additionally, free access to health care was guaranteed for uninsured and vulnerable groups. On the other hand, the pension reform was not reversed despite the government's wishes, and new legislation continued to cut and freeze pensions as well as implementing a unified social security system (EFKA). However, the lowest pensions and the current pensioners (rather than future generations) were now protected and some of the cost was passed on to freelance professions (e.g. lawyers) (Kazakos, 2019 and Law 4387/2016). Another set of reforms passed in light of the first review involved the implementation of a fiscal mechanism that ensured additional measures would automatically be implemented to address any divergence from macroeconomic targets, and the transformation of the semi-autonomous public revenue administration to a fully autonomous agency (the AADE) (Dimitrakopoulos and Passas, 2020, and Law 4389/2016). The first review was successfully concluded and the Greek banks regained access to regular refinancing from the ECB in June 2016.

The second review of the Third Programme was also long and often turbulent, taking another year to complete (European Commission, 2017a). Although the government was making progress with some actions, such as combating tax evasion and preparing the ground for privatisations, there were often conflicts between the government and the Institutions on areas like the labour market (Kazakos, 2019). However, conflict was also the dominant *modus vivendi* between the Institutions, where the IMF and Germany were adamant about the strict implementation of the austerity measures while the IMF and EC continued to disagree about debt sustainability. A Greek government official describes the tension: 'One of the Heads of the Institutions told me: "For each hour that I am negotiating with you, I need another four hours with the rest of the Institutions."'[58]

Interestingly, the Institutions were also tired of Greece and of pushing for the implementation of all the measures during the period of the Third Programme, so they were concentrating on the most important reforms. This was not because the levels of trust in the Greek government had improved but was largely due to reform fatigue on the part of the lenders as they had been calling for these reforms since 2010. An official from the Institutions recalls: 'At this moment, to be absolutely honest, the development plan has ended up a mix of various things that the government wants to reverse and for which the Institutions and especially the Commission has given up and says, "OK, go ahead", especially as far as the labour market is concerned. "Do what you think is right."'[59]

Tension with the Institutions emerged again when the government decided to distribute part of the surplus achieved to pensioners and other vulnerable groups in the form of a one-off benefit, without prior agreement. However, further pensions cuts and tax increases were then implemented and the second review was concluded in June 2017 (Law 3372/2017 and European Commission, 2017a). The terrorist attack injuring the ex-Prime Minister Papademos on 25 May proved a gloomy reminder of the country's continued instability.

The second review of the programme was followed by two positive events. First, the country successfully managed to borrow from the market at the end of July 2017 for the first time since 2014. Secondly, the European

Council decided to close the deficit procedure for Greece in September as the deficit had fallen below the 3 per cent threshold. Meanwhile, the government's privatisations continued and included Piraeus port, railways, regional airports and parts of the energy sector, while others, such as the gold mines in Halkidiki and the Ellinikon (old airport) regeneration, were delayed (Kazakos, 2019). In January 2018, the vote on a final law of austerity and other pending measures led to the closure of the third review (Law 4512/2018). The economy was recovering, although the excessive surpluses of 2017 and 2018 were related not only to growth but also to high taxation.

The international feeling towards Greece was also improved by the signing of the Prespes agreement in June 2018; this resolved a long-lasting dispute regarding changing the name of FYROM, Greece's northern neighbour, to North Macedonia. The European partners wanted this situation resolved because of the positive political and economic impact it would have on the Balkans generally; however, many Greeks saw it as yet another compromise, for which they blamed the SYRIZA–ANEL government (Dendrinou and Varvitsioti, 2019; Tzifakis, 2019). SYRIZA's popularity fell and the coalition with ANEL was shaken. Despite the domestic political turbulence, Alexis Tsipras announced the end of the Third Programme on 21 August 2018 in a highly symbolic speech made from the island of Ithaca. Greece was finally entering the post-Memorandum period.

During the implementation of the Third Programme, the government gained limited room for manoeuvre to alleviate some measures, such as free access to health care for uninsured and vulnerable groups. It also managed to delay and water down reforms including the labour market reform and some of the privatisation measures. However, the conflict with the lenders and the lack of implementation during the negotiation phase had damaged the government's credibility and did not allow for much leverage (see Proposal Three). The governing coalition, which was led by a radical left-wing party, was keen to show that its governance made a difference but it only managed to very marginally change the mix of the policies. The cost of the very few reversals was low, as it was generally passed on to a different group or alternative measures with the same cost had to be taken. This was the case of the pension system in which the partial reversal passed some of the cost from employees to independent professionals. In line with Proposal Two, partisanship does matter to the mixture of measures implemented, though not massively. By the time the Third Programme for Greece was implemented, the Institutions were a little more flexible as they were also tired of pushing Greece to make reforms. It can be argued that lenders' reform fatigue can also lead to some increased room for manoeuvre. However, it is significant to note that in the end the SYRIZA government implemented most of the reforms in the programme and, to a large extent, continued the work started by the previous governments.

After conditionality: August 2018–June 2019

Despite celebrating the end of the Third Economic Programme, the government realised there could not be any dramatic changes to its economic and social policy as the lenders' scrutiny of Greece would be even greater than that of other countries that had exited their programmes.[60] The total Greek loan was significantly larger than that of other countries (€241.6 billion was disbursed) and there had been marked fluctuations in trust between the Greek governments and the lenders during the crisis years. Indeed, Greece entered an enhanced surveillance mechanism that included visits from the Institutions and quarterly reports on the progress made with reforms and the macroeconomic targets (European Commission, 2018a).

Although this meant the government's policies did not change significantly, it gave it more room for manoeuvre in some priority areas. After negotiating with the EU Institutions, the government was able to freeze pensions rather than make further cuts as previously stipulated in 2017 legislation. This was seen as a success even though it was agreed to make cuts in the public investment programme, among others, in return (Koratzanis and Pierros, 2019). Additionally, the minimum wage and the sub-minimum wage for young people were increased despite the lenders' concerns. Finally, the collective bargaining framework came into operation again to limit private companies' ability to change collective agreements for the worse. A further concern for the EC was the Council of State's rulings that the cuts in pensions and benefits since 2012 were unconstitutional. Compensatory fiscal measures were requested to avoid this impacting fiscal targets (European Commission, 2018a; Kazakos, 2019). An appeal from EFKA (public sector pension fund) means that no money has been returned to pensioners yet and at the time of writing this is an ongoing battle with the Council of State (National Herald, 2020).

In January 2019, Greece managed to successfully draw funds from the markets and the economy was showing signs of recovery. On the other hand, the government had been politically weakened by ANEL's withdrawal from the coalition government following the ratification of the Prespes agreement. Nevertheless, six ANEL MPs continued to support SYRIZA and ANEL was split (BBC, 2019). SYRIZA's defeat in the European elections of 25 May 2019 not only confirmed that SYRIZA's narrative was no longer convincing but also the political cost of the implementation of the Third Programme and the Prespes agreement. Indeed, in the early election called for 7 July SYRIZA was again defeated. New Democracy managed to gain 39.85 per cent of the seats, which meant a coalition was unnecessary as it had secured the absolute majority (Ministry of Interior, 2019). Kyriakos Mitsotakis became Prime Minister, with a liberal and reformist agenda very similar to that of Greece's lenders.

In line with Proposal Four, the government did revert some policies in the post-programme period but reversals were only partial and selective. As expected, the reversals aimed at electoral benefits from specific parts of the population that traditionally supported SYRIZA. They generally diffused cost to the population at large and not to a specific group. Alternative measures were often agreed to avoid an imbalance of the macroeconomic situation and under the pressure of EU Institutions. While most reversals were to cost-cutting reforms, the collective agreements were reintroduced as this was symbolically and ideologically very important to the SYRIZA electorate.

Conclusions

The case of Greece demonstrated that governments have some room for manoeuvre even when a country is at its weakest (Proposal One). However, the key to exploiting this leeway is credibility, which is directly linked to the pace of implementation of reforms (Proposal Three). Greece was the only country in our sample where the crisis was so long-lasting (almost ten years), where parties with different ideologies governed on their own or in coalitions, and where three Economic Adjustment Programmes were implemented. Interestingly, despite the changes in government and the intense negotiations with the lenders, there was continuity in the measures and reforms introduced in the three programmes, but they often deepened and became more ambitious with each programme, for example pension reform. Some cases of reversal were also identified but they were the exception and not the rule (Proposal Four).

Like the other case studies herein, Greece therefore offers evidence of the government's capacity to define policies, insert new measures and avoid the insertion and/or implementation of specific measures. Some of these policies, such as public administration reforms, had been on the government's agenda for some time and the economic crisis was a window of opportunity for the government to include them in the MoU (Proposal One). The Greek case shows that when a new government was taking office, it had an opportunity to influence the negotiations and the mix of policies to be included in the MoU or the sequence of reforms to be implemented. The Papandreou and the Samaras governments are both examples of this. As time passed, this room for manoeuvre diminished, mainly because credibility was also declining due to the lenders' dissatisfaction with the governments' implementation rates. The Tsipras government did not have this room for manoeuvre at the start of its term because it totally rejected the Second Programme, refused to implement reforms and thus lost its credibility early on (Proposal Three).

The Greek case allows us to further link our Proposal One about a government's room for manoeuvre to our Proposal Three, which claims that the more willing/able a government is/was to implement the policies agreed, the greater its credibility, and the more its capacity to insert its own preferences in the MoU. This was the case in Greece all along and in all governments during the three programmes. When the governments of Papandreou (2010), Samaras (2013) or Tsipras (2017) were implementing the agreed reforms, the levels of trust rose and the Greek governments gained greater room for manoeuvre. However, the significant exception to this norm was in 2014, when the Samaras government was given little leeway by the lenders despite implementing reforms and managing to borrow from the markets. The most likely explanations are that Samaras was asking too much (to exit the programme in 2014 without completing all the reforms), together with the clash of personalities between the negotiating teams, especially between Samara's team and the IMF team, which created a climate of mistrust that could not be overcome. It can thus be argued that credibility is not only linked to the implementation of reforms and positive macroeconomic results but also to levels of trust that can be affected by other factors such as personal relationships. The Greek case also showed that leeway may also be given because of lenders' 'reform fatigue', as happened during the implementation of the Third Programme.

The effect of partisanship could also be clearly observed in the case of Greece. We had the opportunity to analyse the alternation from a socialist government to a coalition government led by a conservative Prime Minister and then to another coalition government led by a radical left Prime Minister. Our theoretical chapter proposes that partisanship matters and governments with different persuasions will implement different policies during a bailout. We expected that the election of a new government would lead to changes in the terms of conditionality and/or reversals to some of the measures passed by its predecessor (Proposal Two). The Greek case showed that this is only partially true. The conditionality of the three programmes for Greece remained largely unchanged irrespective of the colour of the government in power. When reversals took place during the implementation of the programmes, it was mainly because measures were not working and/or had significant electoral costs (e.g. labour reserve, EETHDE). Despite fierce negotiations, the SYRIZA government's attempts to change the mix of policies included in the MoU to bring it more in line with its ideology were in vain. It implemented parts of its 'parallel programme' to alleviate some of the effects of austerity on the poorest in the population but with limited impact because of the lack of funds and the limitations posed by the Third Programme's conditionality.

Our Proposal Four on the post-programme period can only be partially discussed in the case of Greece since the Third Programme was concluded in August 2018, much later than in the other cases. We expect governments in the post-programme period to reverse what has been done since the crisis, but to do so only partially and selectively. This is confirmed in the case of Greece since SYRIZA reversed some cost-cutting measures but did so carefully and usually after consultation with the European partners. Costs were largely diffused to the general population and instances of structural reform reversals were rare.

Notes

1 See www.europarl.europa.eu/elections2014-results/el/country-results-el-2009.html (accessed 17 March 2021).
2 Interview GR 15, Minister, Athens, 13 December 2017.
3 Interview GR 15, Minister, Athens, 13 December 2017.
4 Interview GR 15, Minister, Athens, 13 December 2017.
5 Interview GR 15, Minister, Athens, 13 December 2017.
6 Interview GR 15, Minister, Athens, 13 December 2017.
7 Interview GR 1, political advisor to Minister, Athens, 27 November 2017 and Interview GR 56, Member of Parliament and political and economic advisor, Athens, 19 June 2018.
8 Interview GR 1, political advisor to Minister, Athens, 27 November 2017; Interview GR 15, Minister, Athens, 13 December 2017; and Interview GR 56 Member of Parliament and political and economic advisor, Athens, 19 June 2018.
9 Interview GR 15, Minister, Athens, 13 December 2017.
10 A type of bonus payment for all private sector employees.
11 Also Interview GR 16, journalist, Athens, 13 December 2017.
12 Interview GR 3, Minister, Athens, 28 November 2017.
13 Interview GR 4, Minister, Athens, 30 November 2017.
14 Interview BR 35, official from the IMF, Skype call, 16 March 2018.
15 Interview GR 15, Minister, Athens, 13 December 2017.
16 Interview BR 35, official from the IMF, Skype call, 16 March 2018.
17 Also Interview GR 3, Minister, Athens, 28 November 2017.
18 Interview GR 9, political advisor to Minister, Athens, 4 December 2017.
19 Interview GR 1, political advisor to Minister, Athens, 27 November 2017 and Interview GR 8, Minister, Athens, 4 December 2017.

20 Interview GR 15, Minister, Athens, 13 December 2017.
21 Interview GR 4, Minister, Athens, 30 November 2017.
22 Interview GR 15, Minister, Athens, 13 December 2017.
23 Extraordinary Special Fee for Constructed Surfaces with Electric Power Supply.
24 Interview GR 3, Minister, Athens, 28 November 2017.
25 Interview GR 4, Minister, Athens, 30 November 2017.
26 Interview GR 51, Minister, Athens, 23 April 2018.
27 Interview GR 17, political advisor, Athens, 15 December 2017.
28 Interview GR 51, Minister, Athens, 23 April 2018.
29 Interview GR 51, Minister, Athens, 23 April 2018.
30 Interview GR 51, Minister, Athens, 23 April 2018.
31 Interview GR 9, political advisor to Minister, Athens, 4 December 2017 and Interview BR 27, Official from the EC 2, Brussels, 30 January 2018.
32 Also Interview BR 35, official from the IMF, Skype call, 16 March 2018.
33 Interview GR 9, political advisor to Minister, Athens, 4 December 2017.
34 Interview BR 35, official from the IMF, Skype call, 16 March 2018.
35 Also Interview GR 9, political advisor to Minister, Athens, 4 December 2017 and Interview GR 25, Minister, Athens, 19 January 2018.
36 Interview GR 14, Member of Parliament and Minister, Athens, 7 December 2017.
37 Also Interview GR 18, political advisor, Athens, 18 December 2017 and Interview GR 34, Minister, Athens, 27 February 2018.
38 Interview GR 18, political advisor, Athens, 18 December 2017.
39 Interview GR 15, Minister, Athens, 13 December 2017.
40 Interview BR 28, official from the EC 1, Brussels, 30 January 2018.
41 Interview GR 23, Secretary of State, Athens, 11 January 2018.
42 Interview GR 9, political advisor to Minister, Athens, 4 December 2017; Interview GR 34, Minister, Athens, 27 February 2018; and Interview BR 32, official from the IMF, Athens, 5 February 2018.
43 Interview GR 24, government official, Athens, 16 January 2018.
44 The term 'Institutions' is used for the remainder of the chapter since this was the term officially used by the government and the lenders. Apart from the symbolic significance for SYRIZA, it also reflects a change in the composition of the Troika. The Institutions were the EC, the ECB, the ESM and the IMF with limited power since it was not contributing financially to the Third Programme.
45 Interview GR 24, government official, Athens, 16 January 2018.
46 Interview GR 24, government official, Athens, 16 January 2018.
47 Interview GR 31, Secretary of State, Athens, 2 February 2018.
48 Also Interview BR 29, official from the EC 3, Brussels, 30 January 2018 and Interview BR 33, political advisor, phone call, 9 February 2018.
49 Interview GR 31, Secretary of State, Athens, 2 February 2018.
50 Interview GR 7, Minister, Athens, 1 December 2017 and Interview GR 52, Member of Parliament, Athens, 26 May 2018.
51 Interview GR 24, government official, Athens, 16 January 2018 and Interview GR 36, Minister, Athens, 21 March 2018.
52 Interview BR 53, official from the ECB, Skype call, 30 May 2018.

53 Interview GR 24, government official, Athens, 16 January 2018.
54 Interview GR 31, Secretary of State, Athens, 2 February 2018 and Interview GR 54, Minister, 31 May 2018.
55 Interview GR 20, Minister, Athens, 5 January 2018.
56 Interview BR 28, official from the EC 1, Brussels, 30 January 2018.
57 Interview GR 7, Minister, Athens, 1 December 2017.
58 Interview GR 54, Minister, 31 May 2018.
59 Interview BR 53, official from the ECB, Skype call, 30 May 2018.
60 Interview GR 31, Secretary of State, Athens, 2 February 2018 and Interview GR 54, Minister, 31 May 2018.

3

Ireland[1]

Introduction

Ireland was the second country to ask for a bailout. This is an interesting case study, insofar as the country is different from the Southern European bailed out countries in a number of significant respects, particularly with regard to the distinct causes of the national crisis, the broader socio-political context and the extent of its subsequent recovery. A first important difference is that of the growth model: whereas Southern European countries were aligned to a demand-led growth model, Ireland had been oscillating in the previous decade between different models. From the 2000s, as Johnston and Regan (2016, p. 324) clearly explain, the Irish export-led growth model in place for a decade was progressively replaced by a domestic demand-driven model fuelled by lenient banking policies, a construction boom and public sector expansion. After the onset of the crisis, however, Ireland re-prioritised its export-led growth model through policies aimed at attracting foreign investment in high-tech sectors. Furthermore, in many respects the Irish economy, long known as the Celtic Tiger, had followed the Anglo-liberal trend of expanding into finance and the export of high-value goods such as pharmaceuticals (Dukelow, 2015; Tooze, 2018).

Secondly, Ireland's economic path was different. On the one hand, the growth of the finance and real estate sectors meant the economy was particularly susceptible to global shocks and notably the fall in inter-bank lending that came in the wake of the 2008 financial crash (Riain, 2014; Tooze, 2018). On the other, the traditional indicators of Irish economic health began to display positive trends within a relatively short space of time, thanks to the pro-investment policies described above. In 2010, for example, GDP grew 1.8 per cent, and the deficit was back within EU fiscal guidelines by 2015 (European Commission, 2015b). This was reflected in the yield on Irish bonds which dropped to pre-crisis levels from 2012 onwards.

This chapter is organised in six sections. The first section analyses the period leading up to the bailout in 2010. It focuses on the initial reaction of Irish authorities to the crisis, the early negotiations with the EU and the decision to request the bailout. The second section discusses the negotiations between Ireland and the Troika on the terms of the adjustment programme set out in the MoU. Sections 3 and 4 examine the three main dimensions of the programme's implementation: banking, fiscal consolidation and structural reforms. The fifth section looks into the post-programme phase and assesses the extent to which the softening of conditionality brought about reversals of the measures implemented during the programme phase. Finally, the last section concludes and summarises the main findings.

September 2008–November 2010: before the bailout

When speaking to Ministers about the crisis in Ireland, it was repeatedly emphasised that Ireland was primarily a victim of the 2007–2008 credit crunch, unlike other bailout countries, whose economies were only peripherally or tangentially linked to the broader global financial crisis.[2] The Irish economic growth model was based on the Anglo-American vision of liberalised financial markets and had produced spectacular economic growth through the 1990s and early 2000s, leading to GDP growth of around 10 per cent per year; this was well ahead of other Western European economies, earning Ireland the nickname of the 'Celtic Tiger' (Brazys and Hardiman, 2015). Opening up the banking sector to foreign competition had forced Irish banks to become more competitive and substantially increased the risk posed by the banking sector to the broader, productive economy. In particular, it encouraged the growth of the 'big 3' Irish banks – Anglo Irish Bank, Allied Irish Bank and Bank of Ireland – which dominated the financial industry. In order to be competitive within their field, the banks engaged in increasingly aggressive lending practices based predominantly on the commercial and residential real estate markets, funded by liabilities accrued in the wholesale credit markets (Tooze, 2018). This involved banks engaging in the risky markets of subprime mortgages and credit default swaps and expanding their own business into the lucrative American market. Taken together, the liabilities of the 'big 3' banks grew to over seven times the annual GDP of the country as a whole (Tooze, 2018) with the vast majority of these liabilities accrued in the wholesale credit market, that is, taken from global, inter-bank lending markets rather than domestic creditors.

At the same time, the lending practices of the banks went hand in hand with record low interest rates, producing a housing/asset boom in Ireland which led to the construction industry becoming an increasingly important component of the Irish economy. Not only was the industry a significant employer, with nearly a quarter of a million employed in the sector at the height of the boom (Nugent, 2018), but the taxes raised during the property boom also contributed significantly to the Irish treasury. As one former Minister explained: 'the rule of thumb at the time was every 10,000 new houses built generated €1 billion in tax revenue'.[3] Another former Minister agreed: 'taxes from construction were, at their peak, around twenty per cent of the economy'. This made the Irish economy particularly susceptible to a liquidity crisis in the case of any downturn in the housing/property market, and public spending commitments would become increasingly dependent on the Irish state being able to borrow money from the market to make up any discrepancy.

The failure of Lehman Brothers in the US in 2008 and the subsequent drying up of credit in the wholesale markets left both the Irish banking and real estate markets massively exposed to failure (Tooze, 2018). The overriding feeling within the Irish government was that the banking sector in particular was 'too big to fail', as the economic consequences of failure would be catastrophic for the Irish economy.[4] On the night of 29–30 September 2008, when the situation had reached the point that it was believed that at least one of the big banks would default the following morning, the Irish executive took decisive action. A meeting was convened by Brian Cowen, the Taoiseach (Prime Minister) to discuss options for saving the banks. Attending were Brian Lenihan, the Minister of Finance, and John Hurley, the Governor of the Irish Central Bank, as well as other actors from the Irish Ministry of Finance and executives of the banks involved (Oireachtas, 2016, pp. 243–244). The result of this meeting was a mechanism called 'the bank guarantee' – a blanket promise from the Irish state to assume all liabilities of the indebted banks. The measure was designed to assure external confidence in banks but in fact served to dramatically undermine confidence in the national balance sheet given the precarious nature of the banks involved, with potentially billions of euros being added to the national deficit in the case of bank failure.

While bank executives joined the government and the Irish Central Bank Governor in making the decision regarding the bank guarantee, other political actors, such as opposition politicians and civil society figures, were excluded from the process. A former Minister from the Labour party (in opposition at the time) succinctly described the exclusion of these actors:

> I remember when the bank guarantee happened, … I got a phone call, I was still in bed, getting up, from the Minister of Finance, Brian Lenihan, to tell me what had happened at this all-night session. The banks were at risk, they were going to put forward emergency legislation and gave me the general gist of what they were going to do and asked for our cooperation. [5]

International actors had limited direct involvement in the bank guarantee. Nevertheless, talks with the ECB had been ongoing throughout the process (Oireachtas, 2016, p. 247). In his evidence to the Irish Banking Inquiry (a cross-parliamentary public inquiry into the circumstances of the Irish bailout), ECB President Jean-Claude Trichet distanced the ECB from the decision-making process: 'We were not kept abreast of any development in Dublin by the Irish authorities, and as regards the Guarantee, we learned of the Guarantee through the media' (Oireachtas, 2016, p. 247). However, Irish actors point to greater involvement with Europe, as David Doyle, Secretary General in the Ministry of Finance, recalled, 'On the core question [whether the ECB would allow a bank failure] the view of the ECB as quoted to the meeting by the Governor on the night was that Mr Trichet had advised him that no bank failure could be allowed, or words to that effect' (Oireachtas, 2016, p. 246).

It was in a spirit of national ownership of the problems that, after the bank guarantee in September 2008, the Irish government began to implement fiscal measures to deal with what was increasingly understood as an interrelated banking *and* fiscal crisis, with fears over the banks driving a general lack of confidence in the Irish economy, resulting in higher borrowing costs for the Irish state.[6] The interrelated series of crises that afflicted Ireland between 2008 and 2010 was summed up well by a former Minister: 'it started as an economic crisis, became a fiscal crisis, became a banking crisis and that was self-evident by 2009'.[7] It was not merely that these cases were sequential but the fact that they fed off each other to make matters worse that indicated to many that Ireland should call in the Troika. As a senior civil servant put it, 'I often think … if we had the fiscal crisis which was extraordinarily deep or if we had the banking crisis we could have managed probably without a programme. But not by having both.'[8]

In this context, the government introduced income and pension levies and additional taxes on items such as second homes, air travel and car parking. The VAT rate was increased by 0.5 percentage points. These measures had begun tentatively from June 2008, even before the guarantee, but were accelerated in an early budget in October of that year and through seven fiscal interventions in 2009 (Organisation for Economic Co-operation and Development, 2009).

In addition to the legislation introducing the fiscal measures during this early period, the Fianna Fáil (FF) government embarked on a sustained series of negotiations with trade unions to ensure the measures had broader social legitimacy.[9] In February 2009, after the failure to renegotiate the existing wage agreement, the government implemented unilateral pay cuts in the public sector (Dellepiane and Hardiman, 2012, p. 39); this led to what commentators have called the collapse of the social partnership model (Doherty, 2011, p. 375). After a demonstration in November 2009, the government sought the unions' agreement to introduce further cuts in public sector pay in the 2010 budget. A few months later, in March 2010, the Public Service Agreement (2010–2014), known as the 'Croke Park' agreement, was signed. Trade union members approved the agreement in June 2010 by a large majority (Doherty, 2011, p. 380). In the negotiated trade-off, the government agreed not to unilaterally implement further pay cuts until 2014 in exchange for a non-strike clause, a pay cut for new public employees, an embargo on public sector recruitment, detrimental changes to the bonus system (Hardiman and Regan, 2013, p. 8) and a constant monitoring of reforms to increase efficiency in key sectors (Regan, 2017, p. 160).

The fiscal consolidation measures and labour agreements did not manage to substantially reduce the state's debt, which rose by 61.5 per cent of GDP in 2009 to 86 per cent in 2010. Half of this increase was due to the state's assistance to the banks since the bank guarantee (Considine and Dukelow, 2014, p. 261). The difficult situation of the Irish banks was particularly 'reflected in their borrowing heavily from the ECB, unable to secure market funding' (Considine and Dukelow, 2014, p. 261). As debt increased, financial markets became more concerned about Ireland's economic situation, with yields on Irish ten-year bonds rising from 5 per cent at the beginning of 2010 to around 8 per cent towards the end of the year (European Stability Mechanism, 2016).

In order to calm the markets, the Irish government started working in late 2010 on a comprehensive fiscal consolidation plan. The original idea was to 'buy time' in order to convince the ECB to publicly support Irish banks and hence avoid the need for a bailout (Oireachtas, 2016, p. 339). On 19 November, however, Ireland's situation took a hard turn. Mr Trichet, President of the ECB, wrote to the Irish Minister of Finance, Brian Lenihan, to say the ECB would not continue to augment the emergency liquidity it had been providing unless Ireland sought a rescue programme. At that point, Irish banks had borrowed more than €75 billion from the ECB (Considine and Dukelow, 2014, p. 262). Two days after Trichet's letter, the government gave in and requested the bailout.

One of the factors shaping crisis responses that is well demonstrated by the Irish case is the importance of relationships between national governments and international actors. In Ireland, the relationship between the national government and the EU had already been under strain.[10] As one former Minister said, 'Ireland had kind of disengaged from involvement in European Councils, its attendance in the Council of Ministers by ministers was low so there was a lot of bridge building to be done and a lot of winning back of friends and allies.'[11] Another former Minister agreed: 'It was no secret, for instance, that ministers from the Irish government during the so-called Celtic Tiger felt it beneath themselves to attend Council meetings and they sent officials. So we hadn't got a great relationship.'[12] Re-engagement at the European level was therefore one of the most important early tasks for the Irish:

> We had a job to do in rebuilding the country's reputation and that was at a number of levels. First of all, immediately it was with the rest of the European Union. Two, you know, I think there was a view of Ireland that it had got its just deserts, that there had been a degree of hubris during the years of the Celtic Tiger in particular. There had been arrogance. And that a lot of Ireland's problems were of Ireland's own making.[13]

In the days after the bailout request, the Irish government made public the National Recovery Plan (NRP), a set of fiscal and banking measures that the government had been working on in the previous weeks. The plan failed its initial goal and was only published after the bailout request on 24 November. It included an anticipated €10 billion in public spending cuts and €5 billion in tax increases in order to minimise the anticipated rise in budget deficit, along with other measures, including the introduction of property tax and reforms to welfare. The latter included the Universal Social Charge, a tax on income that replaced both the income levy and the health levy, which the government had previously been unable to introduce.[14]

As with the bank guarantee, the decision to bring the Troika in was made unilaterally by FF, the senior party of government, and came as a surprise to politicians from other parties – including its partners in government. The government's decision to request the bailout was prompted by the continued deterioration of market conditions and the ability of the Irish to fund their own public spending commitments, as well as the failure of the EU to provide instruments for safeguarding the banks. However, not all sides were in agreement with the need for the bailout.[15] One former Labour Minister, in opposition at the time, described the lack of cross-party engagement: 'On the programme there was no consultation ... the public position of Fianna Fáil right up until the announcement was complete denial that they were even contemplating [bringing them in], but there was no concrete, no discussion with the opposition parties and we didn't have any engagement with it really until ... until we met the Troika.'[16] Going further than this, the same former Minister explained that at the time the feeling was that the lack of consultation and discussion was a deliberate political tactic on the part of FF in order 'to bind the hands of the incoming government. So we opposed it very strongly in the Dail [the lower house of the Irish Parliament], you know, we fought it.'[17]

The decision to bring in the Troika and negotiate the bailout therefore provoked strong protests both from the junior coalition partner, the Green Party, and even from some Ministers within Fianna Fáil. In late 2010 and early 2011, there was a wave of resignations from the government from both the Green Party and FF. One Minister described it as 'The government began to collapse. They were in coalition with the Green Party, they had serious rows among themselves. Irish governments normally have a Prime Minister and fourteen Ministers. At the end, before the election of early 2011, with resignations and sackings they were down to seven Ministers, which is the absolute minimum constitutional position.'[18] After the collapse of the FF/Green coalition, the bailout was therefore negotiated in a situation of both economic and political instability.

December 2010: drafting and negotiating the Memorandum

Despite the internal political problems, the government managed to reach an agreement with the international lenders on the terms of the bailout programme in less than two weeks after asking for financial assistance from the EU and the IMF (Rehn, 2020, p. 99). It entered into force in December, following the approval of the European Council and of the IMF Board. The €85 billion bailout, which ran for a three-year period, was conditional on the Irish state undertaking fiscal consolidation, banking reforms and other structural reforms as outlined in the MoU agreed upon with these institutions (European Commission, 2011c). In terms of fiscal consolidation, the goal was to reduce the fiscal imbalance by €15 billion over the term of the programme, which amounted to about 10 per cent of GDP (Henning, 2017, p. 113). While the goal was clear, the strategies to achieve it were, with a few exceptions, loosely stated. In their study about the Greek and Irish MoUs, Clifton *et al.* (2018) point out that Ireland's MoU was half the length of the first Greek MoU. In our comparative chapter, we show that the Irish document was not only shorter, but also vaguer than that of its counterparts (see Table 7.1 chapter 7). Whereas the Portuguese MoU, for example, contained seventy-five policy statements, the Irish one included only nineteen. This was the case because the Irish MoU contained more objectives to be reached than specific measures.

Even though the intention was that the adjustment fell primarily on the expenditure side, various measures were also included to increase fiscal revenues, notably a large increase in personal income tax through the broadening of the tax base. In terms of banking, the main goal was to fundamentally downsize, reorganise and de-risk the sector. Lastly, the MoU was relatively vague on structural reforms, providing only general guidelines in terms of labour market reforms (reduction of the minimum wage and changes to the unemployment, activation and collective bargaining systems), competition (opening up of sheltered service sectors) and privatisation of public assets (the preparation of a study to examine opportunities). According to an informant, 'what we were looking for in structural reforms was very much at the margin'.[19] This position was generally agreed on at the European level, who acknowledged it in the post-programme analysis, 'The structural reforms in the programme were appropriately limited, as Ireland is a relatively competitive and flexible economy' (European Commission, 2015b, p. 12).

As indicated by various interviewees and academics, the negotiations for the general terms of the MoU were unproblematic.[20] Indeed, when the Troika arrived in Ireland its interlocutor was a government ideologically aligned with pro-cyclical measures and structural reforms (Clifton *et al.*, 2018; Dukelow, 2015; Hardiman and Regan, 2013; Robbins and Lapsley, 2014), eager to distance itself from Greece's image of a 'bad manager' (Allen, 2012, p. 3). As shown in the previous section, in contrast with other European governments that initially attempted to respond to the crisis with fiscal stimulus, the centre-right FF-led government adopted fiscal correction as its early and enduring priority (Laffan, 2016, p. 185).

The Troika readily accepted the plans proposed by the FF and Greens coalition government, especially the NRP, which, according to various informants, became the blueprint for the MoU.[21] As shown by Clifton *et al.* (2018), this was because the Troika was generally sympathetic to the Irish situation and considered the economic crisis a short-term 'blip' in an otherwise healthy economy. Therefore, it was open to accepting Irish strategies on how to overcome the crisis. Furthermore, the Troika saw Irish national policy-makers' commitment to own the problem and 'do "whatever it takes" to ensure deficit-reduction' (European Commission, 2012b, p. 26). As pointed out by a senior Irish civil servant, 'by the time we went into the programme, we were at a point where you were actually at the tail end. It was not insignificant but it was the tail of the fiscal effort. We took early ownership.'[22] For a high official, 'the key was to realise that we needed to get these loans, we needed to move forward on them, so we all pulled together'.[23] There was therefore a strong closeness-of-fit between the Troika and Irish authorities.

Not only was the government clearly aligned with the Troika, but the negotiations were also largely unproblematic because, as noted by various interviewees, there was broad-based consensus across the main political parties that fiscal retrenchment was necessary.[24] According to the literature, this is an expression of the historical absence of a strong left-right cleavage in Irish politics and of the traditional clustering of support to the centre-right (Hardiman and MacCarthaigh, 2017). Preston and Silke (2014) point out that FF and Fine Gael (FG) can both be described as occupying conservative centre-right or Christian democratic political spaces.

In addition to the terms of the NPR, and in line with our expectations regarding the government's room for manoeuvre, various informants told us that the government took the opportunity offered by the bailout to propose measures they had been personally favouring beforehand, such as a reduction in the minimum wage and the introduction of a property tax. A high state official, for example, noted that 'any good finance ministry will look at what are all the things that we would like to do that we haven't been able to do for a number of years and there's a crisis moment in which you can do them, for example taxation on property'.[25] Another senior civil servant told us that it was not the Troika but the government that had requested the reduction in the minimum wage.[26]

One high official also added, 'the Irish side had many "red lines" which demarcated things that we wouldn't agree on – however these were not public and were not crossed'.[27] One of the red lines was, for example, green diesel, as explained to us by a former senior civil servant in the Department of Finance,

> The Commission wanted us to abolish green diesel, [subsidised agricultural fuel] and that would just not work ... we couldn't have signed off on it because you've always got one eye on social stability and economic stability and not having people in the streets protesting about it and so we substituted it for an equal value ... 5c on a pint of beer.[28]

Another red line was the corporation tax rate. Despite pressure from European governments, especially France and Germany, the Irish government resisted increasing it (Henning, 2017, p. 114; Rehn, 2020, p. 100). Irish authorities argued that this was key to the economic recovery. According to a senior civil servant, the Troika accepted the argument because 'they operated as creditors, you know, you don't lend to somebody and then break the economic model that allows them to repay what you've lent them'.[29]

The fact that the Troika took on board the government's requests (corporation tax and green diesel) shows that the measures included in the MoU cannot be fully considered an imposition. Given that most measures were drawn from previous plans put forward by the government, the MoU can actually be considered mostly an Irish national product. The government's room for manoeuvre was also visible in its capacity to include measures that had long been on the agenda but had not been possible to implement, such as the property tax. Finally, and interestingly, a senior official in the Department of Finance (DoF) also told us that the Irish strategy was to under-promise and over-deliver.[30] By doing this, Irish authorities hoped to gain credibility vis-à-vis the Troika and have more room to influence the strategies and timings required to fulfil the measures agreed upon in the MoU. In line with our theoretical expectations, this conscious strategy of the Irish authorities shows that, for debtor countries, credibility is key to achieving leverage in negotiations with lenders.

March 2011: renegotiation of the MoU

In March 2011, just months after the MoU was signed, FF lost the general election, realising its lowest ever share of the vote (17.4 per cent). Voters vented their displeasure with a government that had presided over the emergent stages of the financial crisis and the blanket state guarantee to the banks (Preston and Silke, 2014). FG won the elections with 36.1 per cent of the popular vote. The party returned to office after many years in opposition, forming a government with the support of the Labour party, which had won an unusually high 19.5 per cent of the popular vote – hence shifting the government slightly to the left. The responsibility for implementing the MoU negotiated by its predecessor fell upon this new coalition, led by FG's Enda Kenny.

The incoming government accepted the programme in general terms, though not fully. On the one hand, both parties agreed on the need to continue the adjustment programme. This intention was clearly mentioned in their electoral manifestos (Fine Gael, 2011; Labour, 2011) and was confirmed by several country experts (Hardiman *et al.*, 2019; Murphy, 2014; Preston and Silke, 2014). For example, Hardiman and MacCarthaigh (2013, p. 31) note that the greater reliance on spending cuts rather than tax rises to reach fiscal consolidation did not fundamentally change with the election of a new government in February 2011. This is also confirmed by the Troika's official statements: notably, the IMF's seventh review noted that the 'political commitment to [fiscal] consolidation has been a welcome constant, as reflected in the affirmation by the new government of the medium-term fiscal targets in the EU–IMF supported programme agreed in December 2010' (International Monetary Fund, 2012b, p. 20).

On the other hand, despite accepting the general terms of the agreement signed with the Troika, the new FG/Labour government sought to change some specific measures in the programme. In fact, both FG and Labour had made the renegotiation of parts of the MoU a central plank of their platforms (Fine Gael, 2011; Labour, 2011). According to a former Labour Minister, they largely accepted the MoU but did not want to implement it as it stood since they did not agree with some parts of it.[31] When meeting the Troika after the elections, the new Irish Ministers started by arguing that, by accepting their predecessors' programme and its punishing fiscal contraction, Ireland was being a good team player and that this should be acknowledged in various ways (Henning, 2017, p. 115).

One of the new government's main requests was a bail-in of remaining senior bondholders. As explained above, the FF/Green government had made the decision to bail out senior guaranteed bondholders through the 2008 bank guarantee[32] (Henning, 2017, p. 117). The new government wanted to force losses on the remaining unguaranteed senior bondholders, which by 2011 totalled some €16.4 billion (International Monetary Fund, 2012b); hence the government's push for a bail-in instead of a bailout. Although both FG and Labour had campaigned for this (Lütz *et al.*, 2020), it was promptly rejected by the ECB, which threatened to cut its liquidity support for the Irish banking sector if the government allowed the senior bondholders' bail-in to take place (Henning, 2017, p. 117). According to the IMF, the major concern was possible cross-border euro area spillovers resulting from the Irish senior bondholders' bail-in. The institution felt this could happen in two ways: the bail-in could be seen as precedent-setting in the Eurozone and adversely affect Eurozone banks and their funding markets; and it could unleash a contagion effect given the extensive cross-holdings by banks of other Eurozone bank senior bonds (International Monetary Fund, 2012b, p. 28). Eventually, the government complied and accepted the senior bondholders' bailout.

Even though the government was constrained on the bail-in, it was certainly freer in other areas. In fact, it was successful in renegotiating some measures, notably the speed of fiscal consolidation. While the programme stipulated that the adjustment should be made over three budgets, the government wanted to do it in four,[33] and the Troika agreed to this. Another change, promptly requested by the new government, was to reverse the 12 per cent cut in the minimum wage adopted by the previous government. The new government was able to reverse this cut by making an equivalent and agreed change to the Pay Related Social Insurance (PRSI) between 2011 and mid-2013 (European Commission, 2011d, p. 23). A third change had to do with the expansion of the applicability of the 'inability to pay' clause. In law, a firm could only invoke this clause once to adjust wages. In the MoU, it was agreed that the Irish authorities would consider enlarging it to permit firms to invoke the clause more than once. However, the new government argued that as the clause had never been used in practice, it should be dropped from the MoU, which the Troika agreed to do.

These initial changes to the programme achieved by the new FG/Labour government show that even though Irish decision-makers were under conditionality, they still enjoyed room for manoeuvre vis-à-vis the Troika. For two senior civil servants we interviewed, the Troika readily accepted these changes because they were not central to the programme and, some of them, such as the minimum wage, were not even a Troika request.[34] One of them explained that these adjustments were made at the margins with the aim of showing that the new government *could* change some things.[35] This indicates that our expectations regarding partisan turnover and ideological change are observed, but also that the changes are relatively marginal.

April 2011–December 2013: implementation of the MoU

In terms of implementation, the DoF was at the centre of the process since all policy coordination was concentrated there (Regan, 2013, p. 17). Various interviewees mentioned that the department was the key negotiator with the lenders and also the main manager of the fiscal consolidation process.[36] It hosted all negotiations with the Troika and centrally led all the public sector pay cuts and reductions. Furthermore, according to MacCarthaigh and Hardiman (2020), the DoF took the lead in driving the prioritisation of reforms, negotiating approval for the substitution of measures deemed more important by the Irish authorities than the Troika's own agenda, and securing Troika support for the revised delivery dates.

The strengthening of the DoF was consolidated with the creation of the Department of Public Expenditure and Reform led by the Minister of Public Expenditure and Reform (Brendan Howlin, 2011–2016) in 2011. This new department was spun off from the Finance department, and its objective was to address the specific challenges of structural reforms brought about by the Eurozone crisis (Hardiman *et al.*, 2019). In practice, this meant an upgrading of the departments related to finance, giving them two Ministers and more influence over decision-making processes.

The Ministers of Finance and of Public Expenditure were part of the newly created Economic Management Council, which also included the Prime Minister, Enda Kenny, and the Deputy Prime Minister, Eamon Gilmore. This elite – all male – council centralised all decision-making regarding the management of the crisis and the negotiations with the Troika (Murphy, 2014). As one of the informants said in the interviews, it functioned like a 'war Cabinet'.[37]

In order to oversee the fiscal consolidation effort, the government also established a five-member Fiscal Advisory Council in 2012 (European Commission, 2011e). The council worked as an independent body on a statutory basis to advise the government on how to respect the existing multi-annual expenditure ceilings (European Commission, 2012c). Besides being monitored by external authorities, the Irish government started to be overseen by a national non-elected body, similar to what happened in Portugal. The creation of the institution was first mentioned in the 2010 National Recovery Plan and then included in the 2010 MoU. Reference was also made to the need to set up such bodies in the EU Directive 2011/85 on requirements for national budgetary frameworks of the member states.

Based on this institutional arrangement, the FG/Labour coalition worked to observe the fiscal consolidation goals included in the MoU. The government closely continued the path of fiscal consolidation initiated even before the bailout by the previous government. Between 2011 and 2012, the government approved a minimum 10 per cent reduction in pay for new entrants to the public service as well as an effective pay freeze until 2014 (European Commission, 2011e). Additionally, the government secured extra savings via a reduction in teacher numbers, school funding and student grant systems (European Commission, 2011f) and, going beyond what was outlined in the MoU, via salary reductions for policy-makers. For example, the Prime Minister's salary was reduced by €14,000. It phased out various tax reliefs, credits and exemptions. Furthermore, in line with the MoU guidelines on the revenue side, the main measures included a 2 per cent increase in VAT to 23 per cent, the introduction of an early €100 household charge on principal residence, which was later converted into the local property tax, capital gains tax (2012) and capital acquisition tax; an increase in carbon tax as well as in motor tax and in the excise on tobacco and alcohol (European Commission, 2011f). The government also decided to keep the Universal Social Charge created by the previous government as a temporary measure to replace the income levy and health levy (Finn, 2016). Maternity, adoptive and health benefits started to be taxed for all claimants from 2013. This measure was not mentioned as such in the MoU. There was an overall instruction to broaden the tax base, but this specific measure was not in the document; it resulted from the implementation process.

The government also approved massive reductions in welfare benefits. The FF/Greens coalition had already reduced rates of job seeker payments and introduced sanctions for beneficiaries not in compliance with job-search conditionality (European Commission, 2011d). The FG/Labour coalition further reduced various social benefits allowances and supplements including child allowance, Jobseeker's Allowance and Supplementary Welfare Allowance and rent and fuel supplements (European Commission, 2011f; Smyth, 2011). It also largely maintained the cuts carried out by the previous government, notably the elimination of the Christmas bonus for pensioners and those receiving social welfare and disability payments. There were also substantial changes to the pension system, including the increase in the state pension age (to 66 years in 2014, 67 in 2021 and 68 in 2028) and the introduction of a new maximum retirement age of 70 years (European Commission, 2011d). On the revenue side, the PRSI was progressively expanded and increased; and many of the exemptions in place were abolished.

Although the reduction in these expenses enabled the government to bring its budget deficit down from the record level of 2010 (30 per cent), it remained high at 8 per cent of GDP (European Stability Mechanism, 2016). This decrease had an impact on the yields of Irish government bonds, which dropped from their peak of around 14 per cent in June 2011 to 6 per cent in June 2012 (European Stability Mechanism, 2016). In July that year, the National Treasury Management Agency sold a five-year bond marking the country's re-engagement with financial markets (European Stability Mechanism, 2019, p. 100). According to Kevin Cardiff (2019), former Head of the Department of Finance, there were signs halfway into the programme that the Irish economy was stabilising, making the country's gradual return to the markets possible.

These good economic signs were, however, tempered by the continuous increase in Irish debt, which reached 117 per cent of GDP in 2012 (European Stability Mechanism, 2016). That is perhaps why the government pursued the strategy of continued state spending cuts, despite the positive news on the yields and budget deficit. In 2013, disregarding the promise made by the previous government, the FG/Labour government cut public employees' salaries further. These new cuts were part of the Public Service Stability Agreement 2013–2016, commonly known as the Haddington Road agreement, which replaced the Public Service Agreement signed before the programme. This agreement introduced longer working hours, changes to overtime rates and pay cuts for those earning over €65,000 per annum (Boyle, 2016).

Simultaneously with the introduction of the Public Service Stability Agreement, the government enacted the Financial Emergency Measures in the Public Interest Act 2013. This legislation gave effect to reductions in pay and pension rates and enabled far-reaching changes to pay and working conditions for members of unions that had not signed up to the Public Service Stability Agreement. Despite opposition, the government unilaterally imposed the measures.

While the government diligently observed the MoU's terms on fiscal consolidation, the same cannot be said for structural reforms. This is highlighted by the EC in its ex-post evaluation report which stated that 'the implementation of structural reforms has been less consistent than other parts of the programme, particularly in regulatory reforms that affect vested interests' (European Commission, 2015b, p. 107).

Indeed, various measures included in the structural reforms section of the MoU were not fully implemented during the programme. The most emblematic of these was water charges. In 1997, Ireland abolished water charges for households, becoming one of the few EU countries that did not charge for water usage. There are different views on the reasons behind the introduction of the measure in the MoU. According to some respondents, the measure was imposed by the Troika, which saw the programme as an opportunity to bring Ireland in line with the rest of the EU on water charges.[38] Others claimed the crisis was an opportunity to move forward with a measure that had long been on the Irish policy-makers' agenda.[39] This second view is supported by media reports which show that Fianna Fáil planned water charges before the Troika bailout (Ryan, 2015, p. 20).

This measure was strongly resisted by Irish society, which took to the streets in protest (Newstalk, 2017). The government slowly moved ahead with the change. It passed the Water Services Act 2013, which established a 100 per cent publicly owned company to manage Ireland's water services, called Irish Water, and started the process of installing water meters. Despite the strong social reaction, the Troika insisted on the importance of the measure, as the review reports indicate (European Commission, 2013a). However, social resistance to the measure continued during the programme, and only a fraction of Irish households effectively paid the charges (Newstalk, 2017).

Another structural change not fully implemented by the government was the liberalisation of protected legal professions. Responding to the terms of the MoU, the government initiated the Legal Services Regulation Bill in October 2011, a new regulatory framework for the legal professions that would enhance competition and lower costs (European Commission, 2011f). After overcoming several hurdles, the bill obtained the necessary approval and was implemented, but only at the end of 2015 when Ireland had exited the programme; moreover, according to the European Commission (2015b), it was less ambitious than had initially been expected. As pointed out by respondents, powerful vested interests were fundamental in blocking the government's proposals in this area.[40] The Law Society and Bar Council were two of the most active actors in this regard. As in the case of water charges, the EC report shows that the Troika repeatedly insisted on the need to get this reform approved and, as shown before, was sceptical about the final result (European Commission, 2013a).

The third structural reform not fully implemented by the Irish government during the adjustment programme was the privatisation package. Despite ambitious privatisation plans and pressure from the Troika, as the report reviews show (European Commission, 2013b), the government only sold the National Lottery in 2014 for €400 million and the 50 per cent stake held by the Electricity Supply Board in two overseas power plants for around €200 million in 2014. According to a former Minister in Kenny's government, large-scale privatisation was 'something that we were not prepared to countenance. So, we had to negotiate around that.'[41]

The variation in implementation between fiscal consolidation and structural reforms is explained by the following factors. First, structural reforms were not as salient as fiscal consolidation either to the government or to the Troika which gave the former more room for manoeuvre in these areas. As indicated by a senior civil servant, 'once they [the Troika] saw that the big picture things were done, particularly in terms of the fiscal consolidation stuff and making progress on that and then on the banking side … they're probably not going to argue about some of the smaller structural reforms'.[42] Furthermore, the European Commission (2015b, p. 76) and three respondents noted[43] that the Troika saw Ireland as a fairly open economy where structural reforms were not as necessary as in other cases (see also Clifton *et al.*, 2018; Hick, 2018).

Secondly, the government's credibility was also vital to the variation in the government's room for manoeuvre. As mentioned by a former Labour Minister, the Troika was initially very reluctant to renegotiate, particularly on privatisations, and it was only with the passage of time and as confidence grew between the negotiators that they felt the government was trustworthy and credible.[44] According to a senior civil servant, the credibility the government acquired was due to the early ownership and diligent application of the austerity measures in the programme.[45] Both the Troika and EU members praised Irish authorities for their handling of the crisis. For example, Angela Merkel, Germany's Chancellor, pointed out in 2011 that Ireland was a 'superb example of how a country can work its way out of a debt crisis' (AAP, 2011). In the tenth review report, the EU Commission mentioned that 'on the back of strong political ownership, coupled with appropriate programme design, the steadfast implementation of the Irish adjustment programme is increasingly delivering in terms of regaining market access and making progress towards sustainable economic growth' (European Commission, 2013a, p. 5). Hence, in addition to economic conditions, and confirming our theoretical expectations, the credibility of the government of a bailed out country vis-à-vis lenders, which in fact derives from the capacity to reduce deficit, also seems to be an important condition for negotiation leeway.

The government's room for manoeuvre was also visible in its capacity to go beyond what had been agreed with the Troika. This was the case, for example, of the reform of the public administration. As shown by MacCarthaigh and Hardiman (2020), the crisis and the presence of the Troika provided a window of opportunity for the implementation of a domestically generated administrative reform agenda that went further than the initial plan in the MoU; and which comprised the introduction of system-wide coordination and collaboration measures and the pursuit of standardisation in matters ranging from terms of public service employment to department–agency relationships.

2013–2019: post-conditionality

Ireland exited the programme in December 2013. The European Commission considered the programme a success, pointing out that Ireland met the fiscal targets and that the reforms made the economy more sustainable (European Commission, 2015b, p. 108). By the end of the programme, Ireland registered GDP growth of 1.8 per cent and the budget deficit had fallen from 30 per cent of GDP in 2010 to 7.2 per cent in 2013, still above the Stability and Growth Pact limit (3 per cent), but in line with the Troika expectations (European Commission, 2015b). Thus, even though Ireland left the programme, it remained under the EDP until May 2016, and was closely scrutinised by EU authorities. Plus, until 75 per cent of the financial assistance was repaid, Ireland was put under post-programme surveillance and received six-monthly visits and recommendations from the EC and the IMF. This shows that conditionality continued after the end of the programme, albeit less stringently.

As economic conditions improved, Ireland's GDP grew by 26 per cent in 2015 and the budget deficit fell below 3 per cent (Inman, 2016), giving the government more room to unwind some of the measures adopted during the crisis. The first step in this direction was taken in late 2015 with the adoption of the Financial Emergency Measures in the Public Interest Act 2015, which introduced a phased restoration of pay for most public sector workers between 2016 and 2018 (Eurofound, 2015). Civil servants in Ireland represent 10 per cent of registered voters (Department of Public Expenditure & Reform – Databank, accessed 2020). As in the other cases analysed in the book, and confirming our theoretical expectations, Ireland seized the post-conditionality context to reverse measures adopted during the crisis.

A general election took place in February 2016 with Kenny's FG remaining the largest party despite losing twenty-six seats. Labour, which had been the junior coalition party with FG, was reduced to just seven deputies. This result made it impossible for FG and Labour to have an absolute majority of seats and repeat the government solution in place since 2011. After several rounds of negotiations, FG formed a minority government facilitated by FF and with the support of independent deputies (McDonald, 2016). The confirmation in May 2016 of Ireland's exit from the EDP put the new government in a stronger position to enact reversals; and in 2017 it secured the passage of the Public Service Pay and Pensions Act, which broadened the scope of public cut reversals started in 2015.

However, those measures would not completely unwind until July 2022. The government justified the slow pace of reversals on the grounds that, given the 'UK's decision to exit the EU, an increase in protectionist measures and changes in other jurisdictions, Ireland needs to make sure that public finances continue to be managed in a prudent fashion' (D'Arcy, 2018). This was stressed by several of our interviewees.[46] For example, a former Minister told us that 'the UK is still a very big part of Irish economic activity. In many ways, our whole market is directed towards the UK.'[47] Furthermore, according to a former member of government, the goal after the programme was to achieve and sustain increasing budget surpluses.[48] At the time of writing (April 2020), the pay freeze in the public sector, the 10 per cent reduction in pay for new entrants to the public service and the cuts in civil servant salaries above €65,000 have all been reversed.

Regarding welfare policy, many of the measures adopted during the crisis were reversed in the post-crisis period, including the dismantling of the reductions in unemployment, child, maternity, illness, health and injury benefits. The elimination of the Christmas bonus for pensioners and the reduction of fuel and rent allowances for social beneficiaries were also partially reversed in the post-conditionality phase.

In contrast, most of the fiscal policy measures remained in place. The new taxes, the tax rises and the cuts in tax credits, exemptions and reliefs were not reversed. The Universal Social Charge was the most controversial measure in this regard (Finn, 2015). Though it was adopted as a temporary measure in 2010 within the scope of the National Recovery Plan and despite the social pressure to scrap it, the government has insisted on keeping it, arguing that it cannot afford to have a €3.9 billion hole in the budget due to Brexit and all the other uncertainties (Finn, 2019). The fact that reversals have been made mostly to public pay and welfare policy and less to fiscal policy gives credence to our proposal, namely that more reversals are expected when the benefits of those reversals are concentrated; and when the costs are diffused.

The privatisation of state assets during conditionality was not reversed after the programme ended. This is also the case of the Legal Services Bill, which was implemented only after the end of the programme (2015) and has since remained in place. In line with the theory, the Irish case shows the reversal of structural reforms is more costly for governments and therefore less likely to happen. The water charges were an exception to this, as the government decided to reverse them in April 2016 (European Commission, 2016b). This was a reform that was never fully implemented, socially unpopular and therefore an area where the government could claim credit for reversing it.

To sum up, many measures were reversed in the post-conditionality period. Most of them addressed the cuts in the public sector and in social benefits. This can be explained by the concentration of benefits, the electoral gains the government could reap from these reversals, plus the fact that they were temporary measures. There were fewer reversals in fiscal policy and of structural reforms. With the exception of water charges, all the measures reversed by the government were temporary and therefore easier to undo. The uncertainties related to Brexit, together with the fact that there was no clear partisan turnover in the post-conditionality period in Ireland, favoured the continuity of most measures adopted during the crisis.

Conclusion

The analysis of the Irish case indicates that, similar to other cases in the book and in line with our Proposal One, decision-makers in Ireland also had room for manoeuvre under conditionality. First, we showed that the government took the window of opportunity opened by the bailout to propose measures that had been on the agenda but which had not been implemented before, specifically property tax and wage-setting changes. Secondly, our analysis demonstrated that the Irish government was able to limit the Troika's ambitions, both in the negotiation and the implementation phases. For example, the FF/Labour coalition was able to persuade the Troika not to include the abolition of green diesel in the MoU and not to change the corporation tax rate. In the implementation phase, we showed that partisan turnover in 2011 led to the renegotiation of some of the measures in the MoU, specifically the reversal of the minimum wage cut and the extension of the period of fiscal consolidation (from three to four years). Still in the implementation phase, we demonstrated that Ireland implemented far fewer structural reforms than had been agreed in the MoU. This was largely due to the fact that the priority for both Ireland and the Troika was to achieve the fiscal consolidation goals. Structural reforms were secondary to them. The Irish economy was already fairly open and although these reforms were important, they were not central to the programme.

Furthermore, the fact that the Irish government managed to continuously reduce the budget deficit may have given the government the room it needed to avoid implementing all structural reforms. This is in line with our theoretical expectation that credibility was an important condition for negotiation leeway (Proposal Three). This credibility preceded the actual bailout. On the one hand, the Troika saw Ireland's crisis as a hiccup in an overall positive economic trajectory and structural context. On the other, the Irish governments understood that regaining credibility was a fundamental strategy to increase their leverage vis-à-vis the lenders. Ireland had taken austerity measures early, which was understood by the Troika as proof that the country would do whatever it took to fix the situation. This indication of early ownership fostered mutual trust. Furthermore, the FF/Greens coalition intentionally adopted an attitude to 'under-promise and over-deliver' so that they would seem more credible in the eyes of the lenders. Lastly, the ideological proximity between the main parties meant that negotiations with Irish authorities were relatively unproblematic and the implementation, with just a couple of exceptions, was carried out with little social unrest. This leverage was severely limited whenever the issue was very salient to the lenders, for example the bail-in of senior bondholders in 2011. Therefore, our proposal on the room for manoeuvre needs to take into account the saliency of the issue under negotiation.

Regarding the post-conditionality period, the analysis shows that despite several reversals in the public sector and social benefits cuts, most of the measures adopted in other areas (fiscal policies; structural reforms) were not reversed post-crisis. This confirms our Proposal Four, according to which governments partially reverse policies when a bailout terminates. The profile of reversals in Ireland gives credence to our expectation that more reversals are likely to occur when their benefits are concentrated; when the costs are diffused and when the government can reap electoral benefits from them. The analysis also shows that Brexit and its consequences for Ireland also made the Irish government more risk-averse, which resulted in a conservative approach to reversals.

Lastly, the overall bailout experience represented a significant change in the nature of the relationship between Ireland and the EU. Before the crisis, Ireland's relations with the EU were relatively distant. The crisis proved a turning point in this respect, with Ireland integrating more closely in the European order and demonstrating to Irish elites the limitations of their economic model as well as the importance of their European links. This has only been emphasised in the post-crisis period as Brexit appears to herald a new crisis for the Irish economy and is therefore another consideration when analysing the Irish government's response in the wake of the bailout.

Notes

1 With Adam Standring.
2 Interview IR 11, Minister, Dublin, 15 January 2019; Interview IR 13, Minister, Dublin, 16 January 2019; and Interview IR 15, Minister, Dublin, 17 January 2019.
3 Interview IR 13, Minister, Dublin, 16 January 2019.
4 Interview IR 15, Minister, Dublin, 17 January 2019.
5 Interview IR 15, Minister, Dublin, 17 January 2019.
6 Interview IR 10, senior civil servant, Dublin, 15 January 2019 and Interview IR 13, Minister, Dublin, 16 January 2019.
7 Interview IR 13, Minister, Dublin, 16 January 2019.
8 Interview IR 10, senior civil servant, Dublin, 15 January 2019.

9 Interview IR 12, Minister, Dublin, 16 January 2019.
10 FF's history of involvement in Eurosceptic party groups was also indicative of their reluctance to engage at the European level. Between 1999 and 2009, they were a participant and founder member of the Union for Europe of the Nations, along with Italy's Lega Nord and Poland's Law and Justice Party. In 2009 they switched allegiance to the pro-European ALDE.
11 Interview IR 15, Minister, Dublin, 17 January 2019.
12 Interview IR 12, Minister, Dublin, 16 January 2019.
13 Interview IR 15, Minister, Dublin, 17 January 2019.
14 Interview IR 10, senior civil servant, Dublin, 15 January 2019.
15 Interview IR 10, senior civil servant, Dublin, 15 January 2019; Interview IR 11, Minister, Dublin, 15 January 2019; and Interview IR 12, Minister, Dublin, 16 January 2019.
16 Interview IR 15, Minister, Dublin, 17 January 2019.
17 Interview IR 15, Minister, Dublin, 17 January 2019.
18 Interview IR 15, Minister, Dublin, 17 January 2019.
19 Interview IR 10, senior civil servant, Dublin, 15 January 2019.
20 Interview IR 14, senior civil servant, Dublin, 16 January 2019 and Interview IR 15, Minister, Dublin, 17 January 2019.
21 Interview IR 10, senior civil servant, Dublin, 15 January 2019 and Interview IR 5, trade union representative, Dublin, 18 January 2017.
22 Interview IR 10, senior civil servant, Dublin, 15 January 2019.
23 Interview IR 4, high official, Dublin, 18 January 2017.
24 Interview IR 4, high official, Dublin, 18 January 2017; Interview IR 6, party leader, Dublin, 19 January 2017; and Interview IR 8, senior civil servant, Dublin, 20 January 2017.
25 Interview IR 10, senior civil servant, Dublin, 15 January 2019.
26 Interview IR 8, senior civil servant, Dublin, 20 January 2017.
27 Interview IR 4, high official, Dublin, 18 January 2017.
28 Interview IR 10, senior civil servant, Dublin, 15 January 2019.
29 Interview IR 8, senior civil servant, Dublin, 20 January 2017.
30 Interview IR 10, senior civil servant, Dublin, 15 January 2019.
31 Interview IR 15, Minister, Dublin, 17 January 2019.
32 A guaranteed bond offers a secondary guarantee that interest and principal payments will be made by a third party, should the issuer default due to reasons such as insolvency or bankruptcy. Senior bondholders have priority in the repayment.
33 Interview IR 13, Minister, Dublin, 16 January 2019 and Interview IR 15, Minister, Dublin, 17 January 2019.
34 Interview IR 8, senior civil servant, Dublin, 20 January 2017 and Interview IR 14, senior civil servant, Dublin, 16 January 2019.
35 Interview IR 14, senior civil servant, Dublin, 16 January 2019.
36 Interview IR 2, senior civil servant, Dublin, 16 January 2017 and Interview IR 8, senior civil servant, Dublin, 20 January 2017.
37 Interview IR 5, trade union representative, Dublin, 18 January 2017.

38 Interview IR 3, civil servant, Dublin, 16 January; Interview IR 10, senior civil servant, Dublin, 15 January 2019; and Interview IR 13, Minister, Dublin, 16 January 2019.
39 Interview IR 7, trade union representative, Dublin, 19 January 2017 and Interview IR 14, senior civil servant, Dublin, 16 January 2019.
40 Interview IR 11, Minister, Dublin, 15 January 2019.
41 Interview IR 15, Minister, Dublin, 17 January 2019.
42 Interview IR 14, senior civil servant, Dublin, 16 January 2019.
43 Interview IR 4, high official, Dublin, 18 January 2017; Interview IR 11, Minister, Dublin, 15 January 2019; and Interview IR 14, senior civil servant, Dublin, 16 January 2019.
44 Interview IR 15, Minister, Dublin, 17 January 2019.
45 Interview IR 10, senior civil servant, Dublin, 15 January 2019.
46 Interview IR 11, Minister, Dublin, 15 January 2019 and Interview IR 12, Minister, Dublin, 16 January 2019.
47 Interview IR 11, Minister, Dublin, 15 January 2019.
48 Interview IR 13, Minister, Dublin, 16 January 2019.

4

Portugal

Introduction

Portugal is an interesting case to assess the room for manoeuvre of governments during a bailout and the factors influencing this leverage. In particular, it shows the importance of credibility and that, to some extent, elections do matter during a bailout. Indeed, Portugal experienced quite distinct government configurations in the period under study, and with different degrees of external credibility.

This chapter is organised in six sections. We first look at the period just before the bailout. A second section covers the episode during which a minority Socialist government negotiated the MoUs during the electoral campaign. The third section looks at the implementation of these documents by a rightist coalition composed of the Social Democratic Party (PSD) and the Social Democratic Centre–Popular Party (CDS–PP). Although their names suggest otherwise, both parties were clearly on the right of the political spectrum at this time (Freire and Santana-Pereira, 2012; Lisi, 2010, pp. 137–138).[1] The fourth section focuses on what happened under two distinct governments when the lenders had left town, the last being a minority Socialist government governing with the parliamentary support of the three radical left-wing parties. A sixth section concludes.

September 2008–April 2011: before the bailout (centre-left government)

After the fall of the Lehman Brothers in September 2008, there was a dramatic slowdown in the Portuguese economy. In line with the EU's initial neo-Keynesian approach to the crisis, the first Sócrates government (Socialist – majoritarian: 2005–2009) adopted a policy of fiscal expansion. However, when the extent of the Greek deficit became publicly known a few months later, the EU started to worry about the credibility of national bonds and the European Council urged Portugal to rapidly engage in policies aimed at medium-term fiscal consolidation (De Giorgi *et al.*, 2015). The national government was thus forced to make a huge U-turn in its expansionary policies, taking back what it had just given. The Ministers from the Socialist Party (PS) interviewed testified to the enormity of this task, which obliged the government to renege on past commitments and, when not possible, to make extra savings to compensate for the increased investment and spending commitments.[2]

In April 2010, the interest rates on government bonds soared to their highest level since entry into the euro. As the incumbent PS had lost its absolute parliamentary majority in the September 2009 elections, it needed the support of opposition parties to pass budgetary measures. Despite an increasingly critical stance towards the government, PSD abstained and let the 2010 budget pass in March. In May and September 2010, PSD abstained on two more additional austerity packages. The draft package included measures on both spending and revenue, a written commitment to freeze the minimum wage until the economy recovered and amendments to liberalise the Labour Code (De Giorgi *et al.*, 2015). The announcement of these measures led to waves of protest, including a general strike on 24 November 2010, the first in twenty-two years to be called jointly by the two union confederations, namely the General Union of Workers (UGT) and the General Confederation of Portuguese Workers (CGTP) (Campos Lima and Artiles, 2011).

The EU was not convinced by these cuts and reforms, and Portugal faced mounting pressure from the financial markets. As Ireland began its adjustment programme with the Troika in November 2010, all eyes turned to the Portuguese economy. On 9 March 2011, two days before the special Brussels summit of euro area leaders, Portuguese bond yields had risen to 7 per cent. European institutions, together with individual member states such as France and Germany,[3] urged the Portuguese government to ask for financial assistance. The Prime Minister, José Sócrates, refused to do so but agreed to negotiate what was known as a 'shadow programme' with the EU. The idea was to get the Eurogroup and the ECB to agree on a fourth austerity package so that the Eurogroup would publicly back the plan and the ECB would announce its commitment to buy Portuguese bonds in the secondary market – in the hope that the moves would relax financial speculation.[4] This led to the intervention of a group of EC and ECB representatives in Portugal to draft the plan in conjunction with the government (Dinis and Coelho, 2012; Moury and Standring, 2017).

The measures included further tax rises and cuts in public sector wages, unemployment benefits and the highest pensions, among other things (Távora and González, 2014); however, no changes were made to the labour market legislation. Since it was not possible to achieve a compromise with the social partners in just two days, the Minister of Employment, Helena André, asked them to publicly manifest their acquiescence on a series of reforms, leaving the concrete negotiations for later (Dinis and Coelho, 2012, p. 80). Later that day, all social partners except one (the more lefitst CGTP) signed a declaration that contained fifty measures to improve competitiveness. On 22 March 2011, the Acordo Tripartido para a Competitividade e Emprego (Tripartite Agreement of Competitiveness and Employment) was signed by these same actors. The agreement introduced the reduction of severance payments for new open-ended and fixed-term contracts and made company-level negotiations possible for larger companies.

When asked about the extent of their autonomy in the preparation of these reforms and budgetary packages, all seven participants in the negotiations that we interviewed acknowledged the strong influence of the European Commission.[5] Even before the entry into force of the stricter version of the SGP, Portuguese Ministers were very anxious to placate the Commission when preparing budget plans and structural reforms. They claimed that disapproving feedback from the Commission was taken into account by investors and the ECB, thus potentially increasing yields on sovereign bonds. To avoid EC criticism on their budgetary plans *a posteriori*, experts from the Commission were invited to draft the fourth austerity package together with government members.[6] However, and in a similar spirit to our crisis exploitation hypothesis, all interviewees noted that these austerity packages included many reforms that they had previously supported but had felt unable to push – the reduction of severance payments and cuts in spending on prescription drugs were frequently given as examples.[7]

While Parliament's approval was not formally required, Sócrates announced he would resign if it did not approve the fourth austerity package. The programme, he said, was the only alternative to the bailout (Ferreira, 2012). PSD – clearly leading in the polls at the time – announced it would vote against the government; the package was rejected and Sócrates immediately resigned. At the start of the election campaign, the Socialist caretaker government requested the bailout and called in the Troika on 6 April.

After the rejection of this fourth austerity package, PSD sent an official letter to the Prime Minister and the President on 31 March 2011 defending the 'bailout' option.[8] One day later, on 1 April, they received another letter in defence of the bailout, but this time signed by the Governor of the Bank of Portugal, Carlos Costa. On that same afternoon, the *Jornal de Negócios* published declarations from the Socialist Finance Minister, Teixeira dos Santos, saying that the circumstances were such that it was impossible to avoid bringing in the Troika. It was only then that Sócrates announced to the country that Portugal had decided to request international financial assistance.

May 2011: drafting the Memorandum (centre-left and centre-right parties)

In May 2011, the Portuguese authorities reached agreement with the European Union and the International Monetary Fund on the Financial Assistance Programme. Two separate Memoranda (one with the EU and another with the IMF) were signed by three parties: PS, PSD and CDS–PP, on 17 May 2011. The bailout comprised €78 billion, two-thirds of which was financed by the EU and the final third by the IMF. It foresaw actions on deficit reduction (notably by cutting spending in education, pensions and health; lowering transfers to regional and local authorities; and reducing public sector employment); competitiveness (reduction of severance payments, labour reforms and liberalisation of the public sector); deleveraging of banks, and reforms to the judicial system. While the Memoranda included most measures signed in March, the envisaged decentralisation of collective bargaining was pushed further. It defined tougher goals for the reduction of severance pay to bring it in alignment with the EU average (a bigger reduction for new hires and the extension to current employees) and added new rules to facilitate dismissals.

It must be noted that, though harsh, the programme included some measures to protect the poorest segments of the population. For example, the lowest pensions and salaries remained untouched; the minimum duration of contributions for eligibility to unemployment benefit was shortened; unemployment benefits were extended to include a specific category of self-employment; and benefits were increased by 10 per cent for unemployed couples with children, and unemployed single parents (Cardoso and Branco, 2018).

According to our interviewees, the negotiations were first prepared at a technical level: Portuguese academics and top civil servants were invited to join IMF and EC working groups with the aim of diagnosing and proposing possible remedies to the country's macroeconomic problems.[9] In this phase, benchmarking and consultations with stakeholders were important devices.[10]

After this preparatory work, Socialist Ministers were the Troika's main interlocutors.[11] These negotiations were led by the Minister of Finance and the Prime Minister's Office.[12] While the international lenders also consulted regularly with the two centre-right parties (leading in the polls at this time), the radical left parties refused to enter into discussions with the Troika.

When asked about their room for manoeuvre while negotiating the MoU, members of the government and the Troika unanimously recognised the change in '*rapport de force*' vis-à-vis when the fourth austerity package was being drafted; this meant that their margin of negotiation was smaller.[13] The difference between the two waves of negotiations is of course that failure was much more costly for the government in the case of a bailout request. As a Secretary of State explains:

> It is always different ... negotiating when ... negotiating as people who are in a position of strength, because at the end of the day the country may not accept [the agreement] ... as opposed to negotiating with the Troika after requesting financial assistance and the administrative officials negotiating with us are negotiating with a sense of superiority ... because in the end the country will have to accept if they do not concede, that is the major difference.[14]

In fact, there were many situations in which the government had to concede to requests from the international lenders. This was what happened, for example, with the size of the loan (the government wanted an extra €10 million), the freezing of the minimum wage (which the government opposed), the timing of privatisations (the government wanted a clause allowing it to sell public companies only when the market conditions were good, which was not included),[15] and the speed with which public and private debt was to be reduced (the government wanted it to be slower).[16] According to interviews, the international lenders' preferences for these measures were the most salient.[17] A Minister gives the example of the minimum wage:

> When we negotiated the Stability and Growth Pact 4, the European Central Bank and the European Commission wanted us to include a reference on freezing the national minimum wage. The government said 'no' various times until it was actually not included in the SGP 4. When it came to the Troika memorandum, this was an example of a measure they said was not even worth discussing, they told us to include the freezing of the minimum wage or they would not give us financing.[18]

Many government members also refer to the fact that the EC took the opportunity of the MoU to foster the implementation of Directives, sometimes going beyond the original legislation.[19] The regulation of energy tariffs[20] and prohibiting the state to ask companies for 'compensation' (e.g. the promise to invest in the country) when they acquire military equipment[21] were cited as examples.

Despite these constraints, and in line with our theoretical premise, none of the participants saw the negotiation as a diktat from the international lenders. They describe the negotiations as an 'intelligent game'[22] in which the Troika representatives listened to the Ministers' arguments about the feasibility or desirability of reforms and were willing to accept alternative solutions.[23] Indeed, government members reported many instances in which the government managed to convince international lenders. Examples of this include the dismissal of some public servants (not included), maintaining lower pensions, applying the reduction of severance payments only to new contracts,[24] cuts to severance payments (lower than the Troika wanted)[25] and the duration of the unemployment benefit (not shortened immediately).[26] As a member of the government explains:

> There is obviously not a lot of room for manoeuvre, but my experience from matters that I negotiated with the Troika is that if we [were] able to put forward a counter-argument to what was initially proposed, and to have alternative proposals, there would be a willingness to be flexible on some points. If we look at the initial proposal that the Troika put on the table, for example in the area of the labour market, as opposed to the end result of the agreement signed in May ..., great advances were made ... The Memorandum was negotiated word for word, almost every comma ... everything was negotiated to the last detail.[27]

Additionally, Ministers reported being given great autonomy to find solutions to reach the targeted cuts in the sectors which lenders considered less salient. In the health sector, for example, a government member says that the large majority of the measures to cut spending had been proposed by the government itself.[28]

The four representatives of the lenders we spoke to claim this government leverage is explained by the fact that their institutions value ownership and need insider knowledge to design efficient policies.[29] An agent from the IMF notes: 'It's not like the Troika comes with a list of things and says that they have to do these things and then get the money. It doesn't make sense partly because only the government knows how things work.'[30] Similarly, government officials noted in interviews that they had more leverage on the definition of diagnostics and solutions in both the technical meetings and negotiations because their expertise on Portugal was greater than that of the IMF and EC representatives.[31] Related to this, interviewees from the government and the EC consider that the state capacity (in particular, the fact that both Ministers and the civil service could be trusted) was an important factor to strengthen the government's bargaining position.[32] As discussed in our theoretical approach, insider knowledge and ownership are crucial for a government's credibility, contributing to some room of manoeuvre in negotiating with external lenders. The statements by the lenders' representatives shed light on the relationship between these factors in practice.

Many interviewees also noted the occasional divergence of views between the Troika members, although they did not refer to this as a source of leverage. The question of the provision of liquidity (encouraged by the IMF but viewed more cautiously by the ECB), the speed of deficit reduction (the IMF, more concerned about external competitiveness, was pushing for a slower reduction, unlike the EC and ECB)[33] and the EC's relative lack of flexibility on competition policy[34] were given as examples. One government member also noted that the IMF was much more 'pragmatic' and 'independent' than the EC, which was more dependent on member states' instructions.[35]

As expected, many Socialist Ministers we talked to spontaneously mentioned that the bailout sometimes opened a window of opportunity for reforms they had long desired but could not have passed beforehand.[36] For example, a Socialist Secretary of State gives the example of some justice reforms:

> For example, in urban renewal, the Memorandum includes a rapid eviction process that takes place out of the courts; this is strongly contested by lawyers and the legal professions because they make money from the processes and the lengthy proceedings. It was included in the Memorandum to give it the force of an agreement with the Troika and so something that had to be done.[37]

Another government member, speaking about health reforms:

> There is here a window of opportunity that allows us to bypass the resistance of stakeholders, professions, industries, pharmacies, and of our administration, to make reforms that were necessary ... Portugal had the highest per capita spending on medicines in Europe – something wrong in a country with a relatively low GDP ... prescriptions for generic drugs were minimal in Portugal, we all knew something had to be done; but we could not pass reforms, doctors opposed them, the industry was blocking them ... We asked to have this measure inserted in the Memorandum.[38]

Our interviewees from the EC and the IMF also share the view that the bailout could open a 'window of opportunity' to pass necessary reforms.[39] An IMF official additionally explains that the bailout allows the reforms valued by government to be implemented more efficiently:

> Portugal has been in a permanent reform mode since before the official start of the crisis. However, ... many of these reforms were headline reforms ... In a crisis, there is some control and checks and balances in the implementation process because you have people looking over your shoulder ...It's an opportunity for the country to do things that couldn't normally be done.[40]

Interviewees further noted that some Ministers strategically used the Commission's influence to push forward measures that were facing opposition from their colleagues. When talking about spending cuts in various areas, a former Secretary of State remembered: 'On more than one occasion, policy proposals that had come, for example, from the Minister of Finance, and which weren't accepted by the Cabinet, appeared again in the Commission's proposals.[41] The reduction of corporate tax and the duration of unemployment benefit were given as examples.[42]

Related to this, a Minister noted how the Troika's dialogue with the rightist parties in opposition weakened the government's bargaining hand.[43] 'One example of the latter is the controversial reduction in the social security contribution paid by employers ['Single Social Tax'], which was to be offset by an increase in the VAT rate [by raising the low and intermediate rates]. Another is privatisation, which the PS wanted to limit more than the international lenders and the PSD.'[44] These examples also show that the division in the Portuguese camps weakened the country's bargaining position; more specifically, the Troika's discussion with the main opposition party allowed it to push for reforms that the government had previously managed to take off the table.

June 2011–May 2014: implementation of the Memorandum – centre-right government

In the June 2011 elections, the right-wing PSD/CDS–PP coalition obtained an absolute majority of seats and the leader of PSD, Passos Coelho – known at the time for belonging to the neoliberal section of the party (Lisi, 2010) – became the new Prime Minister. He immediately brought together a group of five experts to form the Monitoring Structure of Memoranda,[45] under the leadership of Carlos Moedas, the Minister of State to the Prime Minister; this group was charged with the internal coordination of Ministers' implementation of the MoU. Some Ministers told us that, for some areas that were less salient for lenders, they were given a free rein to make their preferred amendments to the MoU right away. For example, a government member explained to us how the Justice section of the MoU was entirely redrafted by the Ministry.[46]

During the programme, Carlos Moedas (and his team) and the Minister of Finance (or his Secretary of State) were the interlocutors with the Troika. In addition to the six-monthly visits from the Troika, they spoke to each other weekly (Santos Pereira, 2014, pp. 95–112). Additionally, regular meetings took place for each sector between experts from the IMF and the EC, and the respective Portuguese Secretary of State, sometimes accompanied by members of the Bank of Portugal.[47] The Troika representatives also met regularly with MPs from the PS and trade union leaders, meetings that all interviewees from those groups described as a 'mere formality' in which nothing substantial was disclosed, let alone negotiated.[48]

The government immediately started to implement the MoU, and rarely stepped back despite general strikes and demonstrations. There was one notable exception, however: in September 2012, the government proposed financing a reduction in employers' contributions to social security by increasing the contribution paid by workers, because an additional increase in VAT did not seem feasible. According to the Troika's mission chief, this was the Finance Minister's idea (Faria and Aníbal, 2012). This announcement, seen as particularly unfair because it directly transferred the burden from employers to workers, prompted not only one of the largest demonstrations in Portuguese history (Accornero and Ramos Pinto, 2015, p. 493) but also widespread opposition including from many employers. The government eventually withdrew the measure. To pay for the reduction, there was a further increase in tax, a solution the Troika did not welcome but eventually accepted.[49]

Other significant revisions to the Memorandum were agreed upon during the regular progress assessments. The difficulty in achieving the planned reduction to the deficit (3 per cent) was the first clear reason for the revisions to the original MoU, given that fiscal multipliers were substantially higher than forecasters had assumed. Similarly, the Constitutional Court's veto of some spending cuts (e.g. the suspension of the 13th and 14th month salaries for public workers and pensioners; and the increase in social security contributions from 5 to 6 per cent for the beneficiaries of unemployment subsidies) obliged the government to find alternative solutions.[50] As a consequence, new taxes and spending cuts were introduced; these included additional cuts to public wages at all levels and new and higher taxes.[51]

Those additional efforts led to disagreement between coalition partners. Notably, the leader of the junior party in the coalition, Paulo Portas, went head to head in summer 2013 with the Finance Minister, Victor Gaspar, largely because Portas did not agree with further pension cuts. This first triggered the resignation of the Finance Minister, and then that of all CDS–PP Ministers (Rodrigues, 2017). After the mediation of the President, Cavaco Silva, the government was reshuffled and the junior party members, including the leader, were reintegrated. Thereafter, the new Vice-Prime Minister from the CDS–PP, Paulo Portas, was also involved in the meetings.[52]

The revisions of the Memoranda also encompassed structural reforms.[53] Goals that had been left vague in the original MoU were now specified; moreover, the existing provisions were amended and new ones added. These revisions paved the way for new rounds of bargaining with the Troika. As with the drafting of the original Memoranda, these negotiations were perceived as a two-sided process in which both parties took initiatives to propose new measures and exerted some influence.[54]

Interestingly, none of the Ministers we spoke to could recall any examples of policies they were asked to adopt against their will.[55] In fact, all six interviewees from the Passos Coelho government stressed that the lenders' position was in congruence with their own. They also reported that the lenders generally accepted their arguments when they explained that a certain reform was not feasible either politically (e.g. on reimbursement to the state by the energy sector, which could endanger privatisation;[56] or further changes to the Labour Code which could jeopardise the signing of the Social Pacts[57]) or constitutionally (e.g. further cuts in pensions).

As observed earlier, and in agreement with the theoretical expectation, government members also reported many examples of how the bailout allowed them to pass measures that they deemed necessary but could not previously have passed. An interesting case is the reform of the Labour Code and labour-related legislation. For example, the MoU provides that severance payments should be decreased to the 'European average', which, according to experts, ranges between twenty and twelve days in line with seniority (Prandeka, 2013). This objective was included in the Social Pact (Comissão Permanente da Concertação Social, 2012) signed by the government and social partners (again with the exception of the CGTP) on 18 January 2012, but with the specification that it would be for new contracts only. The government and the external lenders favoured the most stringent calculation, and the fifth and sixth reviews (International Monetary Fund, 2012c, 2013d) extended the reduction of severance payments to all employment contracts in force and reduced them to an average of twelve days per year of employment.[58] As a former Secretary of State remembers:

> The Memorandum established a second reduction [of severance payments] to align Portugal with the European Union average, but it did not specify the average. It was necessary to calculate it. And it can be calculated in various ways, can't it? And each way has its own merit and, maybe, UGT's preference was for a higher number. We thought that, in order to make the labour market more dynamic, perhaps a lower number would be more advantageous.[59]

Another interesting example of the exploitation of external constraints is the reduction of the excessive rents enjoyed by the energy sector. Here, the Troika's interest in reducing rents was shared by the Minister of the Economy.[60] On the other hand, the Minister of Finance feared that these efforts might scare off possible buyers of the main energy company, Electricidades de Portugal– (Portuguese Electricity), which was about to be privatised (Santos Pereira, 2014). As a compromise, rents were reduced by only one-third (Dinis and Coelho, 2012; Santos Pereira, 2014). Even though the reduction was lower than it might have been, it was resisted by the sector. The Minister of the Economy used the following strategy to obtain agreement:

> I spoke to the leaders of the mission and told them we were in favour of advancing with more measures to cut the excessive rents but that we needed

> their support to do so ... We engaged in meetings with all the energy producers on the pretext that the Troika was being very fundamentalist on the matter. We also told them that if they did not agree with our proposed cuts, it was likely that the Troika would end up being even tougher on them. That was how we decided that one way to cut the revenues was to completely eliminate capacity payments, and reduce those payments after the adjustment. (Santos Pereira, 2014, pp. 231–232)

A third example is related to the whole section on deregulation (around a thousand words, two pages) that was included in the fifth revision (International Monetary Fund, 2012c). Among other things, this section prohibited the government from creating new regulations generating costs for businesses without the elimination of an existing regulation with an equivalent cost. In his memoir, the Minister of the Economy confirms how the Troika members went beyond what was written in the initial MoU and introduced this new measure (Santos Pereira, 2014, pp. 101–102).

During the negotiations, the government's leverage was very dependent on whether the issue was salient to the lenders. For example, the Commission monitored very closely the drafting of the new competition law (this strengthens the Competition Authority's powers of inspection, sanction and supervision), as well as the framework for professional bodies (removing several restrictions on matters of recognition of professional qualifications, advertising and access to regulated professions) and the framework for national regulatory authorities (which strengthens the independence of public regulatory and supervisory bodies). The reforms of the Labour Code were supervised closely (and solely) by the IMF.[61]

Additionally, and in line with the literature that states that credibility increases the leverage of bailed out executives, Ministers also reported that the lenders' position evolved over time,[62] and that their leverage was greater towards the end of the programme when growth picked up and yields declined. Notably, the Minister of the Economy notes in his memoir that:

> It is important to note that even the position of the Troika changed over the years. At first, the Troika was extremely demanding and intransigent on certain matters; indeed, there had been a lot of mistrust on the part of international creditors ... However, at a certain point the Troika started to be much more flexible and very understanding. (Santos Pereira, 2014, p. 103)

Pension cuts are a good example of the government's increasing leverage. Towards the end of the programme, the Constitutional Court blocked the introduction of permanent cuts in pensions and public wages. The government decided not to propose alternative measures. The lenders were not happy about this and refused to give the last loan instalment (Dinis and Coelho, 2012); however, there was not much they could do as the programme was coming to an end and Portugal could return to the markets to get funding.

This section thus lends support to our expectation that bailed out governments have leverage, that elections matter and that some of the policies implemented under conditionality had been on the government's agenda for some time. It also provides evidence for the proposal that the terms of conditionality change after elections. The right-wing government deepened spending cuts (and increased taxes) more than was initially planned, but it is unclear whether the left would have been able to do otherwise. As regards structural reforms, however, centre-right Ministers clearly went beyond what had been negotiated in the initial Memorandum, pushing deregulation further than had been agreed by their left-wing predecessors.

Two final points are worth noting. First, and as observed by Socialist Ministers, the Troika was sometimes divided during the programme.[63] Many government and Troika members we talked to noted that the EC was less pragmatic than the IMF,[64] more insistent on rules and a quick deficit reduction, and that the ECB was quite silent and intervened only in the banking sector.[65] However, and as observed by Lütz *et al.* (2020), we have no evidence that this division was exploited by the government. Secondly, the Constitutional Court was undoubtedly the main veto player over these years, invalidating nine policy proposals. In addition to those mentioned above (rejection of the permanent suspension of 13th and 14th month salaries and of the increase in the contributions made by the unemployed), many other measures were declared unconstitutional (further cuts to pensions and civil servant wages; the convergence of private and public pension schemes, etc.).

After the bailout I: May 2014–September 2015 (centre-right government)

After the exit, and until the repayment of 75 per cent of the financial assistance, Portugal was put under post-programme surveillance and received six-monthly visits and recommendations from the EC and the IMF. Moreover, Portugal was still under an Excessive Deficit Procedure, which had started in December 2009 when the Council issued a recommendation to bring the deficit to below 3 per cent by 2013. This deadline was postponed twice (first to 2015 and then to 2016). Under this procedure, there is closer scrutiny of the country's actions, and failure to meet the goals and deadlines can lead to sanctions. In practice, government members reported that the EC was still concerned about macroeconomic plans and objectives and that regular information should be provided by the Ministry of Finance, but that the government was left to propose and decide on how to reach these goals.[66] Furthermore, government members see the fact that it was civil servants or advisors, rather than the actual Minister or Secretary of State as before, who received the EC representatives[67] as an importantly symbolic change. As for the IMF visits, they were perceived as an obligation to provide information, not as a constraint on member states' actions.[68]

Despite the existing, albeit less stringent, constraints, and in line with our theoretical expectations, the government reversed some structural reforms and budget cuts as soon as Portugal exited the programme. Notably, the representativeness criterion to extend sectoral agreements was partially reversed by the Passos Coelho government, after both employers and trade unions opposed the new law (Afonso and Bulfone, 2019). The government also reversed the 20 per cent cuts in civil servant salaries. The Minister of Finance justified this to the lenders by pointing out the savings made by the significant number of people reaching pension age that year. Following these decisions, international lenders issued the warning that they would have to be called again in the future (Pires and Martins, 2015, pp. 200–208).

In August 2014, again against EC and IMF recommendations, the government ratified the new UGT and employers' agreement that increased the minimum wage by €20. In December 2014, the freezing of early pensions for those with more than forty years of social security deductions was reversed. Furthermore, the 2015 budget abolished the temporary extraordinary solidarity contribution on pensions in place since 2011, except for the highest pensions (Pires and Martins, 2015, pp. 200–208).

Nevertheless, there were also strong elements of continuity. Many spending cuts and structural reforms were maintained; and taxes on wages and goods remained at the same level. The government also went ahead with planned reforms, including the privatisation of the national airline. The Labour Code remained largely unaltered, with the exception of the above-mentioned change.

We thus observe that, as we expected, the return to the markets and the exit from the bailout led to partial reversals, despite the strong congruence of views between the lenders and the coalition. Return to the status quo ex ante occurred when benefits were concentrated in groups that are well organised and traditionally vote rather than abstain (pensioners,[69] civil servants[70]). By contrast, most structural reforms were kept intact.

A break from austerity? The leftist coalition, September 2015–September 2018

The 2015 legislative elections opened the door to a grand coalition of left-wing parties (Fernandes and Jalali, 2017). After all left-wing parties voted against a centre-right coalition minority government on 10 November

2015, the PS signed three bilateral (but similar) coalition agreements with the Left Bloc (BE), the Portuguese Communist Party (PCP) and the Greens. These parties identified a long list of policies passed under the Troika that they would like to be be reversed; however, they also stressed that the European rules of deficit and debt reduction ought to be respected.[71]

These proposals were first met with strong scepticism from the EU, and this period clearly demonstrates the bargaining taking place between the Portuguese executive and the EU. For example, the first draft of the state budget, presented in February 2016, included many reversals of the reforms passed under conditionality. Notably, the income tax surcharge was abolished (for high incomes) and additional tax brackets were reinstalled; the pre-bailout salary, working hours and promotions in the public sector were re-established (but the increase in their contribution to a special health insurance was maintained); the state share in the national airway company was increased again to 50 per cent; and the scope of qualification for minimum income, pensions, child and unemployment benefits enlarged and the amount increased again. Following this, the EC warned that the deficit would be excessive and that Portugal's competitiveness was in jeopardy.

The criticism from the EC was noted with concern by the government.[72] The country was still subject to an EDP at the time and obliged to bring its deficit down to 3 per cent by 2016. As observed in earlier periods, many government members report that their efforts to avoid disapproving feedback from the Commission was driven more by their desire to reassure investors than by the possibility of European sanctions.[73]

As had happened with Socrates before the bailout, EC officials were invited to Lisbon to re-draft the budget. All members of the government we interviewed stressed that the reversals could not compromise Portugal's commitment to European rules and debt reduction. A Socialist Party member put it clearly, saying that the government's biggest challenge was to know how 'to reinstate and recover income and rights in a context where the premise is compliance with European rules'.[74]

The solution found by the budget negotiators, accepted by the radical left partners, was to balance the increase in expenditures with an increase in revenues through higher taxes on vehicles, tobacco, alcohol and banking contributions. This compromise allowed the state budget to pass, with the PS, BE, PCP and the Greens voting in favour in March 2016. It was the first time in Portugal's history that a state budget had been approved with the votes of the radical left.

Although the EC accepted the 2016 state budget, four months later it increased pressure on the government by threatening sanctions as the deficit was 4.4 per cent (including a bank rescue) rather than the required 3 per cent. The Prime Minister pledged to go to the European Court of Justice if sanctions were applied but promised the EC the government would reserve the budget (i.e. spend less than was planned) to keep the deficit on track. In the end, the EC recommended a 'sanction zero', that is, a sanction without a fee to pay; and the Council gave Portugal one more year to reach a budgetary deficit below 3 per cent – stressing again the need to stop reversals, namely in pensions, and warning again against an 'excessive' increase in the minimum wage.

In the next budgets, reversals continued and were deepened or completed, for example the reintroduction of supplementary tax brackets, and a further increase in the lowest pensions and social allowances. VAT on restaurants was brought back to 13 per cent from 23 per cent, social allowances and progressions in the civil service were reinstated, and the hiring of public servants, frozen since 2010, was resumed. As noted by Fernandes *et al.* (2018), these measures distributed benefits to crucial party constituencies of all the parties involved.

This was a period of intense pressure on the government from EU institutions, according to the members of the government that we interviewed. A Secretary of State explains: 'There was a certain stigmatisation not only of the government, but of the country that was under a programme which resulted from incorrect policies ... And, therefore, there was a feeling of great distrust towards Portugal, like, what you are presenting has no credibility.'[75]

By the end of 2016, however, Portugal's economic context was improving as growth started to pick up and yields to decrease. Thanks to this cyclical effect that reduced expenditure and raised revenues, the deficit went down to €3.7 billion in 2016. The good results took Portugal out of the EDP in February 2017, moving from the corrective to the preventive arm of the Stability and Growth Pact. A series of sources – including both ex-lenders (European Commission, 2018b; International Monetary Fund, 2017) and national economists[76] – warned that the deficit was not structural; that private and public debt was only declining slowly; that comparatively speaking Portugal was still not very competitive; and that if interest rates increased or growth declined Portugal would be in trouble. Many critics also noted that the low budget deficits had been possible because of the reserves and, above all, at the expense of investment[77] and financing of welfare state services (see for example Fernandes *et al.*, 2018).

Despite these caveats, all our interviewees note that the announcement of the 2 per cent deficit for 2016,[78] even lower than the 2.3 per cent forecast and the lowest in forty years, was a milestone for proving their credibility to the EC and the investors. As one interviewee explains:

> Portugal was seen with a lot of mistrust ... And so, in the first year, it was really tough. Until we managed to have a deficit in 2016 that was clearly

> going to be below 2.5 per cent, which was the marker imposed by the institutions, and the 2.3 per cent that was in the budget and when it was confirmed to be 2.0 per cent ... Then, I think there was a structural change of attitude. As soon as things started to evolve and the result came and when we started to get results ... the investors were the first to change their attitude.[79]

Interestingly, and as observed in other countries, some Ministers also reported that they had strategically planned the reaching of a lower than forecast deficit. A Secretary of State details this approach:

> There is a great advantage to doing better than you promised to. And so my preference is for a budget with 2.2 per cent growth and then, if it is 2.4 per cent, to have some breathing space and be able to do a slightly less restrictive policy or pay the debt more quickly, rather than the scenario of 2.4 per cent but actually have 2.2 per cent so that then we are in search of measures that allow us to meet the target or to do an amended budget.[80]

Another example of Portugal's increased leverage can be found in the nationalisation of a bank, the Caixa Geral de Depósitos, that the EC resisted but finally accepted in April 2017: 'The EU did not want to allow the exclusively public financing of [the bank]. For our partners, it was unthinkable ... But at the end of the negotiations [they nevertheless] accepted [it]. We put together a proposal that made it possible to convince the European Commission that the exclusive public funding would be done under market conditions.'[81]

The good economic results not only shifted the balance of power to the benefit of Portugal in international bargaining, but also softened the EC's opposition to expansionary policies. Remarkably, for example, in May 2017 the EC shifted its opinion on the impact of an increase in the minimum wage. In its recommendations for the 2018 budget, the paragraph stating that the increase in the minimum wage was prejudicial to the country's competitiveness was removed in subsequent reports (Aguiar, 2017). Although reference was still made to a possible (but not observed) effect on low-skilled employment, it noted that such an increase could help reduce poverty and have a positive impact on domestic demand.[82]

Conclusion

Our analysis of the Portuguese executive's room for manoeuvre during the bailout provides a good illustration of our arguments. First, we show that while Portuguese Ministers were undoubtedly constrained by external actors (in particular during the bailout), they were never powerless as posited in Proposal One. When negotiating with the EC or the IMF, Ministers had some leverage and we found considerable evidence of the fact they were able to use the external constraint to pass measures that had been on their agenda beforehand.

Indeed, even before the bailout the centre-left government of José Sócrates had exploited the strong pressure on the sovereign debt to pass a series of reforms it deemed necessary. At this time, for example, the UGT and employers' associations agreed on a number of reforms, many of which had been previously resisted. After asking for help from international lenders, government members unanimously recognised that their margin of negotiation was smaller. Nevertheless, we show that the terms of the MoU were never the diktat of international lenders. Whereas the government had to cede on some aspects, it successfully opposed the international lenders' wishes on others.

Once in power, centre-right Ministers immediately began to implement the programme. New bargaining took place, and again the government was clearly not powerless. New structural measures were added in the programme revisions, sometimes going further than the original deal. Ministers from the centre-right acknowledged a strong congruence of their views with those of the international lenders and gave many examples of policies that were added to the revisions at their own request. This confirms further our first and second theoretical proposals, according to which government has room for manoeuvre and the terms of conditionality change after elections. In all this, and in line with Proposal Three, credibility matters greatly: the good economic performance and the executive's ability to respect the agreed deals were identified by government members as key assets.

As projected in Proposal Four, we finally observe partial reversals for both governments after the bailout. This holds true for many fiscal reforms, but also for some that were structural. This corroborates our argument that governments are pressured and able to reverse some of the policies adopted under conditionality. However, member states still experience very strong external constraints after a bailout: they have to respect the economic governance rules and seek to reassure investors.

Notes

1 The junior coalition party, the CDS–PP (a conservative party with Christian Democrat origins) also called for a minimal state role in the economy and social services (Lisi, 2016).

2 Interview PT 1, Minister, Lisbon, 22 January 2013; Interview PT 4, Minister, Lisbon, 22 January 2013; Interview PT 5, Minister, Lisbon, 17 January 2013; Interview PT 8, Secretary of State, Lisbon, 29 January 2013; and Interview PT 9, Secretary of State, Lisbon, 30 January 2013.

3 Gago (2018), Interview PT 5, Minister, Lisbon, 17 January 2013.
4 Interview PT 5, Minister, Lisbon, 17 January 2013.
5 Interview PT 3, Minister, Lisbon, 17 January 2013; Interview PT 4, Minister, Lisbon, 22 January 2013; Interview PT 5, Minister, Lisbon, 17 January 2013; Interview PT 6, Secretary of State, Lisbon, 28 January 2013; Interview PT 7, Secretary of State, Lisbon, 29 January 2013; Interview PT 8, Secretary of State, Lisbon, 29 January 2013; and Interview PT 9, Secretary of State, Lisbon, 30 January 2013.
6 Interview PT 5, Minister, Lisbon, 17 January 2013; Interview PT 7, Secretary of State, Lisbon, 29 January 2013; Interview PT 8, Secretary of State, Lisbon, 29 January 2013; and Interview PT 9, Secretary of State, Lisbon, 30 January 2013.
7 Interview PT 3, Minister, Lisbon, 17 January 2013; Interview PT 4, Minister, Lisbon, 22 January 2013; Interview PT 5, Minister, Lisbon, 17 January 2013; Interview PT 6, Secretary of State, Lisbon, 28 January 2013; Interview PT 7, Secretary of State, Lisbon, 29 January 2013; Interview PT 8, Secretary of State, Lisbon, 29 January 2013; and Interview PT 9, Secretary of State, Lisbon, 30 January 2013.
8 One informant from PSD testified that the party defeated the fourth austerity package with the aim of winning elections and bringing in the Troika. However, none of the other informants from PSD confirmed this spontaneously. For a similar interpretation, see De Giorgi *et al.* (2015).
9 Interview PT 14, Secretary of State, Lisbon, 25 January 2013.
10 Interview PT 9, Secretary of State, Lisbon, 30 January 2013 and Interview PT 28, European Commission, Lisbon, 22 February 2013.
11 Interview PT 5, Minister, Lisbon, 17 January 2013.
12 Interview PT 4, Minister, Lisbon, 22 January 2013.
13 Interview PT 3, Minister, Lisbon, 17 January 2013; Interview PT 4, Minister, Lisbon, 22 January 2013; Interview PT 5, Minister, Lisbon, 17 January 2013; Interview PT 6, Secretary of State, Lisbon, 28 January 2013; Interview PT 7, Secretary of State, Lisbon, 29 January 2013; Interview PT 8, Secretary of State, Lisbon, 29 January 2013; and Interview PT 9, Secretary of State, Lisbon, 30 January 2013.
14 Interview PT 7, Secretary of State, Lisbon, 29 January 2013.
15 Interview PT 5, Minister, Lisbon, 17 January 2013; Interview PT 6, Secretary of State, Lisbon, 28 January 2013; and Interview PT 7, Secretary of State, Lisbon, 29 January 2013.
16 Interview PT 9, Secretary of State, Lisbon, 30 January 2013.
17 In particular, the EC was very insistent on competition, privatisation and deficit reduction, while the IMF pushed for internal fiscal devaluation through minimum wage reduction, decentralisation of wage bargaining and lowering taxation on wages, Interview PT 5, Minister, Lisbon, 17 January 2013 and Interview PT 18, Secretary of State, Lisbon, 14 December 2017.
18 Interview PT 9, Secretary of State, Lisbon, 30 January 2013.
19 Interview PT 18, Secretary of State, Lisbon, 14 December 2017 and Interview PT 15, Secretary of State, Lisbon, 25 January 2018.

20 Interview PT 15, Secretary of State, Lisbon, 25 January 2018.
21 Interview PT 7, Secretary of State, Lisbon, 29 January 2013.
22 Interview PT 14, Secretary of State, Lisbon, 25 January 2013.
23 Interview PT 3, Minister, Lisbon, 17 January 2013; Interview PT 4, Minister, Lisbon, 22 January 2013; Interview PT 5, Minister, Lisbon, 17 January 2013; Interview PT 6, Secretary of State, Lisbon, 28 January 2013; Interview PT 7, Secretary of State, Lisbon, 29 January 2013; Interview PT 8, Secretary of State, Lisbon, 29 January 2013; and Interview PT 9, Secretary of State, Lisbon, 30 January 2013.
24 Interview PT 5, Minister, Lisbon, 17 January 2013.
25 Interview PT 14, Secretary of State, Lisbon, 25 January 2013.
26 Interview PT 9, Secretary of State, Lisbon, 30 January 2013.
27 Informant (more information here would threaten anonymity).
28 Interview PT 8, Secretary of State, Lisbon, 29 January 2013.
29 Interview PT 28, European Commission, Lisbon, 22 February 2013; Interview PT 29, European Commission, Brussels, 22 February 2013; Interview PT 30, European Commission, Brussels, 22 February 2013; and Interview PT 27, IMF, Lisbon, 15 February 2013.
30 Interview PT 27, IMF, Lisbon, 15 February 2013.
31 Interview PT 14, Secretary of State, Lisbon, 25 January 2013.
32 Interview PT 8, Secretary of State, Lisbon, 29 January 2013; Interview PT 15, Secretary of State, Lisbon, 25 January 2018; and Interview PT 7, Secretary of State, Lisbon, 29 January 2013.
33 Interview PT 6, Secretary of State, Lisbon, 28 January 2013; Interview PT 28, European Commission, Lisbon, 22 February 2013; and Interview PT 9, Secretary of State, Lisbon, 30 January 2013.
34 Interview PT 28, European Commission, Lisbon, 22 February 2013.
35 Interview PT 8, Secretary of State, Lisbon, 29 January 2013.
36 Interview PT 5, Minister, Lisbon, 17 January 2013; Interview PT 6, Secretary of State, Lisbon, 28 January 2013; Interview PT 8, Secretary of State, Lisbon, 29 January 2013; and Interview PT 9, Secretary of State, Lisbon, 30 January 2013.
37 Interview PT 7, Secretary of State, Lisbon, 29 January 2013.
38 Interview PT 14, Secretary of State, Lisbon, 25 January 2013.
39 Interview PT 27, IMF, Lisbon, 15 February 2013 and Interview PT 28, European Commission, Lisbon, 22 February 2013.
40 Interview PT 27, IMF, Lisbon, 15 February 2013.
41 Interview PT 9, Secretary of State, Lisbon, 30 January 2013.
42 Interview PT 9, Secretary of State, Lisbon, 30 January 2013 and Interview PT 5, Minister, Lisbon, 17 January 2013.
43 Interview PT 5, Minister, Lisbon, 17 January 2013.
44 Interview PT 5, Minister, Lisbon, 17 January 2013.
45 In Portuguese: Estrutura de Acompanhamento dos Memorandos (ESAME).
46 Interview PT 6, Minister, Lisbon, 28 January 2013.
47 Santos Pereira (2014, pp. 99–102) and Interview PT 11, Minister, Lisbon, 5 February 2013.

48 Interview PT 8, Secretary of State, Lisbon, 29 January 2013; Interview PT 9, Secretary of State, Lisbon, 30 January 2013; Interview PT 23, trade union official, Lisbon, 18 December 2017; and Interview PT 24, trade union official, Lisbon, 19 December 2017.

49 Interview PT 4, Minister, Lisbon, 22 January 2013.

50 Interview PT 15, Secretary of State, Lisbon, 25 January 2018.

51 Interview PT 11, Minister, Lisbon, 5 February 2013.

52 Interview PT 10, Minister, Lisbon, 26 February 2013.

53 International Monetary Fund (2011a, 2011b, 2012c, 2012d, 2012e, 2013b, 2013c, 2013d, 2014a, 2014b).

54 Interview PT 28, European Commission, Lisbon, 22 February 2013.

55 Interview PT 10, Minister, Lisbon, 26 February 2013; Interview PT 11, Minister, Lisbon, 5 February 2013; Interview PT 12, Secretary of State, Lisbon, 11 December 2017; Interview PT 13, Secretary of State, Lisbon, 18 January 2018; Interview PT 14, Secretary of State, Lisbon, 25 January 2013; and Interview PT 15, Secretary of State, Lisbon, 25 January 2018.

56 This was the view of the Minister of Finance, Santos Pereira (2014) and Interview PT 15, Secretary of State, Lisbon, 25 January 2018.

57 Santos Pereira (2014).

58 Eighteen days for the first three years in the case of a permanent contract.

59 Interview PT 12, Secretary of State, Lisbon, 11 December 2017.

60 Interview PT 15, Secretary of State, Lisbon, 25 January 2018.

61 Interview PT 12, Secretary of State, Lisbon, 11 December 2017.

62 Interview PT 12, Secretary of State, Lisbon, 11 December 2017; Santos Pereira (2014).

63 Interview PT 15, Secretary of State, Lisbon, 25 January 2018; Interview PT 10, Minister, Lisbon, 26 February 2013; and Interview PT 11, Minister, Lisbon, 5 February 2013.

64 Interview PT 27, IMF, Lisbon, 15 February 2013.

65 Interview PT 11, Minister, Lisbon, 5 February 2013.

66 Interview PT 20, Secretary of State, Lisbon, 11 December 2017; Interview PT 15, Secretary of State, Lisbon, 25 January 2018; and Interview PT 17, Secretary of State, Lisbon, 13 December 2017.

67 Interview PT 17, Secretary of State, Lisbon, 13 December 2017.

68 Interview PT 15, Secretary of State, Lisbon, 25 January 2018 and Interview PT 18, Secretary of State, Lisbon, 14 December 2017.

69 Magalhães (2013).

70 While abstention was 44 per cent in the 2015 elections, for example, 72 per cent of civil servants voted (Sources: Post-electoral Survey data, 2015, Portugal, available here: https://account.box.com/login?redirect_url=%2Ffiles%2F0%2Ff%2F6123588382 (accessed 20 April 2020)).

71 Joint position of the PS and the BE on the political solution, http://cdn.impresa.pt/284/9c2/9700333/BE.pdf; Joint position of the PS and the Greens on the political solution, www.osverdes.pt/media/Parlamento/PosicaoConjuntaPS_PEV.pdf; Joint position of the PS and the PCP on the political solution, http://cdn.impresa.pt/14d/378/9700329/PCP.pdf (accessed 11 February 2020).

72 Interview PT 16, Minister, Lisbon, 13 December 2017 and Interview PT 17, Secretary of State, Lisbon, 13 December 2017.
73 Interview PT 18, Secretary of State, Lisbon, 14 December 2017; Interview PT 20, Secretary of State, Lisbon, 11 December 2017; and Interview PT 16, Minister, Lisbon, 13 December 2017.
74 Interview PT 17, Secretary of State, Lisbon, 13 December 2017.
75 Interview PT 18, Secretary of State, Lisbon, 14 December 2017.
76 See for example Joaquim Sarmento (2018) and Luís Aguiar-Conraria (Bastos, 2018).
77 For example, Eurostat shows that public investment (both in 2016 and in 2017) in Portugal had been historically low – as compared with previous governments but also other European countries. The same observations could be made for spending in key sectors. For example, the level of spending for the health sector and education in 2016 was below that of the Troika years (2011, 2012 and 2013). See https://ec.europa.eu/eurostat/cache/metadata/en/sdg_08_11_esmsip2.htm (accessed 1 December 2019).
78 Interview PT 16, Minister, Lisbon, 13 December 2017; Interview PT 17, Secretary of State, Lisbon, 13 December 2017; Interview PT 18, Secretary of State, Lisbon, 14 December 2017; Interview PT 19, Secretary of State, Lisbon, 15 December 2017; Interview PT 20, Secretary of State, Lisbon, 11 December 2017; and Interview PT 21, Secretary of State, Lisbon, 12 December 2017.
79 Interview PT 18, Secretary of State, Lisbon, 14 December 2017.
80 Interview PT 18, Secretary of State, Lisbon, 14 December 2017.
81 Interview PT 20, Secretary of State, Lisbon, 11 December 2017.
82 Interview PT 17, Secretary of State, Lisbon, 13 December 2017.

5

Spain

Introduction

This chapter investigates the negotiations between European institutions, the IMF and the Spanish governments between 2008, when the first effects of the US subprime crisis on the Spanish economy were felt, and the end of the Financial Assistance Programme in 2014. The chapter also evaluates whether or not Spanish governments reversed the reforms implemented during the crisis from 2014 until 2019. The Spanish case is crucial to evaluate some of the variables that influence the bargaining context. Spain is the fourth biggest European economy, allowing us to analyse the significance of the size of the country when negotiating with external actors.

Moreover, this case is empirically attractive because the Memorandum of Understanding attached to the financial assistance programme, which lasted from June 2012 to January 2014, only included reforms in the banking sector. There was conditionality on fiscal cuts and structural reforms but it was monitored through compliance with Stability and Growth Pact recommendations. This variation is also interesting for comparative purposes to evaluate the margin of manoeuvre of governments negotiating in different contexts.

The chapter is divided into five sections. The first section covers the pre-bailout period, which runs from March 2008 to November 2011, when the centre-left Spanish Socialist Workers' Party (PSOE) was in government. The second section goes from November 2011 to January 2014, namely the centre-right People's Party (PP) period in office, and includes the negotiations of the bailout and its implementation. The third section covers the post-bailout period and evaluates the reversals of the PP government until June 2018, when a no-confidence vote in Parliament led to another change of government and the return of the centre-left PSOE to power. Finally, it analyses the reversals implemented by the centre-left government until May 2019. The final section concludes.

March 2008–November 2011: before the bailout (centre-left government)

The PSOE (Socialist party, centre-left) won the elections on 9 March 2008; although it did not have a sufficient majority to form a government, it obtained enough support from other political parties (all except the centre-right PP, the centre-right Union, Progress and Democracy, and the independentist centre-left Republican Left of Catalonia (ERC)) in the second investiture on 11 April 2008. The formation of the new centre-left PSOE government in 2008 coincided with the onset of the economic crisis in Europe. The subprime mortgage crisis in the USA in 2007 had directly affected the Spanish economy, particularly the banking sector (Banco de España, 2012). Indeed, Spanish economic growth from the mid-1990s had been largely the result of a construction bubble (Fishman, 2012, p. 68) following financial speculation on property prices that rose higher than the consumer price index. The US subprime crisis reduced Spanish bank liquidity and the economy was hit by the fall of internal demand (Banco de España, 2012; Royo, 2013, p. 651). In the third quarter of 2008, the Spanish economy entered a recession that lasted until the first quarter of 2010, bringing economic growth to an abrupt halt.

At first, the PSOE government publicly rejected that there was a crisis (Badell *et al.*, 2019, p. 1320; Molina and Godino, 2013). And when it finally admitted its existence, in autumn 2008, the executive played down the gravity of the situation, calling it 'accelerated deceleration' (Molina and Godino, 2013, p. 110). As a result, the government was harshly criticised for not 'reacting in time and for denying and underestimating its magnitude' (Field and Botti, 2013, p. 5). In November 2008, the Spanish Prime Minister, José Luis Rodríguez Zapatero, launched a series of Keynesian-inspired measures known as Plan E (Spanish Plan for the Stimulus of Economy and Employment), aimed primarily at creating jobs through the investment of €55,000 million (Molina and Godino, 2013, p. 111). At the time, there was consensus in the EU that neo-Keynesian measures were the best way to tackle the crisis through the recommendations of the European Economic Recovery Plan (European Commission, 2008b).

However, the Spanish economy deteriorated rapidly throughout 2009 due to a sharp decline in economic growth that went from 1.1 per cent in 2008 to –3.6 per cent in 2009. In addition, the consensus on the suitability of a Keynesian way out of the crisis started to crumble in late 2009, when Greece announced the actual figures of the public debt and deficit. Thereafter, the European institutions started asking the socialist government to opt exclusively for orthodox fiscal consolidation solutions (European Commission, 2009).

Demands for fiscal consolidation were made through the formal rules on fiscal discipline in the SGP, such as the Excessive Deficit Procedure. In line with the SGP rules, the European Commission started an EDP for Spain in February 2009 as the Spanish deficit stood at 4.4 per cent. The report issued by the Commission demanded that the Spanish government reduce the deficit and address structural problems such as the risk of the unsustainability of pensions (European Commission, 2009). Nevertheless, the socialist government had not implemented any of the EU's recommendations on structural reforms by May 2010. As some studies show, there were no important changes in the welfare system in Spain until mid-2010, and social policy reforms contradicted the policy prescriptions of external actors (Del Pino, 2013; Guillén and León, 2011; León *et al.*, 2015). For example, they included some elements of recalibration such as the increase in unemployment expenses (Del Pino, 2013).

Two factors might explain the PSOE government's inaction. First, there was still little pressure from financial markets at this point as bond yields remained below 4 per cent in 2009. This meant that Spain could easily finance its public debt in the private market. Secondly, there was a lack of goodness of fit between the government's preferences and European recommendations.[1] The socialist government did not agree with the pace or content of the reforms the EU demanded and did not want to implement drastic spending cuts and deregulatory reforms (see Molina and Godino, 2013 for the labour market reform; Morlino and Sottilotta, 2019 for austerity measures).

The situation changed in May 2010, when the Eurogroup agreed to provide financial help to Greece, and at the same time asked for the acceleration of fiscal consolidation measures and structural reforms by all countries in financial difficulties, including Spain (Council of the European Union, 2010a). At the meeting of the European Economic and Financial Affairs Council (ECOFIN) on 9 May 2010, the Spanish Minister of Finance, Elena Salgado, was asked to drastically cut the budget to €30,000 million in one year (La Vanguardia, 2010). Financial speculation also increased over Spain, with bond yields going over 4.5 per cent in June 2010.

This meeting marked a turning point in the PSOE government's economic policy in favour of austerity (Bosco, 2013, p. 27; Field and Botti, 2013, p. 6; Jordana, 2014, p. 232). Nevertheless, despite limited policy options to respond to these demands, external pressures did not determine the government's 'exact response' (Field and Botti, 2013, p. 6). The Spanish government was asked to cut public spending but the executive had the margin of *manoeuvre* to decide how to distribute these cuts. It was Elena Salgado and Rodríguez Zapatero who took the decision on which specific measures to implement to reach this figure after evaluating the reports from other Ministries and suggestions from the Economic Office (Zapatero, 2013, p. 32).

The government had many discussions on public employment salaries and the freezing of pensions. The Prime Minister and the Minister of Finance considered that cutting public employee salaries was a priority given that they represented an automatic cut of €8 million (Zapatero, 2013, p. 33). Also, they were aware of the saliency of this measure to the EU and its importance to the government's credibility, in the eyes of external actors, to deliver reforms.[2] As Rodríguez Zapatero explains in his memoirs, the rise in the salaries of Spanish public servants had been repeatedly used by European institutions to question the competitiveness of the Spanish economy and its fiscal imbalances (Zapatero, 2013, p. 35).

These intra-government discussions resulted in the approval of the 'Immediate Action and Austerity plans'.[3] The plans included the freezing of pensions, cuts in old-age care plans, elimination of tax benefits, measures to control public expenses, cuts in public wages and the elimination of the birth allowance, among others (European Commission, 2010f).

In addition, the centre-left government announced the implementation of the labour market reform, which had been one of the 'most demanded since the beginning of the crisis' (Zapatero, 2013, p. 206). Indeed, external actors had recommended the flexibilisation of the Spanish labour market through measures such as the decrease of dismissal compensation and the prioritisation of firm-level agreements over sectoral agreements of collective bargaining (International Monetary Fund, 2010). In that regard, the government had already started negotiations with trade unions and employer organisations in early 2009 but agreement was hampered by the divergent positions of the social partners (Gago, 2016, p. 56). Consequently, the government decided to implement the labour market reform unilaterally. Royal Decree 10/2010[4] allowed for changes to collective bargaining agreements at the firm level and reduced severance pay in the case of fair dismissal from forty-five to thirty-three days per year of employment but maintained the severance pay for unfair dismissal (El Mundo, 2010).

In the end, the reform fell far short of what external actors had recommended for Spain and was criticised by the IMF (2010) because it still prioritised high-level agreements over firm agreements. The EU also showed its disapproval of the reform. The 2011 country-specific recommendations therefore asked the Spanish government to take further measures. The EU recommended a complete reform of the collective bargaining system because 'the predominance of provincial and industry agreements leaves little room for negotiations at firm level' (Council of the European Union, 2011, p. 3). In addition, informal pressures through 'backroom diplomacy' (De la Porte and Natali, 2014, p. 735; chapter 1 of this volume) increased in the second half of 2010 and in 2011. For example, on 18 June 2010 the former IMF chief, Dominique Strauss-Kahn, asked the Spanish Prime Minister to request a bailout but Zapatero was opposed to the idea (Zapatero, 2013, p. 120).

At that time, the government decided to launch another important structural reform: the transformation of the pension system. Rodríguez Zapatero explains in his memoirs that the government chose to implement the pension reform because it was 'among the international organisations' strongest demands as one of the pillars of public finance sustainability' (Zapatero, 2013, p. 208). Moreover, some members of the government explained to us that the pension reform had long been on the government agenda, but they had been unable to implement it.[5] As one of our interviewees told us: 'The pension reform should have been implemented in 2006 but it was postponed because the economic situation was good back then'.[6] Therefore, members of the PSOE had already warned about the need to implement changes to guarantee the sustainability of the pension system but this type of measure was very unpopular in times of economic growth.[7]

At the end of 2010, the centre-left government negotiated the pension reform with the social partners because the Prime Minister wanted to respond to the crisis using social democratic strategies, which meant a commitment to social dialogue (Hamann, 2013, p. 126). The specific measures of the reform were not negotiated directly with the EU, but they were inspired by the European recommendations in the Green paper on pensions.[8] The Green paper was launched by the European Commission in July 2010 to provide member states with measures to reform European pension systems (European Commission, 2010g). The Spanish commission that created the legislative proposal at the Congress of deputies, which is made up of parliamentarians of all political parties and known as the Toledo Pact, took the Green paper as a reference (Commission Toledo Pact, 2010).

Some participants in the negotiations explained to us that they had room for manoeuvre to decide on specific measures, and that they avoided the implementation of some measures proposed by the Commission with which they disagreed.[9] One example was the increase in the retirement age from sixty-five to sixty-seven years, which was implemented with long phase-in periods as opposed to the European recommendations that had requested an immediate implementation. The creation of the sustainability factor to delink pensions from inflation, another EU recommendation,[10] was also avoided. The final reform was contained in the Social and Economic Agreement for Growth, Employment and the Guarantee of Pensions, which in this case was signed in February 2011 by the trade unions, employer organisations and the government. Although European leaders welcomed the reform, they asked the government for further measures such as the delinking of salaries from inflation and the introduction of a constitutional ban on increasing the deficit over the maximum of 3 per cent, known as the golden rule (Council of the European Union, 2011).

The credibility in the PSOE government's capacity to deliver reforms among external actors started to weaken at the start of 2011. There was increasing financial speculation about Spain and bond yields reached 5.37 per cent in January 2011. Several other factors contributed to the loss of PSOE's credibility. First, the reform episodes described above revealed that there were differences between government preferences and European recommendations. The centre-left government watered down structural reforms to avoid confrontation with trade unions and their constituencies because its objective was to achieve the maximum consensus.[11] As Jordana (2014, p. 232) claims, 'reforms were moderate to avoid compromising "insider" electoral support'.

Secondly, political instability increased when the Prime Minister announced in April 2011 that he was not running in the next general elections (Bosco, 2013, pp. 29, 36). In addition, the election polls started shaping the main opposition party, the PP, as the winner[12] of the next general elections. Political contestation against the government also increased in the streets with the emergence of the anti-austerity movement known as movement 15-M (because it started on 15 May 2011), or as the *Indignados* movement. All these factors contributed to a political crisis in the PSOE, which was unable to deliver the necessary reforms (Győrffy, 2018, p. 129). Aware of his inability to provide 'certainty' on the implementation of reforms (Garea, 2011), Rodríguez Zapatero decided to call early elections.

During the run-up to the elections, informal external pressures on the centre-left government continued. For example, the European Commissioner for Economic and Monetary Affairs and the Euro, Olli Rehn, made several declarations to the press urging the Spanish government to implement further labour market and banking sector reforms[13] (Diario de Avisos, 2011). As a result, the government made another change to collective bargaining to increase flexibility but, once again, external actors, notably the ECB, were not satisfied (Badell *et al.*, 2019, p. 1319; European Central Bank, 2011).

The worsening of economic indicators and the increase in bond yields to 5.8 per cent led the Spanish economy to a critical situation in summer 2011. On 5 August 2011, the former President of the ECB, Jean-Claude Trichet, sent a letter to Rodríguez Zapatero after a phone conversation, urging him to implement reforms in exchange for the ECB's purchase of Spanish debt in secondary markets (Zapatero, 2013, pp. 248–254). A part of the letter is reproduced here:

> The Governing Council considers that pressing action by the Spanish authorities is essential to restore the credibility of the sovereign's signature in capital

markets ... at the current juncture, we consider the following measures to be essential:

a) The wage bargaining reform bill adopted by the Spanish government on 10 June 2011 should more effectively strengthen the role of firm-level agreements, with a view to ensuring an effective decentralisation of wage negotiations.
b) Furthermore, we remain very concerned that the government has not taken any measures to abolish inflation-adjustment clauses ... We encourage the government to take bold exceptional steps to exclude the use of such clauses in view of the current crisis.
c) The government should also take exceptional action to encourage private sector wage moderation.
d) We also suggest reviewing other labour market regulations at short notice ... we see strong benefits in introducing an exceptional new labour contract with only very low severance payments, to be applied for a limited period of time. (European Central Bank, 2011)

The letter also contained demands that would ensure the sustainability of public finances (e.g. fiscal consolidation measures of 0.5 per cent of GDP, the transparency of public finances and the introduction of the golden rule), and for the reform of the products market (e.g. increase competition in the energy sector, promote rental market for housing, increase competition in the service sector) (European Central Bank, 2011). The PSOE government responded to the ECB with another letter in which it agreed to implement some of the demands, and openly asked the ECB to purchase sovereign debt bonds (Zapatero, 2013, pp. 236–238).

As promised in that letter, the government approved new regulations on apprenticeship contracts without severance payments.[14] In addition, the Spanish Prime Minister announced new fiscal consolidation measures that amounted to 0.5 per cent of GDP, including an annual reduction of €2.4 million in pharmaceutical expenditures, which was finally approved on 19 August (Zapatero, 2011). The government also passed[15] measures to lower public pharmaceutical spending, including making it obligatory for doctors and pharmacists to dispense the cheapest medicine available to the patient, and price cuts for medication without a generic alternative.

On the other hand, Rodríguez Zapatero was very reluctant to implement further collective bargaining reforms and defended both the previous labour market reform and the bilateral agreements between employers and trade unions on wage moderation. One example of this reluctance was the approval of new regulations[16] on apprenticeship contracts mentioned above, aimed at responding to ECB President Trichet's demands, although the regulations had little impact. As the Prime Minister explains: 'I read the letter with my collaborators and with Elena Salgado various times. There were demands that we had already planned, others we were willing to implement … The letter also included exceptional measures to adopt in the labour market and that I was not willing to accept' (Zapatero, 2013, p. 247).

Despite the timid compliance with labour market demands, the ECB started buying Spanish debt on 8 August 2011. That same month, the bond yields declined from 5.82 to 5.25 per cent. The government also incorporated the golden rule in the Spanish Constitution, which had been one of the last commitments made to the ECB. The golden rule bans the central government and the Autonomous Communities from spending over the fiscal limits imposed by European fiscal rules. The final text, which modified Article 135 of the Constitution, was approved in Parliament with the support of the main opposition party, the PP, and finally implemented on 27 September 2011. The Prime Minister knew that the German Chancellor, Angela Merkel, particularly appreciated this reform (Zapatero, 2013, p. 281).

Nevertheless, external pressures lasted until the end of the socialist legislature. Bond yields started to increase again in autumn 2011 and reached a new high in November (6.19 per cent) coinciding with the campaign for the general elections. Only a few days before these elections, Angela Merkel proposed that Rodríguez Zapatero ask the IMF for preventive financial support of €50 million. He rejected this on the grounds that the economic situation had improved since August and that they could still pay their debt in spite of high interest rates (Zapatero, 2013, p. 290).

In line with our theoretical expectations, this section concludes by showing that the centre-left government had room for manoeuvre on both asking for the bailout and implementing measures that were at odds with their preferences or their constituencies' interests (Proposal One). In the case of labour market reforms, for example, the government did not implement the prioritisation of firm-level agreements in the labour market. Another example was the avoidance of the creation of a pension sustainability factor to unlink pensions from inflation. However, this triggered a political crisis and the call of early elections (Field and Botti, 2013, p. 6). As a consequence, political instability lowered the government's credibility to deliver reforms.

November 2011–January 2014: negotiating and implementing the financial adjustment programme (centre-right government)

The centre-right People's Party led by Mariano Rajoy won the general elections on 20 November 2011 with an absolute majority. The PP obtained 44.63 per cent of the vote (186 seats) and 'gained a tremendous amount of political power' (Field and Botti, 2013, p. 15). The socialist party lost 59 seats and won only 28.76 per cent of the vote. The PSOE got the worst results in its history and had been 'severely punished' for its management of the crisis (Field and Botti, 2013, p. 3). Right after the elections in November 2011, the German Chancellor, Angela Merkel, sent a letter to the newly elected Prime Minister asking him to implement measures 'without delay', mostly on fiscal consolidation and public spending cuts (La Opinión, 2011).

The new government also felt the effects of financial speculation, with bond yields reaching a new historic maximum of 6.19 per cent just five days before the elections. The formation of the PP government led to a slight drop in bond yields to 5.50 per cent but the commitment of the centre-right government to undertake reforms did not consolidate the positive trend, so the spread continued to rise. This contradicted the general feeling within the PP government at the time that the markets would support it by decreasing financial speculation as soon as it started implementing reforms.[17]

The PP's commitment to fiscal consolidation and deregulatory structural reforms was visible in its political programme for the election campaign of November 2011, where fiscal cuts were among the main objectives (Partido Popular, 2011). A few days after the elections, the centre-right government launched a comprehensive austerity package to comply with fiscal objectives. At that moment, the fiscal deficit was 8 per cent and the executive announced that it had to cut €9 million (Cué, 2011). The urgent measures to reduce the fiscal deficit included: increases in income tax and property tax; the freezing of pensions and of new hiring of public employment; an increase in working hours of public employees; 20 per cent cuts in political party funding; cuts in rent subsidies for youth; and the delay of implementation of the 'Law to regulate old age care programme' – a programme that had been introduced by the socialist government in 2006 to provide public care services for old people (Martín *et al.*, 2013, p. 17). The centre-right executive also approved a €10 million cut in the health and education sector in April 2012.

Additionally, the PP government approved a new labour market reform[18] which gave 'absolute priority to enterprise-level agreements over higher-level agreements and allowing firms to opt out of a collective agreement, even in the absence of consensus between the two sides of industry' (Horwitz and Myant, 2015, p. 6). As we have seen above, the prioritisation of firm-level agreements over sectoral agreements was a long-standing demand from external actors that the socialist government had refused to implement. The labour market reform was also included in the PP's political programme for the 2011 elections: 'firm-level agreements will have prevalence on wages and working conditions' (Partido Popular, 2011, p. 38). Evidence also shows that the PP had tried to implement this labour market reform previously.[19] For example, in the early 2000s the PP government of Jose Maria Aznar implemented two labour market reforms that fell short of their initial objectives due to lack of political consensus with trade unions and other political parties (El País, 2010; Otxoa, 2007, p. 14).

In agreement with our theory, the PP's willingness to implement reforms increased its credibility with the EU institutions and, in turn, gave the government more leverage to negotiate with external actors (Proposal Three). This coincided with the negotiations of the fiscal deficit with the EU in March 2012. Although the Spanish government had agreed with European authorities to reduce the deficit to 4.4 per cent under the EDP, Mariano Rajoy declared that the projections pointed to a deficit of 5.8 per cent (BBC, 2012). This was unacceptable to the European Commission and, at the Eurogroup meeting on 12 March 2012, it exerted great pressure on the Minister of the Economy, Luis de Guindos, to implement further cuts (De Guindos, 2016, p. 83).

Nevertheless, the Spanish government finally succeeded in getting an agreement of a 5.3 per cent fiscal deficit, less than the Prime Minister had announced (5.8 per cent) but well above what had been previously agreed with the EU during EDP negotiations (4.4 per cent; Botti, 2013, p. 55). As the Minister of the Economy, Luis de Guindos, explains in his memoirs, there was no need to exercise so much pressure over a country that 'achieved reform records in two months' (De Guindos, 2016, p. 83).

However, despite the government's commitment to austerity, the economic situation worsened due to the banking crisis. The construction bubble had led to the flow of easy credit characterised by long-term loans at low interest rates. When the recession started, many people could not afford to pay their mortgage. This, together with a lack of adequate regulation, left the Spanish banks in a vulnerable position to external shocks (Coller and de Luis, 2020, p. 136; Morlino and Sottilotta, 2019, p. 5). The centre-left government had already partially bailed out some banks in 2009 through the creation of the Fund for Orderly Bank Restructuring (FROB),[20] but those measures had proven insufficient to solve banking problems (Huerta, 2019, p. 28).

In response to this situation, the PP government approved a plan for financial sector restructuring[21] which had three main objectives: to inject €52 million into the Spanish banking system, to modify the FROB and to simplify the organisational structure of the Savings Banks. Despite those measures, in May 2012 the commercial brand of the Financial and Savings Bank and Bankia, Spain's fourth largest bank, announced that they needed a bailout of €19 billion. The European Commission reported that the banking reforms implemented by the government[22] were not enough to resolve the situation (Euractiv, 2012). In addition, the President of the ECB, Mario Draghi, criticised the government for underestimating Bankia's solvency problems (Pérez, 2012a).

In fact, the lack of transparency was one of the problems in the banking sector because the profit and loss forecasts were often incorrect (Banco de España, 2011). In conjunction with increasing financial speculation that took Spanish bond yields to 6.12 per cent, this made it very difficult to get funding from private markets (Reuters, 2012). As De Guindos explains in his memoirs, 'during the first days of May, I started to assimilate that it was difficult to go on without help' (De Guindos, 2016, p. 105). At this time the Treasury Minister, Cristóbal Montoro, also declared: 'the risk premium says Spain doesn't have the market door open' (Reuters, 2012).

In the end, the government started negotiating the conditions of the Financial Adjustment Programme with the EU on 5 June 2012 during the meeting of G7 Ministers of Finance, before making the public request (Pérez, 2012a). The centre-right government wanted to avoid a full programme associated with macroeconomic conditionality and asked for financial assistance to be injected directly into the banks. This was considered a better strategy as it would avoid the loss of sovereignty and the stigma that follows a full bailout (Financial Times, 2012; Spiegel Online, 2012). As De Guindos explains:

> My concern was to state very clearly that it was not a full bailout like in Greece, Ireland or Portugal, but a programme of financial assistance destined exclusively to the banks. It worried me that ... the loan was going to be linked with macroeconomic conditions ... about issues not related to the financial sector such as pensions or unemployment allowances. (De Guindos, 2016, p. 109)

On the other hand, European leaders were divided on where the money should go. The German, Finnish and Netherlands governments were in favour of the Spanish government taking full responsibility with a full bailout (De Guindos, 2016, p. 109; Spiegel Online, 2012). In contrast, other European Commission officials were concerned about the 'destructive potential' of a bailout and favoured other options, such as issuing public debt or recapitalisation by private investors (Doncel, 2012a).

The Spanish government used the size of its economy as its main argument against a full programme. At a conference with other European Ministers of Finance of the Eurogroup on 9 June, De Guindos argued that Spain was 'too big to fail' (De Guindos, 2016, p. 110; Doncel, 2012b). He recalls this in his memoirs: 'If Spain, in fact a big country, was completely rescued, the project of the euro would fail. The threat was very clear: Too big to fail' (De Guindos, 2016, p. 110). Similarly, the Treasury Minister, Montoro, also stated that: 'from a technical point of view, Spain cannot be rescued' (Sérvulo González and Garea, 2012). As a Secretary of State explained to us in interview: 'A total bailout would have meant €750,000 million. There was not enough money for that.'[23]

The final agreement between the Spanish government and the EU was reached on 9 June 2012. Spain made a formal request to the Chairman of the Eurogroup to access the European Stability Mechanism on 25 June 2012, and the Eurogroup signed the MoU on 23 July 2012. Partial bail-in mechanisms were also put in place but only affected junior debt and not senior unsecured debt holders or deposits (Schäfer *et al.*, 2017, p. 18). The trade-off agreed between the government and the EU was that the financial assistance would be given to the Spanish government (and not to the banks), and that the IMF's role would be limited to providing technical support without monitoring the government. In exchange, the MoU would be restricted to reforms of the banking sector and would not include macroeconomic conditions (De Guindos, 2016, p. 110). The European Commissioner, Olli Rehn, confirmed that 'no new conditions on fiscal policy or on structural reforms are needed' (Pop, 2012). Also, the Spanish centre-right government's public announcement avoided using the word 'bailout' and referred to the programme with euphemisms like 'loan with favourable conditions' (De Guindos, 2016, p. 109).

Conforming to our theoretical proposals, Spain's economic size and significance in European institutions gave the government leverage to negotiate with the EU (Badell *et al.*, 2019; Baerg and Hallerberg, 2016). Moreover, the PP government reaffirmed its willingness to implement reforms on many occasions, which undoubtedly strengthened the government's credibility and therefore helped it to avoid a full bailout (Pérez and Doncel, 2012). As the Eurogroup statement confirmed:

> Spain has already implemented significant fiscal and labour market reforms and measures to strengthen the capital base of the Spanish banks. The Eurogroup is confident that Spain will honour its commitments under the Excessive Deficit Procedure and with regard to structural reforms, with a view to correcting macroeconomic imbalances in the framework of the European semester. (Eurogroup, 2012e)

Nevertheless, the exclusion of macroeconomic conditions from the Memorandum did not free Spain from fiscal cuts and structural reforms. The statement above continues: 'Progress in these areas [structural reforms] will be closely and regularly reviewed also in parallel with the financial assistance' (Eurogroup, 2012e).

Spain therefore had to commit to implementing the country-specific recommendations attached to the Stability and Growth Pact (Badell *et al.*, 2019, p. 1312). What the Spanish government achieved during negotiations was that the monitoring of macroeconomic reforms would be done in a parallel process (De Guindos, 2016, p. 110). This was also contained explicitly in the Memorandum:

> Spain will have to comply fully with its commitments and obligations under the EDP and the recommendations to address macroeconomic imbalances within the framework of the European Semester. Progress in meeting these obligations under the relevant EU procedures will be closely monitored in parallel with the regular review of programme implementation. (European Commission, 2012d, p. 1)

Once the agreement on the form of the programme was reached, the centre-right government started new negotiations with the EU on the content of the Memorandum. At this time, investors were still uncertain about whether the programme would resolve all Spain's banking problems (Lafont, 2012), and the bond yields increased to 6.79 per cent (De Guindos, 2016, p. 119).

Given that government debt stood at 86.3 per cent, well above the European limit, the European Council decided to start another Excessive Deficit Procedure for Spain on 6 July 2012, two years after the termination of the preceding one. The Commission forecasted a fiscal deficit of 6.3 per cent of GDP for 2012, higher than the Stability Programme projections in 2012 of an estimated deficit of 5.3 per cent of GDP. Again, the government managed to negotiate a relaxation of the deficit goal with the Commission (Badell *et al.*, 2019). In exchange, the PP government agreed to increase VAT from 18 to 21 per cent, and to eliminate both the Christmas allowance for public employees and fiscal benefits for home purchases, among others (Badell *et al.*, 2019, p. 1317; De Guindos, 2016, p. 124). Cuts in unemployment benefits and a reduction in public employees were also announced in July 2012 (Botti, 2013, p. 56).

In this context, negotiations with the European Commission on the banking reforms to be included in the Memorandum proved difficult (De Guindos, 2016, p. 115). Although the government was able to define the technical aspects of most reforms due to its insider knowledge of the banking sector,[24] there were strong disagreements on two matters (De Guindos, 2016). First, the European Commission wanted the immediate transformation of the banking system and much smaller banks. On its side, the government wanted the liquidation of the banks to be phased in. In the end, the government decided to comply with the calendar imposed by the Commission and approved the restructuring of credit entities[25] (De Guindos, 2016, p. 109). However, it managed to get an agreement on the size of the reduction of the banks. As a member of the government explained to us: 'The Troika also wanted to reduce the size of the banks very much but we did not because that would have meant a drastic loss of value. In the end, we managed to get an agreement.'[26]

The issue of Bankia preferred stock – that is, the dividends some bondholders receive before others – was the second major source of disagreement between the external actors and the government (De Guindos, 2016, p. 143). The Commission did not want all public funds to go to compensating the loss of Bankia's preferred stockholders. The problem was that most of these preferred stockholders in Spain were pensioners who had been encouraged by the banks to convert their savings into preferred stocks without being informed of the risks this entailed (Torres, 2014); hence the government did not want them to lose all their savings. Despite not reaching an agreement with the Troika on this, the government implemented an alternative solution, namely an arbitration mechanism to guarantee that the stockholders could get all or part of their money back.[27] In this case, and in congruence with our theory, we observe that the government had room for manoeuvre to introduce policies to compensate the preferred stockholders (De Guindos, 2016, p. 143).

Further examples of the government's leverage are found in the 'Law on budget stability' (2012) and the setting up of a central fiscal institution, the Spanish Independent Authority for Fiscal Responsibility, in 2013. Although it was the EU that proposed this authority to guarantee financial sustainability, the specific measures implemented by the PP involved the re-centralisation of financial competences of the Autonomous Communities (Muro, 2015, p. 32), which was in line with the ideas of the centre-right party (Mendizabal, 2014, p. 5). Thus, some measures were used by the government as an 'opportunity to regain decision power from periphery administrations' (Kasperskaya and Xifré, 2019, p. 2).

There were no formal negotiations between the government and the external actors on structural reforms, that is, they were not included in the Memorandum. However, the government held discussions with external actors to define priorities, which were then included in the country-specific recommendations and the national reform programmes. The two most salient structural reforms to the EC were reforms of the pension system and the labour market (Expansión, 2012). The analysis of country-specific recommendations for Spain in 2012 and 2013 also shows that the Commission continued to insist on the measures that had not been implemented by the previous centre-left government; these included the delinking of wages and pensions from inflation and the creation of the sustainability factor by linking pensions with life expectancy (European Commission, 2012e, 2013c). In fact, the ECB and IMF had already asked the Spanish government in July 2012 to eliminate the link between inflation and pensions (Pérez, 2012b).

The PP responded to these demands by implementing various reforms to the pension system. It suspended the General Social Security Law that stipulated an annual increase in pensions in line with inflation.[28] The PP also modified the conditions of early retirement by limiting access and excluding a large part of the workforce[29] and approved the law to regulate the sustainability factor to calculate pensions,[30] but postponed its implementation until 2019.[31] As we expected theoretically, this shows that the government had a certain room for manoeuvre that allowed it to avoid implementing measures that were not in its political programme (Cioffi and Dubin, 2016, pp. 441–442).

In other policy fields, the government had even greater room for manoeuvre in the design of specific measures. Although the European Commission had asked for the rationalisation of public administration, for example, the government was responsible for defining the specifics. It thus had total room for manoeuvre when deciding on policy changes in education (e.g. increase teacher–student ratio per class; Lucas, 2012) and the health system[32] (e.g. exclusion of non-regularised immigrants). These two examples demonstrate the centre-right government's ability to choose which policies they wanted to dismantle (Jordana, 2014, p. 224). Similarly, the specific measures used to reform the housing market[33] and the electricity sector also reflected the government's preferences. The Commission wanted both markets to be made more competitive[34] but it was the government's decision to protect the owner over the renter and to 'transfer to consumers any increases in costs' (Jordana, 2014, p. 231). This again demonstrates the centre-right government's ability to define measures.

January 2014–December 2015: after the programme (centre-right government)

In January 2014, Spain exited the adjustment programme after eighteen months. However, it was still under post-programme surveillance and the EDP for Spain was also reactivated. After the Financial Assistance Programme ended, the European Commission made two visits a year (spring and autumn) to assess the implementation of reforms, and published twelve reports. Just before the end of the programme, in December 2013, the European Council told Spain to reinforce fiscal consolidation measures (European Council, 2013). In addition, the Commission indicated in 2014 that there were still problems with the banks and asked for further reforms including the privatisation of nationalised banks, an adjustment of the tax system and the deepening of the labour market reforms (Pérez, 2014).

Good news started to emerge from the Spanish economy in early 2014. The exit of the programme coincided with low bond yields (3.78 per cent), a return to economic growth and a decrease in unemployment (Organisation for Economic Co-operation and Development, 2014). The government saw that the reforms implemented during the programme had led to economic growth. As a parliamentarian from the PP explained to us: 'Those who are trying to reverse the reforms are doing so just for political propaganda, because in fact we can see that the reforms have worked. We reduced unemployment from 27 per cent to 17 percent, 10 points less.'[35]

As a result, the centre-right government's policies were no different from those implemented under conditionality. It continued in 2014 with fiscal devaluation reforms, such as the freezing of the minimum wage to €645.30. Nevertheless, with the European elections around the corner (in May 2014), and municipal and general elections in 2015, the government decided to reverse some austerity measures. This confirms our hypothesis that as soon as the bailout terminates, even governments that wanted to implement reforms were also willing to partially reverse some measures. In this vein, the centre-right government decided to pass some reforms favouring public employees. For example, the freezing of complementary pensions was lifted (as long as this was compensated by a reduction in hiring), half of the Christmas allowance was gradually reinstated and extra holidays that had been cancelled were replaced. In line with our argument, this demonstrates that governments are more prone to reverse cuts that benefit a concentrated group of citizens (public employees) and with diffused costs, in this case among all taxpayers.

Moreover, during the December 2015 campaign for the general elections, the PP government announced a progressive increase in public employees' salaries (that had been cut by 5 per cent in 2010), starting with 1 per cent in 2016. Additionally, the government reinstated half of the Christmas allowance, and authorised the hiring of public employees for the first time in some years.

On 20 December 2015, the PP won the general elections again but this time without a majority to form a government. The elections brought about the 'breakdown of the Spanish two-party system' (Orriols and Cordero, 2016, p. 469). The fragmentation of the political system and the emergence of new political parties such as Podemos and Ciudadanos (Rodon and Hierro, 2016, p. 339) made it impossible to form a government, and new general elections were called for June 2016. However, PP won those elections on 26 June 2016 without an absolute majority. After various negotiations to form a government, PP finally managed to do so on 30 October 2016 with the support of Ciudadanos and the regional Coalición Canaria, and the abstention of the PSOE for the first time in Spanish history (Bosco and Verney, 2016, p. 402).

Economic growth reached 3.2 per cent by the end of 2016, and the unemployment rate had declined steadily to below 20 per cent (Euronews, 2017). Nevertheless, external pressures continued and the European Commission threatened Spain with sanctions if it did not correct the deviation from the SGP; however, as was the case with Portugal, no fine was imposed. Despite the improved economic situation, reversals were rare in this period due to persistent external pressures and PP's belief in the reforms. As the new government had not yet been formed by mid-October 2016, Spain had sent Brussels the same budgetary plan as the previous year, with a commitment to cuts of around €5,000 million (Expansión, 2016).

In fact, the Spanish government did not implement the budget completely.[36] For example, it spent only 6.7 per cent of the budget on active employment policies (Comisiones Obreras, 2016) allocated to job creation. On the other hand, in December 2016 the government decided to end the freeze on the minimum wage, increasing it by €50. The 2017 budget also included a partial reversal of the freezing of transfers to the Autonomous Communities, raised public employees' salaries by 1 per cent, and lowered VAT for bullrings and theatres. In March 2018, agreement was reached with the trade unions to further increase public employees' wages and on the possibility of returning to the thirty-five-hour working week (under certain conditions). As per our expectations, most of these reversals were made to public spending cuts and not structural reforms.

The unexpected turn: June 2018–May 2019 (centre-left government)

On 25 May 2018, the PSOE, led by Pedro Sanchez, presented a no-confidence vote against the PP government that was supported by all opposition parties except Ciudadanos. PSOE won the subsequent elections and Pedro Sanchez became the new Spanish Prime Minister. In a move to recover PSOE's image as a centre-left political party (Khenkin, 2016, p. 105), Sanchez made several declarations stating his intention to reverse austerity measures and structural reforms as well as his commitment to comply with the SGP. As one member of the PSOE explained to us: 'If what they impose from Brussels is against our ideology, it is very complicated to comply with the recommendations because this produces disaffection in our constituencies. In the June 2017 Congress, we decided that we could not implement policies that went against our membership.'[37]

In line with our Proposal Four, the PSOE government decided to reverse some measures. One of the first reforms reversed by the PSOE government was the much criticised (but hardly implemented, see Branco *et al.*, 2019) exclusion of illegal immigrants from the health system. Some other important measures were also reversed: the abolition of the state coverage of social security contributions for non-professional careers, the 'Sun tax' paid by those using solar panels and the additional 7 per cent tax on electricity (hence lowering families' electricity bills by 2 per cent and industry's by up to 40 per cent). The cinema tax went back to 10 per cent (El Confidencial, 2018) and public employees again received full salary when on sick leave. Negotiations began between the government, employers' organisations and trade unions on other reversals in labour regulations and the pension and unemployment system. Nevertheless, the government did not intend to reverse the reforms altogether but only to make a few adjustments.[38]

On the other hand, many fiscal consolidation measures and structural reforms were not reversed, or even discussed, by either the PP or PSOE. This was the case, for example, with the tightening of access to early retirement, the increase in the retirement age from sixty-five to sixty-seven years (Romero, 2020), the cuts in unemployment and family benefits (*cheque bebé*), the increase in VAT on regular goods and the abolition of fiscal deductions for house purchases.

In the case of Spain, the lack of reversals can be explained by weak governments without a parliamentary majority and also by the periods without any government. In the run-up to the Catalan independence referendum in 2017 and beyond, PP and PSOE were unable to get the support of Catalan independence parties to approve central policies. For example, in 2019 the PSOE budget for 2019 did not get the support of the Catalan parties (Catalan European Democratic Party and ERC), which meant that proposed reversals such as the increases in spending on education and the minimum wage were not made. It was so difficult to implement the government programme that Sánchez called general elections for 28 April 2019. Although PSOE won with a simple majority, it was unable to form a government and new elections followed on 10 November 2019 (Ferrándiz and Lobera, 2019). PSOE again won the elections without a sufficient majority and began negotiations with other parties. Finally, a coalition government of PSOE and Podemos was formed on 8 January 2020. Just a few days later, the government approved the law re-establishing the link between pensions and inflation.[39]

Conclusions

The analysis of Spanish governments' leverage vis-à-vis international lenders during the Eurozone crisis offers us empirical support for our arguments. This chapter shows that despite extreme pressure from the financial markets and European institutions, Spanish executives were not powerless. They were able to negotiate with external actors (e.g. fiscal deficit with the European Commission) and avoid the implementation of reforms (e.g. the pension sustainability factor). In line with our theoretical proposal, we demonstrate that the crisis made it easier for both left-wing and right-wing governments to implement reforms that had been on their agenda but difficult to implement in the absence of external constraints (Proposal One).

Nevertheless, we also observe that the socialist government's ability to use the crisis as an opportunity was severely limited by the divergence between the government's preferences and the external actor's demands. The centre-right government was constrained by the need to comply with the Memorandum and the country-specific recommendations but, as this chapter demonstrates, the fiscal cuts and structural reforms it implemented were not only imposed by the external actors. First, the PP government achieved a particular form of bailout for Spain with a Memorandum exclusively for the banking sector. Secondly, it managed to negotiate some of the banking reforms in the Memorandum and, in some cases, was even able to avoid the international lenders' demands through alternative policies (e.g. Bankia preferred stakeholders). Thirdly, the government was able to avoid the implementation of politically difficult reforms (liberalisation of professional services) and to decide the direction of the redistributional costs of some reforms (e.g. housing, electricity).

Moreover, this case clearly illustrates that the PP government's credibility was fundamental to increasing leverage vis-à-vis the external actors. The ideological congruence between the government's preferences and external demands, together with the centre-right executive's commitment to delivering reforms were crucial to obtaining the international lenders' trust (Proposal Three). It also shows that the size of the country was a determinant of leverage, as a country that was 'too big to fail' had more bargaining power than smaller ones.

Finally, this chapter shows that, as expected, all governments partially reversed the reforms implemented during the crisis, and most of the reversals were focused on spending cuts and not structural reforms (Proposal Four). Nevertheless, due to the unstable political situation in Spain in 2018 and 2019, we could argue that the lack of some reversals by the centre-left party resulted from the political impasse, which precluded the implementation of any type of reform in the last years of the period under analysis.

Notes

1 Interview ES 8, political advisor, Madrid, 26 February 2016.
2 Interview ES 8, political advisor, Madrid, 26 February 2016.
3 Royal Decree-Law 8/2010, 20 May, to adopt extraordinary measures to reduce public deficit.

4 Transformed later into Law 35/2010.
5 Interview ES 5, political advisor, Madrid, 14 February 2016; Interview ES 6, Minister, Barcelona, 16 February 2016; Interview ES 7, Minister, Madrid, 25 February 2016; and Interview ES 19, government official, Madrid, 23 November 2017.
6 Interview ES 19, government official, Madrid, 23 November 2017.
7 Interview ES 5, political advisor, Madrid,14 February 2016; Interview ES 6, Minister, Barcelona, 16 February 2016; Interview ES 7, Minister, Madrid, 25 February 2016; and Interview ES 19, government official, Madrid, 23 November 2017.
8 Interview ES 3, trade union official, Madrid, 18 November 2015.
9 Interview ES 3, trade union official, Madrid, 18 November 2015 and Interview ES 5, political advisor, Madrid, 14 February 2016.
10 Interview ES 3, trade union official, Madrid, 18 November 2015.
11 Interview ES 8, political advisor, Madrid, 26 February 2016 and Interview ES 19, government official, Madrid, 23 November 2017.
12 The municipal elections held in thirteen regions in May 2011 gave an overwhelming victory to the Popular Party.
13 Royal Decree-Law 07/2011, 10 June, with urgent measures to reform collective bargaining.
14 Royal Decree-Law 10/2011, 26 August, with measures to promote employment among youth.
15 Royal Decree-Law 1193/2011, 19 August, establishing the procedure for applying the joint scale of deductions to the monthly billing of each pharmacy office.
16 Royal Decree-Law 10/2011, 26 August, with measures to promote employment among youth.
17 Interview ES 10, government official, Madrid, 20 November 2017.
18 Royal Decree-Law 3/2012, of 10 February, with urgent measures to reform the labour market.
19 Interview ES 8, political advisor, Madrid, 26 February 2016.
20 Royal Decree-Law 09/2009, 26 June, on bank restructuring and strengthening of the own resources of credit institutions.
21 Royal Decree-Law 02/2012, 3 February, of financial sector restructuring.
22 A second decree RDL 18/2012, 'Guindos decree 2', was implemented on 11 May 2012.
23 Interview ES 26, Secretary of State, phone interview, 30 October 2019.
24 Interview ES 26, Secretary of State, phone interview, 30 October 2019.
25 Royal Decree of Resolution and Restructuring of Credit Entities on 31 August 2012.
26 Interview ES 26, Secretary of State, phone interview, 30 October 2019.
27 Royal Decree-Law 28/2012, 30 November 2012, with measures to consolidate and guarantee the social security system.
28 Royal Decree-Law 28/2012, 30 November, with measures to consolidate and guarantee the social security system.
29 Royal Decree-Law 5/2013, 15 March, of measures to favour the continuity of the working life of older workers and promote active ageing.

30 Law 23/2013, 23 December, to regulate the sustainability factor of pensions.
31 Law 6/2018, 3 July, postponing the implementation of the sustainability factor until 2023, was the last measure introduced by the Spanish government in that regard.
32 Law 16/2012, 27 December, adopting various tax measures, and Royal Decree-Law 1192/2012, 3 August, regulating the condition of insured and beneficiary for the purposes of health care.
33 Law 4/2013, 4 June, of measures of flexibility and promotion of the housing rental market.
34 Law 24/2013, 26 December, on the electric sector.
35 Interview ES 12, MP, Madrid, 21 November 2017.
36 Interview ES 11, MP, Madrid, 20 November 2017 and Interview ES 13, MP, Madrid, 21 November 2017.
37 Interview ES 23, political party representative, Madrid, 10 October 2018.
38 Interview ES 25, Cabinet Director, Madrid, 11 October 2018.
39 Royal Decree-Law 1/2020, January 14, establishing the revaluation and maintenance of pensions and public benefits of the social security system.

6

Cyprus

Introduction

Our last case study, Cyprus, is particularly interesting insofar as it is the only one where there was a bail-in rather than a bailout during the Eurozone crisis. By the time Cyprus entered the Adjustment Programme, the rescue mechanisms had already been well institutionalised. In fact, it was 2013 when Cyprus signed the Economic Adjustment Programme as a result of delays on the part of both Cyprus and the European partners. Cyprus successfully exited the programme three years later in March 2016. The Cypriot case is also unique due to two characteristics of its politico-economic system that played a significant role in the development of the events and negotiations. First, Cyprus is a very consensual country; the division of the island after the Turkish invasion in 1974 and its colonial history have created a consensual climate in politics and in relations with the social partners that is quite different from the rest of Southern Europe. Moreover, although Cyprus' presidential system gives the President a lot of power, he or she does not always control the Parliament (Ker-Lindsay, 2006). Secondly, Cyprus had a close relationship with Russian investors and there were allegations of facilitating Russian oligarchs' money-laundering; this created a negative image in Western public opinion and impacted the negotiations and final agreement on a bail-in and the subsequent Economic Adjustment Programme. The chapter is organised chronologically in six sections.

Pre-Memorandum mid-2011–June 2012

Cyprus entered the Eurozone in 2008, just a few months before the collapse of Lehman Brothers and the onset of the global economic crisis. Eurozone membership consolidated the trust in the Cypriot economy, triggering an influx of property investors, notably from Britain and Russia. The low interest rates offered by banks and large deposits in euros made by these investors caused excessive growth of the banking and financial sector, while easy access to loans and an attractive tax system led to a property bubble (Charalambous, 2014; Demetriades, 2017). In the first quarter of 2008, real estate and housing loans were growing at an annual rate of 43.9 per cent (Clerides, 2014). As a result, by 2011 the banking system had reached 835 per cent of GDP, the highest percentage in the Eurozone after Luxembourg (International Monetary Fund, 2011c; Pegasiou, 2013).

Soon after Cyprus's entry into the Eurozone in February 2008, a left-wing coalition government came into power formed by AKEL (Progressive Party of the Working People, former communist party, now centre-left), DIKO (Democratic Party, centrist) and EDEK (Social-Democratic movement, centre-left) led by AKEL's Dimitris Christofias (Charalambous, 2014). In the following years, the economy quickly deteriorated. As was the case with Spain and Ireland, the global financial crisis abruptly dried up the flow of foreign capital to Cyprus that had been feeding its housing bubble. Additionally, the Christofias government was still pursuing an expansive economic policy that went far beyond the Eurozone's Keynesian response at the start of the crisis, and this played a negative role, especially once investors started to doubt the peripheral countries' ability to repay their debts (Katsourides, 2019). A Council Decision due to the excessive deficit in Cyprus had been put in place in July 2010 (Council of the European Union, 2010b) and the central bank had already asked for Emergency Liquidity Assistance (ELA) from the ECB to support the Popular Bank.

Although Cyprus lost access to the markets in May 2011, making it very difficult to fund its needs (Orphanides, 2014), it was a domestic event that triggered the worsening of the situation. In July 2011, an explosion at a naval base near Mari resulted in thirteen deaths and damaged a nearby electricity generation plant, causing widespread blackouts (Ladi, 2011). The Mari explosion intensified criticisms of the government's economic policy and ultimately led to the replacement of the Finance Minister, Charilaos Stavrakis (Xiouros, 2016). By this time, all coalition parties had withdrawn from the government, leaving AKEL on its own. Kikis Kazamias became the Christofias government's second Finance Minister in August 2011 and immediately started implementing austerity measures to tackle the worsening economic situation and in response to the Council's Decision on excessive deficit. Four austerity packages were implemented at this time, including cuts in benefits, salaries and pensions in the public sector, as well as tax increases; this was approximately two years before Cyprus entered an Economic Adjustment Programme in 2013 (Charalambous, 2014).[1] These austerity measures were passed with the agreement of the opposition and trade unions in the Cypriot tradition of the cooperative social and labour relations model. The process was perceived as a domestic affair and was facilitated by a general understanding that the measures were timely and necessary to put public finances in order (Pegasiou, 2013).[2] Unlike other Southern European countries, therefore, the austerity measures in Cyprus were calmly received.

However, the situation in the Cypriot banks deteriorated even further in October 2011 with the implementation of the Eurogroup Decision on the Greek PSI. The Cypriot banks had bought Greek sovereign bonds in the secondary market from German and other European banks at the start of the crisis, so were seriously exposed to the haircut (Pegasiou, 2013). Public debt rose to 71.6 per cent of GDP and yields to 5.78 points (Republic of Cyprus, 2012). Relative to other Eurozone countries, these figures were not excessive but they were marked by an upward trend. In December, the government negotiated a €2.5 billion loan from Russia to help with its liquidity and to avoid an EFSF loan which would come with conditionality measures.[3] The Russian loan had no formal conditionality attached to it. The European partners, and especially the Germans, at that point were highly critical of the Cypriot government's decision to turn to Russia.[4]

However, conversations started with the EFSF in early 2012 as the Russian loan was not enough, in part because the Popular Bank, one of the biggest in Cyprus, needed urgent support. In March 2012, Kikis Kazamias resigned as Finance Minister for health reasons and was replaced by Vassos Shiarly. An experienced banker, Shiarly's technocratic background sometimes made him seem like an outsider (Demetriades, 2017). Investors' trust in the system was at its lowest by this time, Cyprus's credit ratings were at junk status and there were excessive outflows from the banks, especially the Popular Bank. The government decided it was necessary to grant the Popular Bank financial support in addition to the ELA support it was already receiving, to avoid the collapse of the whole banking system (Christofias, 2013). On 25 June 2012, the government had no option but to apply for an EFSF and IMF loan (European Stability Mechanism, 2019). Both the banking system and public finances were in such a bad state by this time that the government, which had little leverage, could not justify requesting a bailout of the banks alone. At the start of negotiations, the Cypriot banks' outstanding loans and other money at risk totalled €152 billion – about eight times the size of the country's GDP (Ewing, 2012; International Monetary Fund, 2011d). Moreover, the EU's trust in Cyprus had been negatively impacted by its cooperation with the Russians.

MoU negotiations under the Christofias government (June 2012–February 2013)

Cyprus requested a loan just as it took the EU presidency on 1 July 2012. Soon after the formal request was submitted, the Troika made its first official visit to Cyprus to start negotiations. The estimated total cost of the bailout ranged between €13.5 billion according to the IMF to €10 billion based on press leaks (Demetriades, 2017). It was immediately agreed that the Troika and the Cypriot institutions would appoint an independent consultant to provide an accurate calculation. The resulting report from the investment management company, PIMCO, was submitted on 1 February 2013 after the data had been confirmed by another financial planning and investment management company, Black Rock (Christofias, 2013).[5]

The key political controversy was whether Cyprus had a banking or a sovereign debt problem. Whereas the government said it was a banking debt crisis, the opposition was keen to stress government mistakes so claimed it was also a sovereign debt crisis. Academic research shows the complexity of the question, with both debts rising simultaneously and the banking debt feeding into the sovereign debt and vice versa (e.g. Panayi and Zenios, 2015). Politically, this proved to be a key question as the deflation of the banking sector in Cyprus was largely due to Russian investment, which the German and other European media were presenting as money-laundering by Russian oligarchs (Young, 2013). The Cyprus bailout was therefore much more controversial than those of Ireland and Spain despite their similarity. The Christofias government had little room for manoeuvre because of the worsening economic situation, but it did manage to avoid a bail-in in the rescue of the banks during its term of office. In 2013, public debt in Cyprus reached 104 per cent of GDP and in March that year yields stood at 6.5 points (Demetriades, 2017).

At the end of July, the Troika submitted its proposal to the government for internal negotiations and discussion with the stakeholders. Known as the 'Building Blocks', this included austerity measures and privatisations just as in the other programmes.[6] The government was about to host the September ECOFIN meeting one month later when it presented its counter-proposals. Although it accepted many of the Troika's proposals, privatisations were a key objection. Meanwhile, the government was still trying to secure a second Russian loan, something that the Troika did not openly object to as it would mean the country considered to be partially responsible for the situation would contribute to its solution (Gotev, 2012). The government also favoured a Russian loan as it would not be attached to conditionality, and so would give it more freedom in its tackling of the crisis. However, the loan never materialised. According to government officials, the Russians did not want to be seen funding a country that had already asked for a loan from the EU (Demetriades, 2017).[7]

The key areas of disagreement between the Christofias government and the Troika during the negotiations related to structural reforms. Based on the assumption that Cyprus's problem was mainly in the banking sector, the President was fiercely against privatising semi-public organisations such as the Cyprus Telecommunications Authority (CYTA), the Electricity Authority of Cyprus and the ports, especially since they were profitable.[8] The modification of the Cost of Living Adjustment (COLA) of wages and salaries was another source of disagreement as the government considered it to be a pillar of Cyprus's consensual labour relations that had been working successfully for decades (Pegasiou, 2013).[9] Additionally, the government supported the inclusion of establishing a National Health System (GESY) in the MoU; this had traditionally been part of AKEL's manifesto (AKEL Central Committee, 2010).[10] The negotiations with the Troika were further complicated since agreement was often reached at a technical level with the Ministry of Finance but then blocked by the President, so negotiations were constantly breaking down. There were no major divisions within the Troika during this period. A compromise was finally reached: the government agreed to the freezing of COLA and to the implementation of the GESY, but privatisations would only take place if necessary. In fact, the final MoU only referred to 'a plan for privatisations' and did not include specific targets (European Commission, 2013d).

Although agreement was reached with the Troika by 23 November 2012, the MoU was only signed in April 2013. Due to the pressing economic situation, Parliament unanimously voted through the prior actions necessary for the freezing of COLA as well as other austerity measures on 12 December.[11] On 19 December, the 2013 budget with the calculated benefit from implementing these preliminary actions was also unanimously approved by Parliament in a gesture of goodwill from Cyprus.[12] However, Cyprus was disappointed when the programme was not discussed at the December meeting of the Eurogroup, largely because of Germany's reluctance to proceed until the measures had actually been implemented. Similarly, although welcoming the progress made in negotiations, on 21 January 2013 the Eurogroup decided not to adopt the agreed MoU until after the February presidential elections. We can therefore see that despite the opposition's criticism of the government for the delay in the negotiations, the European partners were also to blame. The reason put forward by the European partners was that waiting until after the 2013 presidential elections would facilitate the new government's ownership of the programme (Demetriades, 2017). Moreover, the levels of trust between the Troika and the Christofias government at the time were low, and public opinion in Germany and Europe was still negative because of both the allegedly close relationship between Cyprus and the Russian oligarchs and accusations of money-laundering (Young, 2013). AKEL's ideology and reluctance to accept a loan from the EU and the IMF until the last minute had also hampered the relationship.

The delay had important consequences for the nature of the agreement reached a couple of months later. Indeed, the Christofias government had negotiated a bailout programme but the PIMCO report submitted on 1 February, just a few days before the elections, painted a very gloomy picture, calculating that the banks' needs were much higher than previously thought. The capital shortfall under the adverse scenario was estimated as €8.128 million for domestic banks, €149 million for foreign banks and €589 million for participating credit cooperatives (PIMCO, 2013). During the electoral campaign, academics and bankers often questioned the calculations, which they deemed exaggerated (Demetriades, 2017).[13] Following the inconclusive first round of elections on 17 February, Anastasiades, the leader of the liberal-conservative Democratic Rally (DISY), was elected in the second round a week later with 57.5 per cent of the vote. Anastasiades had been endorsed by Angela Merkel and other European leaders and officials as he was seen as a pro-European, pro-market leader, and it was thought he would be easier to negotiate with than Christofias who, after all, was the leader of the communist party (AKEL) (Demetriades, 2017). Negotiations to finalise the programme resumed as soon as the new government took office in March 2013.

MoU negotiations under the new Anastasiadis government (March 2013–April 2013)

The first Eurogroup meeting took place on 4 March with the new Finance Minister, Michael Sarris, representing Cyprus. Like his predecessor, Sarris was a technocrat. Although the official Eurogroup statement simply welcomed the new government, in fact the meeting was the start of a new period in the negotiations for the Cypriot programme (Eurogroup, 2013). A journalist following the Cypriot crisis explained how the bail-in became the only acceptable solution for the Troika:

> Basically, they created a communicative framework for Cyprus being a special case. As far as the banking sector is concerned, there should be a bail-in because there is foreign money there. So why should the German taxpayer … pay for the Russian oligarch that has his money in Cyprus? And in Cyprus this felt like the end of the world. We thought that there was going to be no tomorrow. That was the climate.[14]

In light of the ongoing controversy about the Russian oligarchs and the Cypriot banking system, it was agreed that an independent evaluation should be conducted of the anti-money-laundering frameworks of the Cypriot financial institutions (Demetriades, 2017).[15] At the Troika's first meeting with the Cypriot government, the IMF, together with the rest of the Troika, made it clear it would not grant Cyprus a loan that would make its debt unsustainable. A Cypriot bank executive explained: 'In the end it was the political opinions of the Eurozone's hard core that dominated who, with the help of the IMF, imposed the bail-in by saying that no country can borrow more than 100 per cent of its GDP.'[16] Despite some disagreements, the IMF calculations and the PIMCO report were used as the baseline and it was decided that the loan to Cyprus could not exceed €10 billion. This left Cyprus with a bill of €5.8 billion to save its two biggest banks (Popular Bank and Cyprus Bank), which meant a bail-in was becoming unavoidable (Demetriades, 2017).[17] Additionally, the ring-fencing of the Cypriot bank branches in Greece was considered critical given the fragile situation of the Greek economy. Indeed, Cyprus was obliged to sell its bank branches to a Greek bank before it could enter an Economic Adjustment Programme (Demetriades, 2017).[18]

At the next Eurogroup meeting just ten days later (15–16 March), the unprecedented decision was made to impose a one-off 'deposit levy' on all deposits in Cypriot banks in order to concentrate the necessary revenue for the recapitalisation of the two problematic banks. This levy was set at 9.9 per cent for deposits over €100,000 and, for the first time in the Eurozone, deposits of less than €100,000 euros would pay a 6.75 per cent levy. This was the first time that the guarantee for deposits under €100,000 would be broken (European Commission, undated b). Contrary to the norm, President Anastasiades participated directly in these Eurogroup negotiations since both sides recognised the urgency of the situation (Demetriades, 2017; Dijsselbloem, 2018). According to an informant, the President said: 'They put the gun to my head. There was no other solution.'[19] This unorthodox decision was very much the result of the allegedly close relationship between Cyprus and the Russian oligarchs; in other words, European leaders did not want to risk public opinion's disapproval back home (Demetriades, 2017).[20]

Blame-shifting started as soon as the Eurogroup decision was announced. The two sides distanced themselves from the decision after a public outcry, each describing it as rushed and badly calculated with neither of them wanting to take responsibility. The Eurogroup's President Jeroen Dijsselbloem stated that this was a Cypriot proposal while President Anastasiades claimed he was blackmailed by the Eurogroup (Demetriades, 2017; Dijsselbloem, 2018). Just a few days later, on 19 March, the Cypriot Parliament rejected the Eurogroup decision. In the meanwhile, the Finance Minister Sarris was sent to Russia to try to secure a second loan. He stayed in Moscow for almost a week in the hope that the new government would prove more successful in securing a second Russian loan than Christofias. However, Sarris came up against the same hurdles as the previous government and the opposition accused him of not really trying or, in light of the Christofias government's attempts, of already knowing a Russian loan would be impossible.[21] Just two days later, Parliament rejected the Eurogroup agreement and the ECB announced that the ELA for the Cypriot banks would end on 25 March unless a new agreement was reached at the next Eurogroup meeting. According to ECB rules, the ELA could not be granted if it entailed a risk for the European banking system. Of course, the politicians took this announcement as ECB blackmail.[22] At that point, Cyprus was closer than ever to exiting the Eurozone since a collapse of the banking system would also signify the collapse of the Cypriot economy (Demetriades, 2017). Between the Eurogroup decision on 16 March and the next Eurogroup meeting on 25 March, there was a ten-day bank holiday in Cyprus to avoid a bank run.

In preparation for the upcoming Eurogroup meeting and given that the Popular Bank and the Bank of Cyprus were near to collapse, the Central Bank of Cyprus pushed through a resolution law which gave it power to act as a resolution authority over failing financial institutions. The legislation was controversial since it basically gave the Central Bank of Cyprus the authority to lead the closure of the Popular Bank without a parliamentary vote on the issue. There were later claims that everything happened so quickly that the MPs did not even realise what they had voted for (Demetriades, 2017).[23] The negotiations between the Cypriot government and the European partners were tough; Cyprus was in a weak position and Anastasiades was forced to accept almost a full bail-in although with a different arrangement as a prerequisite for the signing of an Economic Adjustment Programme. The new agreement was much closer to the IMF position, as well as that of Germany, Austria, Finland, the Netherlands and Slovakia (Blustein, 2016; Demetriades, 2017) than the government would have wished. The new agreement meant that the Popular Bank was split into a 'good' bank and a 'bad' bank; this financial structure aimed to isolate high-risk assets. The good bank was absorbed by the Bank of Cyprus, which was restructured and saved; on the other hand, the bad bank was immediately dissolved with serious losses for shareholders and uninsured depositors. Bank of Cyprus depositors with deposits of over €100,000 also suffered a haircut close to 47 per cent (Demetriades, 2017). Deposits below €100,000 were safeguarded but everyone else lost a huge amount of money and the Cypriot banking system was shaken. Capital controls were immediately imposed (Blustein, 2016; Demetriades, 2017).[24] According to a government official, this was the peak of the crisis for Cyprus: 'disaster was felt so much with the bail-in that the other aspects of the MoU conditionality mattered much less'.[25] The climate in Cyprus after the 26 March decision was that of a national disaster; nevertheless, most of our interviewees argue that, because of the island's traumatic history, a patriotic feeling of survival emerged that allowed for the smooth implementation of the bail-in despite the big losses of some of the depositors, including the Church.[26] Of course, this did not stop the legal battles initiated by Popular Bank depositors or the Governor of the Central Bank of Cyprus being made a scapegoat on the grounds that he did not protect the Popular Bank (Demetriades, 2017).

The conditionality of the Economic Adjustment Programme took only a few days to finalise as the previous government's agreement remained almost intact. What the Anastasiades government pushed for was for the fiscal adjustment to take place via spending cuts and not via tax rises, which would affect investment.[27] The government was indeed granted room for manoeuvre to keep taxation low. However, the austerity measures included in the conditionality were the same as those Christofias had negotiated, namely fiscal and financial policy measures, cuts in social, health and education provisions, and some public administration and tax system reforms such as the Immovable Property Tax as well as a plan for future privatisations. Unlike the other bailout countries, labour market reforms were not part of the conditionality (European Commission, 2013d) because no one wanted to jeopardise the consensual labour relations already in place. It is important to note that the government immediately took ownership of the programme through the new Finance Minister, Harris Georgiades, who was responsible for the coordination of the different Ministries and for the programme's implementation. A government Minister stated that the MoU 'had our signature. Meaning that it was a political commitment made with our signature. It could thus be considered as part of and indeed as a centrepiece of our governmental programme.'[28]

Immediately after the agreement was finalised on 2 April, Finance Minister Michalis Sarris resigned from his position. In a statement, he said his resignation would facilitate investigations into the Popular Bank since he had acted as its President from January to August 2012 (Iefimerida, 2013). The next day, Harris Georgiadis, a politician from the inner circle of President Anastasiades, was appointed Finance Minister and was responsible for the implementation of the MoU. The programme was finally agreed at the Eurogroup meeting on 12 April. The ESM would contribute with €9 billion and the IMF with €1 billion to the €10 billion loan (European Stability Mechanism, 2019). It was calculated that Cyprus would need €4.1 billion for refinancing, €2.5 billion for bank recapitalisation and €3.4 billion for the macroeconomic part of the programme (European Commission, 2013d). To conclude, during this period efforts went entirely into the negotiation of the bail-in and the government had very limited room for manoeuvre despite its ideological ease with austerity measures.

MoU implementation (April 2013–March 2016)

The implementation of the conditionality of the MoU in Cyprus went smoothly thanks to a general consensus within the government and in the rest of society that most of the reforms were necessary; the programme was completed on time three years later. Even before the first review of the programme, the government established an ad hoc coordination mechanism that formally gave the lead to the Finance Ministry (Pegasiou, 2018). The government also had the backing of a centre-right coalition including Evroko (European Party) and DIKO, giving it an absolute majority in Parliament (Lütz *et al.*, 2019). Unlike in Greece, the Troika visits were kept quiet and received little media attention; press conferences were rare and always well coordinated between the Troika and the government.[29] The opposition enhanced this climate of consent despite their disagreement with some aspects of the MoU, keeping these discussions inside Parliament, where they often abstained from voting on harsh measures. Trade unions did not incite big demonstrations or strikes that would obstruct the government measures.[30] The reasons for this climate of consent go beyond the crisis and are linked with the socio-political system in Cyprus as well as a feeling of national solidarity due to the island's turbulent history and relationship with Turkey (Charalambous, 2014). In fact, almost all our interviewees explained that the bail-in was much more costly, painful and shocking for the Cypriots than the conditionality *per se*.[31]

The government decided to push ahead with the public spending cuts early on to speed up fiscal consolidation and avoid tax increases. A government Minister explains that the government cut public spending by 11 per cent in one year 'in order to minimise [the] Troika's ability ... to tell us what to do in relation to economic policy'.[32] Like Ireland, the government took a proactive stance to minimise the Troika's intervention. For the Finance Ministry, it was of paramount importance to maintain low taxes in order to keep investment coming in; they even managed to lower taxation in some instances in 2015.[33] The banking sector was also put under stricter surveillance and new regulations were put in place for both banks and cooperative credit institutions. The Financial Ombudsman was strengthened (European Commission, 2013d, 2013e, 2015c). During the implementation of the programme, the government also proposed introducing the Guaranteed Minimum Income, which was designed to replace a number of existing social benefits. Although the Troika was reluctant to accept the measure since the cost was calculated at around €40 million, an agreement was reached after negotiations led by President Anastasiades, thanks to the government's good record of implementation.[34] This is in line with our Proposal One, that governments have room for manoeuvre during a bailout, and with our Proposal Three, that when a government implements measures its credibility increases and thus it is easier to push for preferred measures. In February 2014, DIKO left the coalition government over a disagreement on the peace talks related to the long-lasting Cyprus issue; however, as it continued to support the government in Parliament on the legislation linked to the MoU, the implementation was not hampered (Lütz *et al.*, 2019).

By 2014, one year after the start of the programme, the country was already showing signs of financial recovery, which meant that its bargaining power was increasing and some undesirable measures were avoided (Lütz *et al.*, 2019). For example, the privatisation of semi-public organisations had never received much support except from the ruling party DISY. CYTA and the Electricity Authority of Cyprus were seen as state assets, this in a country that perceives itself to be under threat given the northern part of the island is still under Turkish occupation.[35] Although the MoU included a plan for privatisations, they were never a government priority and this is evident in all the progress reviews (European Commission, 2013e, 2013f, 2014a, 2014b, 2014c, 2015c, 2015d). Even though the Third Programme review stipulated prior action on privatisations before the disbursement of the next tranche, in the end only the Ports Authority was privatised (European Commission, 2014a).[36] Eventually, the Troika turned a blind eye and Cyprus exited the programme without completing the final review or the privatisation programme (Lütz *et al.*, 2019).[37]

Similarly, the foreclosure procedures bill aiming to streamline bank foreclosures is also described by interviewees as a 'bill without teeth'.[38] Although it was a prior action for the disbursement of a loan tranche, the actual bill passed was much softer than initially expected but was eventually accepted by the Troika (Lütz *et al.*, 2019). Once again, it was the successful implementation of the austerity measures that made this possible. Two further areas where reforms were not completed were the restructuring of the pension system and the introduction of the GESY (European Commission, 2015c, 2015d).[39] However, neither of these was considered to be salient for the successful closure of the programme as the macroeconomic targets were reached through the government spending cut programme.[40] These examples support our Proposal Three on the increased room for manoeuvre enjoyed by governments once they successfully implement reforms and gain trust.

On 6 April 2015, Cyprus lifted all capital controls and the economy was already in much better shape. The government decided to exit the programme on time in March 2016 without completing all the reforms, leaving €2.7 billion from the initial loan unspent (European Stability Mechanism, 2019). It was decided not to further pursue the privatisations since they did not have the support of Parliament.[41] Although Cyprus's exit from the programme was seen as a success, some still argue that more reforms would have been achieved had the programme lasted a little longer.[42]

The Economic Adjustment Programme in Cyprus shows that, during the implementation phase, governments still have room for manoeuvre and can use the review process to amend conditionality, as in the case of the Guaranteed Minimum Income. They can also partially implement reforms, as happened with the restructuring of the pension system and the privatisation plan. The Cypriot government even managed to end the programme without implementing the final reforms or using the full loan since it managed to get access to the markets. As suggested by our Proposal Three, this was all possible for Cyprus because the most salient issue, namely the bail-in, was concluded before the programme had even started; moreover, the government's credibility was strong due to its rapid implementation of the key austerity measures after the signing of the programme.

Post-MoU (April 2016–2019)

Cyprus's exit from the Economic Adjustment Programme was followed by a Post-Programme Surveillance period, due to last until 75 per cent of the financial assistance received had been paid. Cyprus was also under the EU Macroeconomic Imbalance Procedure as a result of its continued macroeconomic imbalances. During this period, there had been six-monthly visits from the Troika to assess the progress in the Cypriot economy and the implementation of the structural reforms. However, Cypriot policy-makers considered this surveillance much more relaxed than the MoU period since the Troika no longer had the stick of the next tranche of financial assistance. As one Cypriot official put it, 'They come, they observe and they report'.[43] A government Minister adds, 'The judge is no longer the Troika when the programme has ended. The judge is the markets', meaning that the constraint was still there but it had to do with the markets and not the post-programme surveillance itself.[44]

Two months after the exit from the programme, parliamentary elections were held on 22 May. Given that Cyprus has a presidential system, these elections have less salience but they are still indicative of the parties' power. In addition, the elections had gained significance as Parliament had demonstrated its importance during the crisis, through its rejection of the first version of the bail-in, for example. The electoral campaign for both DISY and AKEL revolved around the financial crisis, together with the management of and exit from the Economic Adjustment Programme. DISY claimed victory for the successful exit from the programme, while AKEL launched an anti-austerity campaign. Despite significant abstention, DISY won the elections with the loss of only two seats from the previous term (Triga, 2017). A journalist in Nicosia describes the period after the exit from the MoU as a lengthy electoral cycle between 2016 and 2018, including parliamentary, municipal and presidential elections; in other words, continuing with difficult reforms was not a priority since the economy was improving and the surveillance was light.[45]

However, there were a few reversals during this post-crisis period, and they mainly addressed austerity and cost-cutting measures. The most significant reversal was that of the Immovable Property Tax, which was abolished very soon after Cyprus exited the programme (European Commission, 2016c, 2017b). This was an unpopular tax due to the large numbers of property owners on the island but also because the property market is still a significant economic activity in Cyprus. The benefits and the costs of this reversal were spread across the population. Reversals to the cuts in public sector salaries and pensions were debated but little was done until 2019, despite pressure from the court (Psylides, 2019). The banking sector remained the main concern of both the government and the Troika in the post-programme period, notably measures to limit non-performing loans and finding a solution to the fragmented system of cooperative banks in Cyprus. By 2019, non-performing loans had been significantly reduced and the Cyprus Cooperative Bank sold (European Commission, 2019). Some of the reforms initiated by the MoU, like the establishment of a National Health System, continued slowly, while others, such as public administration reform and the privatisation of semi-public organisations, never took off (European Commission, 2016c).[46] In January 2018, President Anastasiades was re-elected for another five-year term without much difficulty. The crisis period in Cyprus is now perceived to be over.

Conclusions

Cyprus was the last country to enter into an Economic Adjustment Programme in 2013, which it successfully exited in 2016. Similarly to Ireland and Spain, in Cyprus there was primarily a banking crisis which developed into a sovereign debt crisis. The Cypriot case is unique in that it is the only country where a bail-in with significant losses for depositors was implemented as a precondition for the signing of the Economic Adjustment Programme. European public opinion and media allegations of Cyprus's close relationships with the Russian oligarchs certainly played a role in this decision and limited the government's room for manoeuvre.

In line with the findings in all our cases, there is evidence in Cyprus of the government being able to define policies in conjunction with the

Troika, to insert new measures, such as the introduction of GESY, and to avoid implementing certain measures like the privatisation programme. Some policies, like the rationalisation of social benefits, had long been on the government's agenda and were implemented as part of the MoU. Even more than in other cases, there was a consensus among the government, opposition and social partners on most of the MoU reforms. The most telling fact is that the conditionality in the programme signed by Anastasiades was largely negotiated by the Christofias government. However, the negotiation of the bail-in was much more difficult and there were clear asymmetries of power between the Cypriot government and the European partners. In fact, this was the most important battle for Cyprus and neither the Christofias nor the Anastasiades governments managed to improve the situation significantly. Cyprus seemed to lack credibility in the bail-in negotiations and had very limited room for manoeuvre mainly because of the Russian factor.

The negotiation and implementation of the MoU in Cyprus does not offer much evidence on our proposition about partisanship. The conditionality negotiated by the left-wing Christofias government was fully adopted by the right-wing Anastasiades government. It is true that Christofias delayed asking for help from the European partners for as long as possible, and that he only negotiated but did not implement the reforms. The final negotiation, implementation and post-programme period in Cyprus were all led by the Anastasiades government, which managed to be re-elected in 2018 and was not penalised for implementing the MoU or indeed the bail-in.

In line with our proposal about government credibility, on the other hand, there is clear evidence in Cyprus that the government's room for manoeuvre to adjust and implement the programme increased when it took ownership and managed to cut public spending by 11 per cent in its first year. For example, it managed to negotiate the introduction of the Guaranteed Minimum Income and avoided implementing most of the privatisation programme.

There have been few reversals in post-programme Cyprus because most of the measures were adopted consensually and there was no change in government after the end of the programme. Reversals have been made when the costs are diffused and they bring general benefit to the economy, as in the case of the Immovable Property Tax. Reversing some of the cost-cutting measures has also been under discussion but the government did not reverse any of the structural reforms. However, partial implementation can be observed for some of the costly (GESY) or unpopular (privatisation programme) reforms. It can be concluded that, similarly to our other cases, reversals in Cyprus have been partial and selective.

Notes

1 Interview CY 49, Minister, Limassol, 13 April 2018.
2 Interview CY 46, trade union representative, Nicosia, 12 April 2018.
3 Interview CY 44, government official, Nicosia, 12 April 2018 and Interview CY 49, Minister, Limassol, 13 April 2018.
4 Interview CY 49, Minister, Limassol, 13 April 2018.
5 Interview CY 40, senior officer at Central Bank of Cyprus, Nicosia, 10 April 2018.
6 Interview CY 50, government official, Nicosia, 13 April 2018.
7 Interview CY 50, government official, Nicosia, 13 April 2018.
8 Interview CY 41, government official, Nicosia, 11 April 2018.
9 Interview CY 41, government official, Nicosia, 11 April 2018 and Interview CY 50, government official, Nicosia, 13 April 2018.
10 Interview CY 43, journalist, Nicosia, 11 April 2018.
11 Interview CY 42, Minister, Nicosia, 11 April 2018.
12 Interview CY 42, Minister, Nicosia, 11 April 2018.
13 Interview CY 40, senior officer at Central Bank of Cyprus, Nicosia, 10 April 2018.
14 Interview CY 43, journalist, Nicosia, 11 April 2018.
15 Interview CY 42, Minister, Nicosia, 11 April 2018.
16 Interview CY 40, senior officer at Central Bank of Cyprus, Nicosia, 10 April 2018.
17 Interview CY 55, Minister, Athens, 31 May 2018.
18 Interview CY 42, Minister, Nicosia, 11 April 2018 and Interview CY 55, Minister, Athens, 31 May 2018.
19 Interview CY 43, journalist, Nicosia, 11 April 2018.
20 Interview CY 37, senior official at the Central Bank of Cyprus, Skype call, 26 March 2018.
21 Interview CY 49, Minister, Limassol, 13 April 2018; Interview CY 50, government official, Nicosia, 13 April 2018; and Interview CY 55, Minister, Athens, 31 May 20 18.
22 Interview CY 44, government official, Nicosia, 12 April 2018.
23 Interview CY 42, Minister, Nicosia, 11 April 2018.
24 Interview CY 40, senior officer at Central Bank of Cyprus, Nicosia, 10 April 2018.
25 Interview CY 55, Minister, Athens, 31 May 2018.
26 Interview CY 43, journalist, Nicosia, 11 April 2018 and Interview CY 48, Minister, Nicosia, 13 April 2018.
27 Interview CY 45, Minister, Nicosia, 12 April 2018.
28 Interview CY 45, Minister, Nicosia, 12 April 2018.
29 Interview BR 29, official from the EC 3, Brussels, 30 January 2018 and Interview CY 48, Minister, Nicosia, 13 April 2018.

30 Interview CY 44, government official, Nicosia, 12 April 2018; Interview CY 45, Minister, Nicosia, 12 April 2018; and Interview CY 46, trade union representative, Nicosia, 12 April 2018.
31 E.g. Interview CY 40, senior officer at Central Bank of Cyprus, Nicosia, 10 April 2018 and Interview CY 47, government official, Nicosia, 13 April 2018.
32 Interview CY 45, Minister, Nicosia, 12 April 2018.
33 Interview CY 45, Minister, Nicosia, 12 April 2018.
34 Interview CY 41, government official, Nicosia, 11 April 2018 and Interview CY 48, Minister, Nicosia, 13 April 2018.
35 Interview CY 46, trade union representative, Nicosia, 12 April 2018 and Interview CY 55, Minister, Athens, 31 May 2018.
36 Interview CY 37, senior official at the Central Bank of Cyprus, Skype call, 26 March 2018; Interview CY 47, government official, Nicosia, 13 April 2018; and Interview CY 50, government official, Nicosia, 13 April 2018.
37 Interview CY 37, senior official at the Central Bank of Cyprus, Skype call, 26 March 2018.
38 Interview CY 37, senior official at the Central Bank of Cyprus, Skype call, 26 March 2018.
39 Interview CY 45, Minister, Nicosia, 12 April 2018; Interview CY 46, trade union representative, Nicosia, 12 April 2018; and Interview CY 55, Minister, Athens, 31 May 2018.
40 Interview BR 29, official from the EC 3, Brussels, 30 January 2018.
41 Interview CY 45, Minister, Nicosia, 12 April 2018.
42 Interview CY 48, Minister, Nicosia, 13 April 2018 and Interview CY 55, Minister, Athens, 31 May 2018.
43 Interview CY 47, government official, Nicosia, 13 April 2018.
44 Interview CY 45, Minister, Nicosia, 12 April 2018.
45 Interview CY 43, journalist, Nicosia, 11 April 2018.
46 Interview CY 47, government official, Nicosia, 13 April 2018.

7

Capitalising on external constraint: six things you should know about Eurozone bailouts

At the time of writing (mid-April 2020), the world is facing the new public health and economic challenges posed by the spread of COVID-19. This new crisis has understandably been attracting a lot of attention. In our view, our book contributes to this debate as it helps identify lessons to be drawn from the last crisis on the designing of EU economic responses and the pros and cons of conditionality.

In this last chapter, we summarise our main conclusions in light of the comparison between different countries and stress what they bring to the literature. We also present our quantitative data. Finally, we examine the similarities between the Eurozone crisis and the current situation and draw some conclusions.

On the room for manoeuvre of bailed out countries

Bound by European treaties, such as the Stability and Growth Pact, and pressured by the increasing divergence of yields between Eurozone countries, the peripheral countries had little room for manoeuvre during the financial crisis. In all our cases, governments tried to avoid further encroachment on their sovereignty tied to formal conditionality and passed packages of structural reforms and spending cuts to regain investors' trust. We have seen that the effectiveness of those efforts was very dependent on the perceived risks of contagion from other countries and on the actions and declarations of richer Eurozone countries or international institutions. The ECB emerged as an influential actor in this period. The fact that banks in the Eurozone relied on the ECB for liquidity gave the latter the power to pressure national governments. For example, when the Parliament rejected a one-off 'deposit levy' on all deposits in Cyprus, the ECB announced the end of emergency lending to domestic banks. The deposit levy was eventually approved. Using the same strategy, the ECB exerted heavy pressure on Irish authorities to ask for a bailout, which they eventually did.

The package of reforms and spending cuts adopted domestically failed to decrease the yields partly as a result of the delays in and/or lack of coordinated actions at the EU level at the onset of the crisis. Hence, one lesson to be learned when tackling future crises is that delays in common solutions are costly both financially and for the reputation of the EU. History has shown that, institutionally and politically, Europe eventually evolves through crises but the timely nature of decisions remains important.

When the governments of Greece, Ireland, Portugal, Spain and Cyprus perceived interest rates to be unsustainable, they eventually decided to ask the EU and IMF for credit. As Vreeland (1999) and Rogers (2009) show, some governments may ask for an IMF loan without necessarily needing it in order to bypass domestic veto players and pass reforms they deem desirable. This was not the case in the Eurozone, as we have seen that governments tried to avoid requesting a bailout for as long as possible. Doing so, they came under heavy pressure as their European counterparts and the ECB, which feared contagion, insisted that they asked for financial help.

Italy – not covered in this book – never asked for a bailout and coped with the mounting interest rates until the ECB announced its Outright Monetary Programme in 2012. In all cases, the decision to ask for external help was often taken by a few Ministers and was rarely consensual domestically. In some countries bail-in was discussed (Ireland) and/or pursued (Cyprus). This means that the request for a Troika bailout was made under strong pressure and as a solution of last resort but was nevertheless a political choice.

After requesting a bailout, these countries had to negotiate and implement a series of specific reforms for each tranche of the loan. The negotiations of the conditions associated with the loan were generally hasty, lasting no more than a couple of weeks. All countries were constrained to accept policies they disliked, and elections never brought about fundamental changes to the conditions attached to the loans. For example, the centre-left government in Portugal did not believe that internal devaluation was necessary for growth but it was forced to comply. In Greece, various governments considered that spending cuts were going too far but implemented many of them nevertheless, and SYRIZA was unable to introduce the U-turn in policies it had campaigned for during the elections and the referendum. In Cyprus, although privatisations were resented by most of the parties, the Ports Authority was in fact privatised in the end. In Ireland, the government wanted bondholders in two of its banks to foot the bill in 2011, but this measure was not accepted.

However, our book shows that despite these constraints, governments were far from powerless: in all our cases, governments of bailed out countries were able to advocate, resist, shape or roll back some of the policies demanded by external actors. As shown in the various chapters, this influence was not only exerted while the MoUs were being negotiated, but also during their implementation.

Informants from all sides indeed explained to us that negotiations were not a diktat and that the negotiators from the Troika were open to the solutions proposed by governments, as long as they reached general objectives (e.g. the reforms of the health and education systems in Spain and of local government administration in Greece were in fact drafted by these governments). Governments felt they could take the initiative to insert specific policies in the MoU or its revisions (e.g. the Guaranteed Minimum Income or the creation of a National Health System in Cyprus, the property tax in Ireland or a whole section of deregulation in Portugal).

Interviewees from all countries further reported instances of policies that the lenders wanted but which were eventually dropped from the Memoranda. In Portugal, for instance, the negotiators managed to take the reduction in the minimum wage off the table; in Ireland the corporate tax was not targeted, despite the Troika's wish to see it reformed. This was also the case of the subsidised agricultural fuel (green diesel) in Ireland, which the Troika wanted to abolish and the government managed to exclude from the programme.

In a similar vein, we show that domestic actors sometimes successfully resisted the implementation of some MoU policies they disliked; and that lenders were sometimes willing to turn a blind eye and let non-implementation go unsanctioned. This often happened towards the end of the programme when the economic conditions improved and/or when trust was high or even when the Troika was suffering from 'reform fatigue'. In Spain, the pension sustainability factor was approved but never implemented. In Cyprus and Ireland, a privatisation programme included in the MoU was never fully executed and, similarly, many of the privatisations in Greece are still pending. Lastly, the Portuguese government resisted pressure from lenders to find an alternative to the Constitutional Court's annulment of a permanent reform of the pension system.

Given this leeway, domestic negotiators told us that, in some cases, the bailout represented an opportunity to pass reforms that they considered necessary but could not previously have passed. For example, Ministers from Portugal told us that the bailout made the reduction of severance payment possible, as well as the decrease in the rents (excessive profits) enjoyed by the pharmaceutical and Electricity Companies; and that they had been wanting to do this for a long time. In Spain, informants from both centre-left and centre-right governments told us that they welcomed the reform of the pension system. Similarly, almost everybody in Greece, including SYRIZA Ministers, agreed that the pensions system should have been reformed much earlier and, in Cyprus, our interviewees from all major parties stated that the social benefits system needed rationalisation. In Ireland, respondents acknowledged that the liberalisation of legal services had been on their agenda for some time. Interestingly, reports published by the EC, the IMF and the OECD long before the onset of the Eurozone crisis had already acknowledged that many of these reforms were necessary.

This book thus demonstrates that the bailout was, to some extent, 'exploited' by executives as an opportunity to pass policies that they 'privately wish[ed] to do, but [were] powerless to do domestically' (Putnam, 1988, p. 457; see also Dyson and Featherstone, 1996; Featherstone, 2003; Grande, 1996; Vreeland, 1999). This supports the idea that although the bailout weakened the state internationally, it also strengthened the executive domestically (Moravcsik, 1994) and hence allowed the latter to override the veto of domestic actors on their preferred policies. The decision to ask for a loan, the negotiation of the MoU and its implementation were indeed centralised within the executive (and within it, in the Ministry of Finance). Only a small number of people were fully informed of the Troika's red lines, and the government in some instances exploited this asymmetry of information when presenting its plan to the parliamentary opposition or stakeholders. In many instances, this context allowed Ministers to adopt reforms that they deemed necessary but could not previously have passed.

As a result of this leverage, elections during a bailout changed the terms of conditionality, albeit to a limited extent. In Portugal, elections took place immediately after the Socialist party had negotiated the MoU and, during the programme, new measures – such as a new section on deregulation and the further liberalisation of the Labour Code – were added in the reviews at the request of the centre-right government. In Ireland, the change in government formed just after the bailout negotiations led to a reversal of the minimum wage cut and an extension of the fiscal consolidation period. In Greece, the SYRIZA government did not manage to change the conditionality of the programme but attempted to implement a 'parallel programme' focusing on alleviating some of the social inequalities arising from austerity.

This finding consolidates the strand of literature which shows the relevance of national executives during moments of external conditionality imposed by the EU (Afonso *et al.*, 2015; De la Porte and Natali, 2014; Dyson and Featherstone, 1996; Featherstone, 2003; Hardiman *et al.*, 2016; Hick, 2018; Moury and Standring, 2017; Walter, 2016) or by the IMF (Rogers, 2009; Vreeland, 1999). It also supports the idea that it still matters who is in government in times of crisis (for instance, Doyle, 2012; Galasso, 2014; Ha and Kang, 2015; Pop-Eleches, 2008; Starke *et al.*, 2013). This book thus also nuances the argument that the conditions of international loans are a 'diktat' (Hill, 2003; Keaney, 2001); or that democracy 'ended' during the crisis (Davis, 2016; Pianta, 2013). We show that conditionality narrows, but does not annihilate, political choice, and that voting still matters. Even if strongly constrained, governments in all cases had alternatives to balance the accounts and room for manoeuvre as regards the structural reforms.

However, this was true only as long as there was a minimum of trust between the lenders and the bailed out government (see below). We also show that governments rarely acknowledged their leverage in public or in their discourse with stakeholders. This led to a decline in the transparency and openness of policy-making in light of crisis management. Yet these are fundamental dimensions of the quality of established democracies (Altman and Pérez-Liñán, 2002). The reforms implemented during a crisis are highly salient and should be at the centre of public debate and choice (Séville, 2017).

Determinants of bargaining leverage

Our case studies also reveal that in many instances executives agreed with the lenders on the diagnostics and solutions – a phenomenon that was underlined by the fact that technocrats or 'sympathetic Ministers' were often appointed during the bailout (as shown by Alexiadou and Gunaydin, 2019). When there was disagreement, the leverage of the bailed out executives was, according to interviewees, dependent on five interlinked variables: economic fundamentals, the costs for lenders of not granting assistance, domestic governments' credibility and insider knowledge, and the saliency of the issues at stake.

First, the evolution of the economic conditions and the urgency of striking a deal (Finke and Bailer, 2019; Hennessy, 2017; Offe, 2017; Schimmelfennig, 2015) were important determinants of a country's leverage. This is something we are clearly witnessing today during the COVID-19 crisis as Ministers are negotiating on a package to stimulate growth after the lockdown.

Indeed, informants from bailed out countries and from the Troika reported to us that a change in the economic fundamentals of the bailed out countries (principally debt and yields) impacted their bargaining power. When the economic situation of any country deteriorated so much that it had no choice but to ask for a bailout, its bargaining position inevitably weakened. When domestic banks were in trouble, then governments became very vulnerable to the ECB's cutting of liquidity (as happened in Cyprus and Greece) or to the threat of doing so (as in Ireland). Alternatively, if the economy of bailed out countries improved during the programme, they became less reliant on the loan, and their bargaining power was stronger. Towards the end of the programme in Portugal, for example (when the economy was recovering and yields were at their lowest point for a decade), the government was able to say no to the lenders' requests to introduce an alternative to the Constitutional Court's annulment of a permanent reform to the pension system. Similarly, in Cyprus the last review was never concluded since the economy was already recovering.

Secondly, the comparison between cases shows that the bargaining power of domestic executives is positively related to the costs lenders would pay if they failed to grant assistance (Hennessy, 2017; Howarth and Quaglia, 2016). Countries like Spain that were 'too big to fail' were in a better position than smaller ones such as Cyprus. By the same token, Greece was in a stronger position in 2012, when the cost of a default would be high for German and French banks and the Eurozone as a whole, than in 2015 when the Eurozone had already started reforming and it was much more protected from a potential Grexit.

Thirdly, our analysis also stresses that bailed out governments' credibility is important to leverage, a variable which has been understudied (but see Sacchi, 2018). Building credibility during the crisis was a complex, multifaceted issue. The improvement or deterioration of economic fundamentals was one factor, but our research reveals that the *perception* of these changes was also paramount. A good example of this is the successful strategy pursued by the Irish, Portuguese and Cypriot Ministers to 'under-promise and over-deliver', that is, to purposefully keep expectations low as regards the reduction of their deficit so that they could then do better than expected. As they explained to us, the 'surprise effect' had a positive impact on the EU actors' (and investors') evaluation of a given country's efforts, and hence in turn increased their credibility.

Credibility also derived from a given government's capacity to implement the agreed deals, itself facilitated by political cohesion and stability. Credibility also interlinks with personal trust, that is, the good faith and competence of the interlocutor as perceived by the lenders. This was particularly visible in Greece, where the credibility of the government (and hence its leverage) varied at different times depending on the success and speed of the implementation of reforms; and where the 'unorthodox' behaviour of Ministers such as Yannis Varoufakis quickly created distrust among their international partners and annihilated Greek leverage. In contrast, the lenders perceived Ministers and top civil servants in Ireland and Portugal as being qualified and motivated to implement the deals, and this gave extra leverage to the domestic negotiators. Similarly, in Spain the absolute majority of the PP, which guaranteed the approval of all reforms without parliamentary vetoes, and the government's commitment to external demands increased their credibility and room for manoeuvre vis-à-vis the lenders. Finally, Cypriot negotiators were regarded at first with suspicion because of their links with

Russia; but later were considered more credible given the national consensus around the reforms.

In this context, credibility and partisanship are related insofar as the congruence of the international lenders' and domestic Ministers' ideology (and that of top public servants) increases the trustworthiness and consequently the latter's leeway. In Cyprus, Portugal, Spain and particularly Ireland, the lenders and the debtors were generally in strong agreement on the country's problems and how to resolve them. This gave domestic negotiators leeway not only to determine the policies to be followed, but also not to implement some of the measures that had been agreed. The situation was the exact opposite at the start of SYRIZA's governance (2015) when trust between the institutions and the Greek government was at its lowest.[1] However, the relationship between credibility and partisanship is not straightforward: the Portuguese centre-left government was highly trusted after the bailout due to its ability both to keep its radical left partners on board and respect the EU rule. This also happened in SYRIZA's second term of office in Greece, when the government started implementing the reforms without creating strong social unrest.

Finally, credibility seems to increase when experts and technocrats occupy important governing positions. This was definitely the case in Greece during the Papademos interim government, when the negotiations with the Troika are described by our interviewees as easier since Papademos and the lenders spoke the same language and shared the same network. Cyprus and Portugal tried to increase their leverage by appointing technocrats as Ministers of Finance. These results serve as a reminder for governments that, in future crises, building credibility is of paramount importance to strengthening one's hand in negotiations.

Our book shows that insider knowledge is a fourth variable that was crucial to increase the government's leverage in negotiations with the lenders. While the lenders' representatives had specific ideas on policies to be implemented by debtor countries, they lacked information about the domestic context. This opened up the possibility for national governments to influence the design of solutions to the crisis. Nevertheless, we show that insider knowledge was more valued by the lenders when trust between the two parties was high.

Finally, the saliency of the measures was also crucial in determining national governments' room for manoeuvre. Whenever a policy was considered to be a priority by the lenders, the executives' capacity to influence the final outcome was much more limited. For example, all the labour market reform measures were central for the IMF, whereas the liberalisation of services was the priority for the EC; but both lenders insisted on cutting spending to allow for immediate macroeconomic adjustment. Although governments were never powerless, in all those cases they had much less room for manoeuvre and executives were much more likely to be forced to accept measures against their will. By contrast, governments felt much freer to shape the policies for many structural reforms (for instance in the fields of justice, health and education, and in some cases banking reform).

Differences in MoU

Another important observation made in this book is that MoUs for the different countries vary. While all documents are based on the same assumptions (the need to cut spending, privatise, introduce structural reforms, deleverage banks and for internal devaluation), the solutions proposed, the details of the measures and the stringency of conditions all differ. This result then nuances the claim that international organisations use a one size fits all model (Rodrik *et al.*, 1999).

This variety is a direct consequence of the fact that governments had leverage to identify the structural problems the country was facing and to propose solutions addressing those problems. As noted above, governments were indeed relatively free to propose ways of reaching defined goals of deficit reduction. In many cases, structural reforms were proposed by the government itself, and in all our cases entire parts of the MoU were drafted domestically. It would be interesting to further investigate whether EU member states, namely our sample herein, were treated differently from countries from outside the EU in the design of their programmes.

We also observed differences in the precision and the number of conditions. Different explanations for longer MoUs have been advanced in the literature, such as the economic weakness of a country prior to the crisis (Copelovitch, 2010; Dreher, 2004). This appears to be true in our cases, but our process-tracing also uncovered other explanations that had not yet been explored. Again, trust seems to be of paramount importance, insofar as when lenders do not believe the decision-makers in a given borrower country act in good faith they will tend to detail the policies in writing (and hence insert more conditions). Another variable suggested by our process-tracing analysis is the fact that some measures were set out in detail in the original MoU or its review at the request of the government itself, to more easily circumvent the opposition to those reforms. In Spain, for example, the interviewees from the centre-right government mentioned that they included the liberalisation of some professions in the MoU hoping to bypass veto players. In Portugal, some parts of the Labour Code were specified in great detail in one of the reviews at the request of the government and for the same reason. This result is in line with Vreeland's (2004) finding that the greater the number of veto players, the greater the number of conditions in the MoU.

Fulfilment of MoUs

Given that MoUs included policies wanted by the government as well as others imposed by the lenders, to what extent were they implemented? Our research shows that, despite the struggles between national executives and the Troika, the degree of implementation of MoU reforms was very high in all the case studies. Indeed, the spending cuts and structural reforms made by the five countries in our analysis were mostly in line with the MoUs. These findings are congruent with studies that have shown that IMF intervention is efficient when it comes to decreasing public spending on health and education (Nooruddin and Simmons, 2006).

In Table 7.1, we present the number (and percentage) of important conditions included in MoUs, whether or not they were implemented and whether or not measures had been reversed *during* the programme (see next section for post-programme reversals). From the table we see first that measures deriving from the MoUs were occasionally reversed during the bailout. This was the case seven times in Greece, and once in Ireland. For example, in Greece the Hellenic National Broadcasting Corporation reopened when SYRIZA took over. In Ireland, the 2010 minimum wage cut agreed with the Troika was reversed in 2011 by a new government. This, again, testifies to the fact that domestic governments had some degree of room for manoeuvre during the programme.

On the other hand, Table 7.1 also shows that non-implementation is relatively rare: 84 per cent on average and at least 75 per cent of the conditions of the MoUs were at least partially implemented during the bailouts.[2] This is in part because governments 'own' some of the reforms included in the MoUs, but also because not implementing the MoU is costly. We do, however, observe variation in the fulfilment rate: Ireland and Spain are the champions of fulfilment (at least 90 per cent), followed by Greece (86 per cent), Cyprus (85 per cent) and Portugal (75 per cent). The Spanish and Irish rate is easily explained by the fact that there was a great congruence of views between the centre-right governments and the lenders. Moreover, Ireland was already very liberalised. In addition, the Irish MoU contains less specific policy statements than its counterparts (19 versus 75 for Portugal, for example); it focuses more on objectives to be reached than specific measures. And as we have seen, in Cyprus there was a great internal consensus about the need to introduce the reforms.

The results for Greece and Portugal are more surprising. In Greece, although the high fulfilment rate goes against conventional wisdom, it is linked to the fact that the breadth and the duration of the programmes were much greater than in the other countries and, therefore, some reforms started in the first MoU and were completed during the second and third ones.

Table 7.1 Number and percentage of MoU reforms implemented

	Greece	Ireland	Portugal	Spain	Cyprus	Total
At least partial	P1: 39/48, 81% P2: 41/66, 62% P3: 59/64, 92% Total: 106 (86.18%)	18 (94.74%)	56 (74.66%)	46 (93.88%)	64 (85.33%)	290 (84.30%)
Reversed during programme	7 (5.69%)	1 (5.26%)	0 (0%)	0 (0%)	0 (0%)	8 (2.35%)
At least partial (and not reversed during the programme)	99 (80.49%)	17 (89.47%)	56 (74.66%)	46 (93.88%)	64 (85.33%)	282 (82.70%)
Not fulfilled	17 (13.82%)	1 (5.26%)	19 (25.33%)	3 (6.12%)	11 (14.67%)	51 (14.96%)
Total (of all conditions in the MoU)	123 (100%)	19 (100%)	75 (100%)	49 (100%)	75 (100%)	341 (100%)

Source: Own calculation.

Additionally, when conditions were not met immediately, they were broken down into smaller measures so that their fulfilment could be more easily monitored. Finally, the Greek chapter shows that the country's disagreements with the Troika were very often about the pace and depth of the reforms rather than the substance (e.g. there was agreement on the need for the pension system reform but the Greek governments could not fulfil the reform at the fast pace required by the Troika).

Taking a closer look at the Greek data, we calculated the difference between the implementation rates of each MoU. Whereas the fulfilment of the first MoU was high (39/48, or 81 per cent of the conditions were at least partially fulfilled at the end of the first programme), the scores are lower at the end of the second (41/66, or 62 per cent) and very high for the third (59/64, 92 per cent) MoU. The SYRIZA government's good fulfilment of the MoU supports the idea that left-wing politicians may be able to introduce structural reforms or spending cuts more easily than their rightist counterparts, as their proposals might be vested with more credibility and face less opposition – this is the 'it takes a Nixon to go to China' argument (Cukierman and Tommasi, 1998). In the same vein, Gunaydin (2018) shows that left-wing governments reform the labour market more successfully than centre/right-wing governments in the presence of militant labour unions.

Finally, Portugal had the lowest fulfilment score, despite the fact that Ministers generally agreed with the lenders about the country's diagnostics and prognosis (see chapter 4). One obvious reason for this lower fulfilment is the fact that the Constitutional Court blocked the adoption of nine measures in the MoU; if this had not been the case, Portugal's implementation rate would have been more similar to the other countries. In relation to this, our five cases also show that conditions were often only partially met because of the strength of special interests – see for example the liberalisation of professions in Greece, Ireland and Spain; or the decrease in rents in the energy sector in Portugal. Those findings are congruent with the research of Juwana (2005), who stresses the roles of courts, and of Ivanova *et al.*(2003), who state that political systems with strong vested interests are less likely to deliver on externally mandated reform programmes (see also Stolfi and Papamakariou, 2019 for Greece).

Due to our focus on governmental manoeuvring, a limitation of our database is that it addresses only reforms or spending cuts. Deficit reduction objectives have not been included. Also, to increase inter-coder reliability, we have merged partial and full fulfilment in our analysis. Hence, our quantitative findings do not necessarily imply that the conditions fully reached their objectives. Nor do we imply that they were all adequate. As discussed in our country chapters, and as many studies have convincingly shown (e.g. Blyth, 2013), spending cuts are not an effective method to decrease deficit and debt during a recession. What our data shows, however, is that the adoption of MoUs and adjustment programmes – which are to some extent 'owned' by governments – proved to be an effective model for ensuring the adoption of specific policies.

Post-programme reversals

A much neglected question in the conditionality literature is the resilience of reforms after conditionality. In Table 7.2, we present the absolute number and percentage of the measures passed after the crisis that were reversed once the programmes ended (to December 2019). Therefore, Table 7.2 not only shows the reforms included in the MoUs but also those passed by governments just before the bailout, under pressure from external actors.

We can see that reversals occurred in all countries, as we theoretically expected. However, the extent of reversals varies across countries. In particular, post-programme reversals are rare[3] in Greece and Cyprus. This is not surprising in Greece, given that it terminated the third bailout in August 2018, just sixteen months before the end of our analysis. Furthermore, post-conditionality scrutiny has been stricter in Greece than in the other four countries because the Greek loan was the biggest of all and there were many more reforms to be followed up by the government in order to guarantee a long-lasting economic recovery. However, some reversals had been planned in the 2020 state budget prepared by the SYRIZA-led coalition government (and subsequently implemented by the Conservative government led by New Democracy). This is the case, for example, of the reductions in selected VAT rates, the reintroduction of the 13th month payment for pensioners, and a reversal of an earlier reform of survivors' pensions. In Cyprus, the rarity of reversals could also be explained by the fact that the bailout terminated later than in Portugal, Spain and Ireland, but also by political continuity – as Nicos Anastasiades has been the Cypriot President since early 2013. Nevertheless, some reversals were also made there – such as a progressive reversal of the cuts in public servants' wages.

In Ireland, Spain and, above all, Portugal, post-programme reversals were more frequent. In Portugal, in particular, almost 50 per cent of the measures taken under conditionality were later dismantled, mostly by the minority Socialist government that was supported by three radical left parties that had made reversals a condition of their support (De Giorgi and Cancela, 2019; Moury *et al.*, 2019). In Spain, the new minority Socialist government had promised during its campaign to pass many reversals, but political instability prevented it from passing many of them. In Ireland, there were many reversals despite relative political stability (Fine Gael governed both

Table 7.2 Types of reversals (non-exclusive) of the policies implemented during the crisis

	Greece	Ireland	Portugal	Spain	Cyprus	Total
Total no. of reversals	5 (4.67%)	15 (30%)	28 (47.46%)	14 (28.57%)	9 (13.85%)	58 (17.58%)
Passed by new government	5 (4.67%)	15 (30%)	23 (39.0%)	8 (16.3%)	n.a.	52 (15.6%)
Structural reforms	0 (0%)	1 (2%)	7 (11.9%)	2 (4.1%)	0 (0%)	10 (3.03%)
Total no. of measures	107 (100%)	50 (100%)	59 (100%)	49 (100%)	65 (100%)	330 (100%)

Source: Own calculation.

during and after the bailout, first in coalition and then alone): most of the public sector cuts and some social benefits cuts were, at least, partially reversed. In this country, many reforms had been undertaken before the bailout, and hence most of the measures adopted during the crisis were related to fiscal consolidation, which means that they were also easier to reverse in the post-programme period.

Table 7.2 also shows that only a minority of reversals were passed by governments of a different persuasion. This means that reversals will occur even if there is political continuity. Table 7.2 further distinguishes structural reforms and other types of measure and shows that out of the 58 reversals, only 10 were for structural reforms. This number is mainly driven by the Portuguese case (7 out of 10), where many parts of the Labour Code reforms were eventually reversed (although the central parts remain, see Moury *et al.*, 2019). From our data, we also calculated that the great majority (91 per cent) of structural reforms enacted during the crisis remained. For example, the labour market reforms in Spain, the reforms of the banking system in Cyprus, the introduction of the Public Revenue Independent Authority in Greece, and the public administration reform and the pension age increase in Ireland were all kept. These figures and the information in the case studies testify to the governments' unwillingness to reverse structural reforms.

Finally, in Table 7.3 we look at the correlation between the type of policy and the likelihood of reversal. Here, we see that reversals are less likely when the reforms were structural and involved concentrated costs, and more likely when they concentrated benefits and diffused costs. These differences are statistically significant. The findings speak to the conclusion reached in the literature that governments make cost–benefit calculations when deciding which measures to reverse (Branco *et al.*, 2019; Independent Evaluation Office, 2003; Moury and Afonso, 2019; Moury *et al.*,

Table 7.3 Absolute number and percentage (in parentheses) of reversals per type of reform and statistical significance

	Structural	Concentrated benefits and diffuse costs	Concentrated costs	Total
Kept	131 (88.51%)***	111 (69.81%)***	54 (94.74%)***	264 (80%)
Reversed	17 (11.49%)***	48 (30.19%)***	3 (5.26%)***	66 (20%)

Note: *** p-value <0.001.
Source: Own calculation.

2019; Rickard and Caraway, 2019). They are also in the same vein as the findings of Moury *et al.* (2021) that visible reversals in Portugal after the bailout were made to the detriment of other, less noticeable, spending (such as public investment), leading to what the authors call 'austerity by stealth'.

Our analysis thus shows that since the end of Eurozone bailout programmes, executives have been able to reverse what was done during the programme. However, these reversals have been partial and limited. They have mostly concerned visible spending cuts and tax increases, while less noticeable changes in taxation have often been kept. We also show that the great majority of structural reforms have been maintained, and thus that conditionality has at least a medium-term effect. The bailout has therefore brought about a profound and durable change in the socio-economic structure of the society, even though the national growth models persist (Chang *et al.*, 2019). For example, the Labour Code is very different today than it was a decade ago in many countries (Afonso, 2019; Branco *et al.*, 2019; Moury and Afonso, 2019). Pensions have seen profound reforms in some countries and durable spending cuts have been made (in the health sector, for example). The leverage ratio (i.e. the percentage of debt in banks' balance sheet) has decreased significantly. Many professions have been liberalised, rents in the pharmacy and energy sectors have been (at least partially) cut, and various businesses and services have been privatised. Further research should certainly cover the resilience of reforms in a longer time period. These results again show that conditionality can be effective, but also that spending cuts and tax increases are less resilient than structural reforms. This difference is again the product of the varying degrees of ownership by domestic governments which was larger for structural reforms. Not surprisingly, this suggests that reforms are more durable when they correspond to the government's preferences.

Future developments

The unexpected spread of COVID-19, a public health problem, is progressively turning into an economic crisis. In this last section, we discuss the differences and similarities between the two occurrences and their implications.

A first striking similarity between the two episodes is the increased initial public spending. Today, just as in 2008–2009, in a 'neo-Keynesian' spirit, many European countries are increasing their spending to compensate for the economic losses of the lockdown. EU-level investment and pro-growth financial plans are being discussed. As happened twelve years ago, flexibility on fiscal rules was permitted by the Council in mid-April 2020 (Eurogroup, 2020). This rise in public spending, together with the recession, will again lead to a rise in public debt, but this time the figures are much higher: according to IMF forecasts, public debt will on average reach almost 100 per cent of GDP by the end of the year in the Eurozone, with Italy, Greece, France, Spain and Portugal exceeding this figure (Gopinath, 2020).

We know from the past that an important problem associated with this rising debt is the fact that investors can sell the bonds of a given country to buy bonds of a more credible country (e.g. Germany) denominated in the same currency (De Grauwe, 2011). In 2009–2013, this allowed for the skyrocketing of borrowing costs in one member state and their rapid decline in another. Today, the sovereign yields of the weakest countries are still low – although they have increased slightly. This is because this time the ECB, after a brief hesitation,[4] has acted quickly. In early March, it created a 'Pandemic Emergency Purchase Programme', a temporary €750 billion scheme involving both government and private debt. The question is whether this will be enough, and we know from the past crisis that even if countries were pursuing healthy fiscal policies beforehand, that alone will not protect them from speculation.

Member states are currently discussing at the European level how to avoid such speculation. The possibility of risk mutualisation is putting some countries against others, as it was a decade ago (Matthijs and McNamara, 2015). On the one hand, Italy, Portugal, Greece and Spain, but also France, Luxembourg and Belgium, among others, have called for the issuance of joint European debt to finance the fight against COVID-19 (Michalopoulos, 2020). In late May, Germany joined them as Angela Merkel announced, jointly with Emmanuel Macron, a plan to raise €500 billion on financial markets to fund a European Coronavirus recovery plan; that was quickly followed by an EC proposal.

By contrast, the Netherlands, then followed by Austria, Sweden and Denmark, is opposing this option fiercely. Hence, the North–South divide observed in 2009 is less evident today; but it is not clear whether the joint issuance of common debt bonds will happen given the unanimity requirement.

As in 2009, however, joint EU decisions – although somehow insufficient – have been made. A 'Pandemic Crisis Support' fund has been created to provide cheap loans to every country up to 2 per cent of their GDP, but for the exclusive support of direct and indirect health care costs related to COVID-19 The Council also decided to create a temporary recovery fund (SURE) that could issue debt and distribute loans for aid to employers that would otherwise lay off workers, but questions on the size and sources of funding are unresolved and still subject to disagreements between Northern and Southern capitals (European Council, 2020). At the European Council of 24 April 2020, EU national leaders directed European Commission President Ursula von der Leyen to go further and draw up plans for growth, mixing grants (through the budget) and loans (Herszenhorn, 2020).

Consensus was not reached on whether to attach conditions to those loans. Just as a decade ago, countries that would receive the loan are resisting conditionality. In this case, and contrary to what happened during the financial crisis, the Netherlands – that was pushing the most to make lending subject to conditionality – finally dropped its demand. In our view, this was made possible because the narrative has changed. The predominant discourse one decade ago was that of a 'morality tale' that juxtaposed the Northern virtues of 'hard work, prudent savings, moderate consumption, wage restraint, and fiscal stability' to the 'Southern vices of low competitiveness, meagre savings, undeserved consumption, inflated wages, and fiscal profligacy' (Matthijs and McNamara, 2015, p. 135). Today, this discourse has lost some strength; it is much harder (and obviously even more unfair) to blame individual countries for a pandemic. Although the crisis will be felt asymmetrically in the weakest countries, the cause of the crisis is more obviously exogenous and symmetric for all member states. In relation to this, the experience of this past decade has shown that austerity, which had become synonymous with conditionality, was not helpful in stopping the increase in public debt or regaining market trust (Blyth, 2013). What, by contrast, was determinant were the actions, or even declarations, of the ECB and other European actors (Demertzis and Wolff, 2016), and many decision-makers are now aware of that.

However, further reforms and spending cuts or transfers between sectors (to the benefit of the health sector) are not to be excluded, albeit less likely. The new funds will not be sufficient for member states to borrow the extra spending and, unless there is additional funding at the EU level, it is crucial for decision-makers to reassure investors that they will be reimbursed. As noted above, even though interest rates are still low, if the ECB does not or cannot prevent investors from panicking, things might change as they did at the end of 2009. In this case, domestic actors might be obliged to accept austerity or conditionality right now – even if they do not want to do so – if they or their European peers perceive such reforms as a condition for credibility. As we have seen in this book, conditionality is only successful if there is honest cooperation between lenders and member states and if national preferences are taken into account. Austerity cannot be the only game in town, especially because of the magnitude of the current crisis. As we have shown, at the end of the day governments remain strong players even when they are at their weakest.

Notes

1 However, it is important to note that some of the tension was also due to personality clashes (see chapter 2).

2 Important statements are those present in any of the EC or IMF summaries of the MoU reviews (and European semesters in Spain). Only actions are coded (not outcomes). Full and partial fulfilment were merged due to low inter-coder inter-reliability to distinguish between full and partial fulfilment, and in line with choices made by pledges fulfilment scholars.

3 Until the time of writing, mid-April 2020.

4 Ms Lagarde said it was not the ECB's role to 'close the spread' in sovereign debt markets – referring to the gap between Italian and German bond yields that is a key risk indicator for Italy – but quickly apologised after that and announced the buying of bonds (Arnold, 2020).

References

List of interviews

Brussels

Interview BR 27, official from the EC 2, Brussels, 30 January 2018.
Interview BR 28, official from the EC 1, Brussels, 30 January 2018.
Interview BR 29, official from the EC 3, Brussels, 30 January 2018.
Interview BR 32, official from the IMF, Athens, 5 February 2018.
Interview BR 33, political advisor, phone call, 9 February 2018.
Interview BR 35, official from the IMF, Skype call, 16 March 2018.
Interview BR 53, official from the ECB, Skype call, 30 May 2018.

Cyprus

Interview CY 37, senior official at the Central Bank of Cyprus, Skype call, 26 March 2018.
Interview CY 40, senior officer at Central Bank of Cyprus, Nicosia, 10 April 2018.
Interview CY 41, government official, Nicosia, 11 April 2018.
Interview CY 42, Minister, Nicosia, 11 April 2018.
Interview CY 43, journalist, Nicosia, 11 April 2018.
Interview CY 44, government official, Nicosia, 12 April 2018.
Interview CY 45, Minister, Nicosia, 12 April 2018.
Interview CY 46, trade union representative, Nicosia, 12 April 2018.
Interview CY 47, government official, Nicosia, 13 April 2018.
Interview CY 48, Minister, Nicosia, 13 April 2018.
Interview CY 49, Minister, Limassol, 13 April 2018.
Interview CY 50, government official, Nicosia, 13 April 2018.
Interview CY 55, Minister, Athens, 31 May 2018.

Greece

Interview GR 1, political advisor to Minister, Athens, 27 November 2017.
Interview GR 3, Minister, Athens, 28 November 2017.

Interview GR 4, Minister, Athens, 30 November 2017.
Interview GR 7, Minister, Athens, 1 December 2017.
Interview GR 8, Minister, Athens, 4 December 2017.
Interview GR 9, political advisor to Minister, Athens, 4 December 2017.
Interview GR 14, Member of Parliament and Minister, Athens, 7 December 2017.
Interview GR 15, Minister, Athens, 13 December 2017.
Interview GR 16, journalist, Athens, 13 December 2017.
Interview GR 17, political advisor, Athens, 15 December 2017.
Interview GR 18, political advisor, Athens, 18 December 2017.
Interview GR 20, Minister, Athens, 5 January 2018.
Interview GR 23, Secretary of State, Athens, 11 January 2018.
Interview GR 24, government official, Athens, 16 January 2018.
Interview GR 25, Minister, Athens, 19 January 2018.
Interview GR 31, Secretary of State, Athens, 2 February 2018.
Interview GR 34, Minister, Athens, 27 February 2018.
Interview GR 36, Minister, Athens, 21 March 2018.
Interview GR 51, Minister, Athens, 23 April 2018.
Interview GR 52, Member of Parliament, Athens, 26 May 2018.
Interview GR 54, Minister, 31 May 2018.
Interview GR 56, Member of Parliament and political and economic advisor, Athens, 19 June 2018.

Ireland

Interview IR 2, senior civil servant, Dublin, 16 January 2017.
Interview IR 3, civil servant, Dublin, 16 January 2017.
Interview IR 4, high official, Dublin, 18 January 2017.
Interview IR 5, trade union representative, Dublin, 18 January 2017.
Interview IR 6, party leader, Dublin, 19 January 2017.
Interview IR 7, trade union representative, Dublin, 19 January 2017.
Interview IR 8, senior civil servant, Dublin, 20 January 2017.
Interview IR 10, senior civil servant, Dublin, 15 January 2019.
Interview IR 11, Minister, Dublin, 15 January 2019.
Interview IR 12, Minister, Dublin, 16 January 2019.
Interview IR 13, Minister, Dublin, 16 January 2019.
Interview IR 14, senior civil servant, Dublin, 16 January 2019.
Interview IR 15, Minister, Dublin, 17 January 2019.

Portugal

Interview PT 1, Minister, Lisbon, 22 January 2013.
Interview PT 3, Minister, Lisbon, 17 January 2013.
Interview PT 4, Minister, Lisbon, 22 January 2013.
Interview PT 5, Minister, Lisbon, 17 January 2013.
Interview PT 6, Secretary of State, Lisbon, 28 January 2013.

Interview PT 7, Secretary of State, Lisbon, 29 January 2013.
Interview PT 8, Secretary of State, Lisbon, 29 January 2013.
Interview PT 9, Secretary of State, Lisbon, 30 January 2013.
Interview PT 10, Minister, Lisbon, 26 February 2013.
Interview PT 11, Minister, Lisbon, 5 February 2013.
Interview PT 12, Secretary of State, Lisbon, 11 December 2017.
Interview PT 13, Secretary of State, Lisbon, 18 January 2018.
Interview PT 14, Secretary of State, Lisbon, 25 January 2013.
Interview PT 15, Secretary of State, Lisbon, 25 January 2018.
Interview PT 16, Minister, Lisbon, 13 December 2017.
Interview PT 17, Secretary of State, Lisbon, 13 December 2017.
Interview PT 18, Secretary of State, Lisbon, 14 December 2017.
Interview PT 19, Secretary of State, Lisbon, 15 December 2017.
Interview PT 20, Secretary of State, Lisbon, 11 December 2017.
Interview PT 21, Secretary of State, Lisbon, 12 December 2017.
Interview PT 23, trade union official, Lisbon, 18 December 2017.
Interview PT 24, trade union official, Lisbon, 19 December 2017.
Interview PT 27, IMF official, Lisbon, 15 February 2013.
Interview PT 28, official from the European Commission, Lisbon, 22 February 2013.
Interview PT 29, official from the European Commission, Brussels, 22 February 2013.
Interview PT 30, official from the European Commission, Brussels, 22 February 2013.

Spain

Interview ES 3, trade union official, Madrid, 18 November 2015.
Interview ES 5, political advisor, Madrid,14 February 2016.
Interview ES 6, Minister, Barcelona, 16 February 2016.
Interview ES 7, Minister, Madrid, 25 February 2016.
Interview ES 8, political advisor, Madrid, 26 February 2016.
Interview ES 10, government official, Madrid, 20 November 2017.
Interview ES 11, MP, Madrid, 20 November 2017.
Interview ES 12, MP, Madrid, 21 November 2017.
Interview ES 13, MP, Madrid, 21 November 2017.
Interview ES 19, government official, Madrid, 23 November 2017.
Interview ES 23, political party representative, Madrid, 10 October 2018.
Interview ES 25, Cabinet Director, Madrid, 11 October 2018.
Interview ES 26, Secretary of State, phone interview, 30 October 2019.

Secondary sources

AAP (2011), 'Austerity-hit Ireland is poster boy for EU', *News.Com.Au*, 27 November, available at: www.news.com.au/finance/austerity-hit-ireland-is-poster-boy-for-eu/news-story/35cd3c259ffe99c02f308724d566114e (accessed 12 April 2019).

Accornero, G. and Ramos Pinto, P. (2015), '"Mild mannered"? Protest and mobilisation in Portugal under austerity, 2010–2013', *West European Politics*, Vol. 38, No. 3, pp. 491–515.

Afflatet, N. (2016), 'Public debt and borrowing: are governments disciplined by financial markets?', *Cogent Economics and Finance*, Vol. 4, No. 1, pp. 1–14.

Afonso, A. (2019), 'State-led wage devaluation in Southern Europe in the wake of the Eurozone crisis', *European Journal of Political Research*, Vol. 58, No. 3, pp. 938–959.

Afonso, A. and Bulfone, F. (2019), 'Electoral coalitions and policy reversals in Portugal and Italy in the aftermath of the Eurozone crisis', *South European Society and Politics*, Vol. 24, No. 2, pp. 233–257.

Afonso, A., Zartaloudis, S. and Papadopoulos, Y. (2015), 'How party linkages shape austerity politics: clientelism and fiscal adjustment in Greece and Portugal during the Eurozone crisis', *Journal of European Public Policy*, Vol. 22, No. 3, pp. 315–334.

Aguiar, N. (2017), 'Bruxelas já não acha que subida do salário mínimo prejudica a competitividade', *Jornal de Negócios*, 25 May, available at: https://rr.sapo.pt/2018/04/08/conversas-cruzadas/cativacoes-transformam-oe-em-grave-farsa-diz-luis-aguiar-conraria/artigo/110197/ (accessed 14 March 2020).

AKEL Central Committee (2010), *Θέσεις Της Κ.Ε. ΑΚΕΛ Προς Το 21ο Συνέδριο.*

Alcaraz, C., Claessens, S., Cuadra, G., Marques-Ibanez, D. and Sapriza, H. (2019), 'Whatever it takes: what's the impact of a major nonconventional monetary policy intervention?', *European Central Bank Working Paper Series*, BIS Working Paper, No. 02249.

Alexiadou, D. and Gunaydin, H. (2019), 'Commitment or expertise? Technocratic appointments as political responses to economic crises', *European Journal of Political Research*, Vol. 58, No. 3, pp. 845–865.

Allan, J.P. and Scruggs, L. (2004), 'Political partisanship and welfare state reform in advanced industrial societies', *American Journal of Political Science*, Vol. 48, No. 3, pp. 496–512.

Allen, K. (2012), 'Recession and the new resistance', *Irish Marxist Review*, Vol. 1, No. 2, pp. 3–12.

Altman, D. and Pérez-Liñán, A. (2002), 'Assessing the quality of democracy: freedom, competitiveness and participation in eighteen Latin American countries', *Democratization*, Vol. 9, No. 2, pp. 85–100.

Anastasatou, M. and Tsakloglou, P. (2019), *Διαρθρωτικές Αλλαγές Στο Πεδίο Της Δημοσιονομικής Πολιτικής Στα Χρόνια Της Κρίσης*, ELIAMEP and Papazizis Publishers, Athens.

Armingeon, K. (2012), 'The politics of fiscal responses to the crisis of 2008–2009', *Governance*, Vol. 25, No. 4, pp. 543–565.

Arnold, M. (2020), 'Christine Lagarde apologises for botched communication of ECB strategy', *Financial Times*, 15 March, available at: www.ft.com/content/ce39716e-66c0–11ea-a3c9–1fe6fedcca75 (accessed 27 April 2020).

Asensio, M. and Popic, T. (2019), 'Portuguese healthcare reforms in the context of crisis: external pressure or domestic choice?', *Social Policy and Administration*, Vol. 53, No. 7, pp. 1003–1017.

Badell, D., Di Mascio, F., Natalini, A., Ongaro, E., Stolfi, F. and Ysa, T. (2019), 'Too big to fail? The dynamics of EU influence and fiscal consolidation in Italy and Spain (2008–2016)', *Public Management Review*, Vol. 21, No. 9, pp. 1307–1329.

Baerg, N.R. and Hallerberg, M. (2016), 'Explaining instability in the stability and growth pact: the contribution of member state power and euroskepticism to the euro crisis', *Comparative Political Studies*, Vol. 49, No. 7, pp. 968–1009.

Banco de España (2011), *La Reestructuración Del Sector Bancario Español y El Real Decreto-Ley Para El Reforzamiento Del Sistema Financiero*, Banco de España.

Banco de España (2012), *Informe Anual 2012*, Banco de España.

Bank of Greece (2014), *The Chronicle of the Great Crisis*, Bank of Greece, Athens.

Barber, T. (2009), 'Greece vows action to cut budget deficit', *Financial Times*, 20 October.

Barkbu, B., Eichengreen, B. and Mody, A. (2016), 'The euro's twin challenges: political and economic dynamics of the Eurozone crisis', in Caporaso, J. and Rhodes, M. (eds), *The Political and Economic Dynamics of the Eurozone Crisis*, Oxford University Press, Oxford, pp. 48–79.

Bastasin, C. (2009), 'Partisan protectionism: political consensus, the euro and Europe's response to the global crisis', in Micossi, S. and Tosato, G.L. (eds), *The European Union in the 21st Century: Perspectives from the Lisbon Treaty*, Centre for European Policy Studies, Brussels, pp. 7–30.

Bastos, J. (2018), '"Cativações transformam OE em grave farsa", diz Luís Aguiar-Conraria', *Rádio Renascença*, 8 April, available at: https://rr.sapo.pt/2018/04/08/conversas-cruzadas/cativacoes-transformam-oe-em-grave-farsa-diz-luis-aguiar-conraria/artigo/110197/ (accessed 20 December 2019).

Bauer, M.W. and Becker, S. (2014), 'The unexpected winner of the crisis: the European Commission's strengthened role in economic governance', *Journal of European Integration*, Vol. 36, No. 3, pp. 213–229.

BBC (2012), 'Spain to miss 2012 budget deficit target, says Rajoy', *BBC*, 2 March, available at: www.bbc.com/news/business-17235179 (accessed 10 March 2020).

BBC (2019), 'Greek government crisis over Macedonia name change', *BBC*, 13 January, available at: www.bbc.co.uk/news/world-europe-46855088 (accessed 10 February 2020).

Beyers, J., Braun, C. and Klüver, H. (2017), 'Framing between the logic of membership and the logic of influence', in Beyers, J., Braun, C. and Klüver, H. (eds), *Legislative Lobbying in Context: The Policy and Polity Determinants of Interest Group Politics in the European Union*, Routledge, Abingdon and New York, pp. 50–52.

Bird, G. and Willett, T.D. (2004), 'IMF conditionality, implementation and the new political economy of ownership', *Comparative Economic Studies*, Vol. 46, No. 3, pp. 423–450.

Blanchard, O. and Leigh, D. (2013), *Growth Forecast Errors and Fiscal Multipliers*, IMF Working Paper No. WP/13/1, International Monetary Fund.

Blustein, P. (2016), *Laid Low: Inside the Crisis That Overwhelmed Europe and the IMF*, Centre for International Governance Innovation, Waterloo.

Blyth, M. (2013), *Austerity: The History of a Dangerous Idea*, Oxford University Press, New York.

Bonoli, G. and Natali, D. (2012), *The Politics of the New Welfare State*, Oxford University Press, Oxford.

Börzel, T. and Risse, T. (2003), 'Conceptualizing the domestic impact of Europe', in Featherstone, K. and Radaelli, C. (eds), *The Politics of Europeanisation*, Oxford University Press, Oxford, pp. 57–80.

Börzel, T.A. and Risse, T. (2009), *The Transformative Power of Europe: The European Union and the Diffusion of Ideas*, Vol. 1, Freie Universität Berlin, FB Politik- und Sozialwissenschaften, Otto-Suhr-Institut für Politikwissenschaft

Kolleg-Forschergruppe 'The Transformative Power of Europe', Berlin, available at: https://nbn-resolving.org/urn:nbn:de:0168-ssoar-364733 (accessed 15 July 2019).

Bosco, A. (2013), 'The long adiós: the PSOE and the end of the Zapatero era', in Field, B. and Botti, A. (eds), *Politics and Society in Contemporary Spain*, Palgrave Macmillan, New York, pp. 21–39.

Bosco, A. and Verney, S. (2012), 'Electoral epidemic: the political cost of economic crisis in Southern Europe, 2010–11', *South European Society and Politics*, Vol. 17, No. 2, pp. 129–154.

Bosco, A. and Verney, S. (2016), 'From electoral epidemic to government epidemic: the next level of the crisis in Southern Europe', *South European Society and Politics*, Vol. 21, No. 4, pp. 383–406.

Botti, A. (2013), 'From opposition to government: the Popular Party of Mariano Rajoy', in Field, B. and Botti, A. (eds), *Politics and Society in Contemporary Spain*, Palgrave Macmillan, New York, pp. 41–59.

Boyle, R. (2016), 'Public sector reform', in Roche, W.K., O'Connell, P.J. and Prothero, A. (eds), *Austerity and Recovery in Ireland: Europe's Poster Child and the Great Recession*, Oxford University Press, Oxford, pp. 214–231.

Branco, R., Cardoso, D., Guillén, A.M., Sacchi, S. and Balbona, D.L. (2019), 'Here to stay? Reversals of structural reforms in Southern Europe as the crisis wanes', *South European Society and Politics*, Vol. 24, No. 2, pp. 205–232.

Brazys, S. and Hardiman, N. (2015), 'From "Tiger" to "PIIGS": Ireland and the use of heuristics in comparative political economy', *European Journal of Political Research*, Vol. 54, No. 1, pp. 23–42.

Bremer, B. (2018), 'The missing Left? Economic crisis and the programmatic response of social democratic parties in Europe', *Party Politics*, Vol. 24, No. 1, pp. 23–38.

Bulmer, S. (2014), 'Germany and the Eurozone crisis: between hegemony and domestic politics', *West European Politics*, Vol. 37, No. 6, pp. 1244–1263.

Buthe, T., Jacobs, A.M., Bleich, E., Pekkanen, R., Trachtenberg, M., Cramer, K., Shih, V., et al. (2015), 'Transparency in qualitative and multi-method research: a symposium', *Qualitative and Multi-method Research: Newsletter of the American Political Science Association's QMMR Section*, Vol. 13, No. 1, pp. 2–64.

Campos, N.F. and Horváth, R. (2012), 'Reform redux: measurement, determinants and growth implications', *European Journal of Political Economy*, Vol. 28, No. 2, pp. 227–237.

Campos Lima, M. da P. and Artiles, A.M. (2011), 'Crisis and trade union challenges in Portugal and Spain: between general strikes and social pacts', *Transfer: European Review of Labour and Research*, Vol. 17, No. 3, pp. 387–402.

Capelos, T. and Exadaktylos, T. (2015), '"The good, the bad and the ugly": stereotypes, prejudices and emotions on Greek media representation of the EU financial crisis', in Karyotis, G. and Gerodimos, R. (eds), *The Politics of Extreme Austerity: Greece in the Eurozone Crisis*, Palgrave Macmillan, London, pp. 46–68.

Caporaso, J. and Rhodes, M. (2016), 'Introduction', in Caporaso, J. and Rhodes, M. (eds), *The Political and Economic Dynamics of the Eurozone Crisis*, Oxford University Press, Oxford, pp. 1–15.

Cardiff, K. (2019), 'Ireland: back to a different normal', in Chang, M., Steinberg, F. and Torres, F. (eds), *The Political Economy of Adjustment Throughout and Beyond the Eurozone*, Routledge, Abingdon, pp. 94–121.

Cardoso, D. and Branco, R. (2018), 'Liberalised dualisation: labour market reforms and the crisis in Portugal: a new departure', *European Journal of Social Security*, Vol. 20, No. 1, pp. 31–48.

Chang, M., Steinberg, F. and Torres, F. (eds) (2019), *The Political Economy of Adjustment Throughout and Beyond the Eurozone Crisis: What Have We Learned?*, Routledge, Abingdon and New York.

Charalambous, G. (2014), *Political Culture and Behaviour in the Republic of Cyprus during the Crisis*, PCC Report No. 2/2014, Peace Research Institute Oslo, Oslo.

Chatzidakis, K. (2018), Μεταρρυθμίσεων Ανάβασις, Ekdoseis Papazisi, Athens.

Christofias, D. (2013), Όσα Πρέπει Να Ακουστούν, C.C. AKEL Publications, Nicosia.

Chwieroth, J.M. (2015), 'Professional ties that bind: how normative orientations shape IMF conditionality', *Review of International Political Economy*, Vol. 22, No. 4, pp. 757–787.

Cioffi, J.W. and Dubin, K.A. (2016), 'Commandeering crisis: partisan labor repression in Spain under the guise of economic reform', *Politics and Society*, Vol. 44, No. 3, pp. 423–453.

Clauwaert, S. and Schömann, I. (2012), 'The crisis and national labour law reforms: a mapping exercise', *European Labour Law Journal*, Vol. 3, No. 1, pp. 54–69.

Clerides, S. (2014), 'The collapse of the Cypriot banking system: a bird's eye view', *Cyprus Economic Policy Review*, Vol. 8, No. 2, pp. 3–35.

Clift, B. (2018), *The IMF and the Politics of Austerity in the Wake of the Global Financial Crisis*, Oxford University Press, Oxford.

Clift, B. and Ryner, M. (2014), 'Joined at the hip, but pulling apart? Franco-German relations, the Eurozone crisis and the politics of austerity', *French Politics*, Vol. 12, No. 2, pp. 136–163.

Clifton, J., Diaz-Fuentes, D. and Gómez, A.L. (2018), 'The crisis as opportunity? On the role of the Troika in constructing the European consolidation state', *Cambridge Journal of Regions, Economy and Society*, Vol. 11, No. 3, pp. 587–608.

Cline, W.R. and Wolf, G.B. (eds) (2012), *Resolving the European Debt Crisis*, Vol. 21, Peterson Institute for International Economics, Bruegel.

Coller, X. and de Luis, F.R. (2020), 'Unstable preferences and policy changes: Spain', in Morlino, L. and Sottilotta, C. (eds), *The Politics of the Eurozone Crisis in Southern Europe*, Palgrave Macmillan, Cham, pp. 133–171.

Collier, D. (2011), 'Understanding process tracing', *PS: Political Science & Politics*, Vol. 44, No. 4, pp. 823–830.

Comisiones Obreras (2016), *CCOO y UGT Exigen al Gobierno Que Cumpla Los Compromisos Del Programa de Activación Para El Empleo*, Comisiones Obreras, available at https://www.ccoo.es/noticia:125544–CCOO_y_UGT_exigen_al_Gobierno_que_cumpla_los_compromisos_del_Programa_de_Activacion_para_el_Empleo (accessed 15 July 2019).

Comissão Permanente da Concertação Social (2012), *Agreement for Growth, Competitiveness and Employment*, CES, Lisbon.

Commission Toledo Pact (2010), *Informe de Evaluación y Reforma Del Pacto de Toledo*, Spanish Parliament, Spain.

Considine, M. and Dukelow, F. (2014), 'The role of national and international policy actors and influences in the crisis: the case of Ireland', in Hill, M. (ed.), *Studying Public Policy: An International Approach*, Policy Press, Bristol, pp. 254–266.

Copelovitch, M., Frieden, J. and Walter, S. (2016), 'The political economy of the Euro crisis', *Comparative Political Studies*, Vol. 49, No. 7, pp. 811–840.

Copelovitch, M.S. (2010), 'Master or servant? Common agency and the political economy of IMF lending', *International Studies Quarterly*, Vol. 54, No. 1, pp. 49–77.

Council of the European Union (2008), *Presidency Conclusions*, Council of the European Union, Brussels.

Council of the European Union (2009), *Economic and Finance Affairs*, Council of the European Union, Brussels.

Council of the European Union (2010a), *Press Release: Extraordinary Council Meeting Economic and Financial Affairs Brussels*.

Council of the European Union (2010b), *Council Decision of 13 July 2010 on the Existence of an Excessive Deficit in Cyprus*, No. 2010/401/EU.

Council of the European Union (2011), *Council Recommendation of 12 July 2011 on the National Reform Programme 2011 of Spain and Delivering a Council Opinion on the Updated Stability Programme of Spain, 2011–2014*.

Crespy, A. and Ladi, S. (2019), 'In the name of "the people"? Popular sovereignty and the 2015 Greek referendum', *Journal of European Integration*, Vol. 41, No. 7, pp. 871–885.

Cué, C. (2011), 'Rajoy aprueba el mayor recorte de la historia y una gran subida de impuestos', *El País*, 31 December.

Cukierman, A. and Tommasi, M. (1998), 'When does it take a Nixon to go to China?', *American Economic Review*, Vol. 88, No. 1, pp. 180–197.

Cusack, T., Iversen, T. and Rehm, P. (2006), 'Risks at work: the demand and supply sides of government redistribution', *Oxford Review of Economic Policy*, Vol. 22, No. 3, pp. 365–389.

D'Arcy, M. (2018), *Pay Inequality in the Public Service: Statements*, Dáil Éireann debate, 24 May.

Davis, M. (2016), 'Social democracy's last rounds: an interview with Wolfgang Streeck', *Jacobin*, February, available at: www.jacobinmag.com/2016/02/wolfgang-streeck-europe-eurozone-austerity-neoliberalism-social-democracy/ (accessed 1 March 2021).

De Giorgi, E. and Cancela, J. (2019), 'The Portuguese radical left parties supporting government: from policy-takers to policymakers?', *Government and Opposition*, pp. 1–20.

De Giorgi, E., Moury, C. and Ruivo, J.P. (2015), 'Incumbents, opposition and international lenders: governing Portugal in times of crisis', *Journal of Legislative Studies*, Vol. 21, No. 1, pp. 54–74.

De Grauwe, P. (2010), 'Fighting the wrong enemy, 19 May 2010', *VOX CEPR Policy Portal*, 19 May, available at: https://voxeu.org/article/europe-s-private-versus-public-debt-problem-fighting-wrong-enemy (accessed 1 March 2021).

De Grauwe, P. (2011), *Only a More Active ECB Can Solve the Euro Crisis*, Centre for European Policy Studies Policy Briefs No. 250.

De Grauwe, P. (2012), 'The governance of a fragile Eurozone', *Australian Economic Review*, Vol. 45, No. 3, pp. 255–268.

De Guindos, L. (2016), *España Amenazada: De Cómo Evitamos El Rescate y La Economía Recuperó El Crecimiento*, Ediciones Península, Madrid.

De la Porte, C. and Natali, D. (2014), 'Altered Europeanisation of pension reform in the context of the great recession: Denmark and Italy compared', *West European Politics*, Vol. 37, No. 4, pp. 732–749.

De Witte, B. (2009), 'The Lisbon Treaty and national constitutions: more or less Europeanisation?', in Closa, C. (ed.), *The Lisbon Treaty and National Constitutions: Europeanisation and Democratic Implications*, ARENA, Oslo, pp. 25–48.

Degryse, C. (2012), *The New European Economic Governance*, ETUI, Brussels.

Del Pino, E. (2013), 'The Spanish welfare state from Zapatero to Rajoy: recalibration to retrenchment', in Field, B. and Botti, A. (eds), *Politics and Society in Contemporary Spain*, Palgrave Macmillan, New York, pp. 197–216.

Dellepiane, S. and Hardiman, N. (2012), 'The new politics of austerity: fiscal responses to the economic crisis in Ireland and Spain', University College Dublin, Geary Institute Discussion Paper.

Demertzis, M. and Wolff, G.B. (2016), *The Effectiveness of the European Central Banks's Asset Purchase Programme*, Bruegel Policy Contribution No. 2016/10, available at: http://hdl.handle.net/10419/165978 (accessed 11 October 2019).

Demetriades, P. (2017), *Diary of the Euro Crisis in Cyprus*, Palgrave Macmillan, Cham.

Dendrinou, V. and Varvitsioti, H. (2019), *The Last Bluff: How Greece Came Face-to-Face with Financial Catastrophe and the Secret Plan for Its Euro Exit*, Papadopoulos Publishing, Athens.

Diario de Avisos (2011), 'La UE aconseja a Zapatero que culmine con firmeza las reformas', *Diario de Avisos*, 5 August.

Dijsselbloem, J. (2018), Η Κρίση Του Ευρώ, Economia Publishing, Athens.

Dimitrakopoulos, D. and Passas, A. (2020), *The Depoliticisation of Greece's Public Revenue Administration*, Springer, Cham.

Dinas, E. and Rori, L. (2013), 'The 2012 Greek parliamentary elections: fear and loathing in the polls', *West European Politics*, Vol. 36, No. 1, pp. 270–282.

Dinis, D. and Coelho, H.F. (2012), *Resgatados: Os Bastidores Da Ajuda Financeira a Portugal*, Esfera dos Livros, Lisbon.

Doherty, M. (2011), 'It must have been love … but it's over now: the crisis and collapse of social partnership in Ireland', *Transfer: European Review of Labour and Research*, Vol. 17, No. 3, pp. 371–385.

Doncel, L. (2012a), 'Europe braces itself for bailout dilemma: who gets the money?', *El País*, 3 June.

Doncel, L. (2012b), 'La Unión Europea anima a España al rescate financiero', *El País*, 3 June.

Dooley, N. (2019), 'Who's afraid of the big bad wolf? Rethinking the core and periphery in the Eurozone crisis', *New Political Economy*, Vol. 21, No. 4, pp. 62–88.

Doyle, D. (2012), 'Pressures to privatize? The IMF, globalization, and partisanship in Latin America', *Political Research Quarterly*, Vol. 65, No. 3, pp. 572–585.

Drazen, A. (2002), 'Conditionality and ownership in IMF Lending: a political economy Approach', *IMF Staff Papers*, Vol. 49, No. 1, pp. 36–67.

Dreher, A. (2004), 'A public choice perspective of IMF and World Bank lending and conditionality', *Public Choice*, Vol. 119, Nos 3–4, pp. 445–464.

Dukelow, F. (2015), '"Pushing against an open door": reinforcing the neo-liberal policy paradigm in Ireland and the impact of EU intrusion', *Comparative European Politics*, Vol. 13, No. 1, pp. 93–111.

Dür, A. and Mateo, G. (2010), 'Choosing a bargaining strategy in EU negotiations: power, preferences, and culture', *Journal of European Public Policy*, Vol. 17, No. 5, pp. 680–693.

Dyson, K. (1994), *Elusive Union: The Process of Economic and Monetary Union in Europe*, Longman, London.

Dyson, K. and Featherstone, K. (1996), 'Italy and EMU as a "Vincolo Esterno": empowering the technocrats, transforming the state', *South European Society and Politics*, Vol. 1, No. 2, pp. 272–299.

ECOFIN (2009), *Informal Meeting of Finance Ministers and Governors of Central Banks*, ECOFIN, Prague.
El Confidencial (2018), 'El IVA del cine baja del 21 al 10 % con la aprobación definitiva de los Presupuestos', *El Confidencial*, 28 June.
El Mundo (2010), 'Así queda la reforma laboral: despido más barato y mayor control a los parados', *El Mundo*, 10 September.
El País (2010), 'Cronología de las reformas laborales en España', *El País*, 15 June.
Elster, J. (1979), *Ulysses and the Sirens: Studies in Rationality and Irrationality*, Cambridge University Press, Cambridge.
Epstein, R.A. and Sedelmeier, U. (2008), 'Beyond conditionality: international institutions in postcommunist Europe after enlargement', *Journal of European Public Policy*, Vol. 15, No. 6, pp. 795–805.
Euractiv (2012), 'EU explores Spain bank rescue', *Euractiv*, 7 July.
Eurofound (2015), *Ireland: New Public Sector Agreement Passed*, Eurofound, Dublin.
Eurogroup (2012a), *Eurogroup Statement 21/2/12*, available at: https://www.consilium.europa.eu/media/25716/128075.pdf (accessed 1 March 2021).
Eurogroup (2012b), *Eurogroup Statement 12/11/12*, available at: www.consilium.europa.eu/media/24045/133445.pdf (accessed 1 March 2021).
Eurogroup (2012c), *Eurogroup Statement 13/12/12*, available at: www.consilium.europa.eu/media/24051/134270.pdf (accessed 1 March 2021).
Eurogroup (2012d), *Eurogroup Statement 27/11/12*, available at: www.consilium.europa.eu/media/24042/133857.pdf (accessed 1 March 2021).
Eurogroup (2012e), *Eurogroup Statement on Spain*, available at: www.consilium.europa.eu/media/25703/131309.pdf (accessed 1 March 2021).
Eurogroup (2013), *Eurogroup Statement on Cyprus*, available at: www.consilium.europa.eu/media/24039/135809.pdf (accessed 1 March 2021).
Eurogroup (2014), *Eurogroup Supports a Two-Month Programme Extension for Greece*, available at: www.consilium.europa.eu/en/meetings/eurogroup/2014/12/08/ (accessed 4 February 2020).
Eurogroup (2020), *Report on the Comprehensive Economic Policy Response to the COVID-19 Pandemic*, 9 April, available at: www.consilium.europa.eu/en/press/press-releases/2020/04/09/report-on-the-comprehensive-economic-policy-response-to-the-covid-19-pandemic/ (accessed 10 May 2020).
Euronews (2017), 'Spanish economy shows strong 2016 growth', available at: www.euronews.com/2017/01/30/spanish-economy-shows-strong-2016-growth (accessed 1 March 2021).
European Central Bank (2011), *Letter to Mr. José Luis Rodríguez Zapatero*, European Central Bank, Frankfurt and Madrid, available at: www.ecb.europa.eu/pub/pdf/other/letter_mr_zapatero_es.pdf (accessed 1 March 2021).
European Central Bank (2015), *Eligibility of Greek Bonds Used as Collateral in Eurosystem Monetary Policy Operations*, 4 February, available at: www.ecb.europa.eu/press/pr/date/2015/html/pr150204.en.html (accessed 4 February 2020).
European Commission (undated a), *Financial Assistance to Greece*, European Commission, Brussels, available at: https://ec.europa.eu/info/business-economy-euro/economic-and-fiscal-policy-coordination/eu-financial-assistance/which-eu-countries-have-received-assistance/financial-assistance-greece_en#secondeconomicadjustmentprogrammeforgreece (accessed 4 February 2020).
European Commission (undated b), *Deposit Guarantee Scheme*, European Commission, Brussels, available at: https://ec.europa.eu/info/business-economy-euro/banking-and-finance/financial-supervision-and-risk-management/managing-

risks-banks-and-financial-institutions/deposit-guarantee-schemes_en (accessed 25 February 2020).

European Commission (2008a), *State Aid: Frequently Asked Questions Concerning EU Rules*, No. MEMO/08/660, European Commission, Brussels, available at: https://ec.europa.eu/commission/presscorner/detail/en/MEMO_08_660 (accessed 15 January 2019).

European Commission (2008b), *Communication from the Commission to the European Council – A European Economic Recovery Plan*, European Commission, Brussels.

European Commission (2009), *Recommendation for a Council Recommendation to Spain with a View to Bringing an End to the Situation of an Excessive Government Deficit*, European Commission, Brussels.

European Commission (2010a), *Report on Greek Government Deficit and Debt Statistics*, No. COM(2010) 1 final, European Commission, Brussels.

European Commission (2010b), *Commission Assesses Stability Programme of Greece; Makes Recommendations to Correct the Excessive Budget Deficit, Improve Competitiveness through Structural Reforms and Provide Reliable Statistics*, No. IP/10/116, European Commission, Brussels.

European Commission (2010c), *The Economic Adjustment Programme for Greece*, Occasional Papers No. 61, European Commission, Brussels.

European Commission (2010d), *The Economic Adjustment Programme for Greece, First Review – Summer 2010*, Occasional Papers No. 68, European Commission, Brussels.

European Commission (2010e), *The Economic Adjustment Programme for Greece, Second Review – Autumn 2010*, Occasional Papers No. 72, European Commission, Brussels.

European Commission (2010f), *Communication from the Commission to the Council*, European Commission, Brussels.

European Commission (2010g), *Green Paper on Adequate, Sustainable and Safe European Pension Systems*, European Commission, Brussels.

European Commission (2011a), *The Economic Adjustment Programme for Greece, Fourth Review – Spring 2011*, Occasional Papers No. 82, European Commission, Brussels.

European Commission (2011b), *The Economic Adjustment Programme for Greece, Fourth Review – October 2011*, Occasional Papers No. 87, European Commission, Brussels.

European Commission (2011c), *The Economic Adjustment Programme for Ireland*, Occasional Papers No. 76, European Commission, Brussels.

European Commission (2011d), *Economic Adjustment Programme for Ireland Spring 2011 Review*, Occasional Papers No. 78, European Commission, Brussels.

European Commission (2011e), *Economic Adjustment Programme for Ireland Summer 2011 Review*, Occasional Papers No. 84 REVIEW 3, European Commission, Brussels.

European Commission (2011f), *Economic Adjustment Programme for Ireland Autumn 2011 Review*, Occasional Papers No. 88 REVIEW 4, European Commission, Brussels.

European Commission (2012a), *The Second Economic Adjustment Programme for Greece*, Occasional Papers No. 94, European Commission, Brussels.

European Commission (2012b), *Economic Adjustment Programme for Ireland Spring 2012 Review*, Occasional Papers No. 96 REVIEW 6, European Commission, Brussels.

European Commission (2012c), *Economic Adjustment Programme for Ireland Autumn 2012 Review*, Occasional Papers No. 127 REVIEW 8, European Commission, Brussels.

European Commission (2012d), *Spain: Memorandum of Understanding on Financial-Sector Policy Conditionality*, European Commission, Brussels.

European Commission (2012e), *Recommendation for a Council Recommendation on Spain's 2012 National Reform Programme and Delivering a Council Opinion on Spain's Stability Programme for 2012–2015*, European Commission, Brussels.

European Commission (2013a), *Economic Adjustment Programme for Ireland Spring 2013 Review*, Occasional Papers No. 154 REVIEW 10, European Commission, Brussels.

European Commission (2013b), *Economic Adjustment Programme for Ireland Autumn 2013 Review*, Occasional Papers No. 167, European Commission, Brussels.

European Commission (2013c), *Recommendation for a Council Recommendation on Spain's 2013 National Reform Programme and Delivering a Council Opinion on Spain's Stability Programme for 2012–2016*, European Commission, Brussels.

European Commission (2013d), *The Economic Adjustment Programme for Cyprus*, Occasional Papers No. 149, European Commission, Brussels.

European Commission (2013e), *The Economic Adjustment Programme for Cyprus First Review – Summer 2013*, Occasional Papers No. 161, European Commission, Brussels.

European Commission (2013f), *The Economic Adjustment Programme for Cyprus Second Review – Autumn 2013*, Occasional Papers No. 169, European Commission, Brussels.

European Commission (2014a), *The Economic Adjustment Programme for Cyprus Third Review – Winter 2014*, Occasional Papers No. 189, European Commission, Brussels.

European Commission (2014b), *The Economic Adjustment Programme for Cyprus Fourth Review – Spring 2014*, Occasional Papers No. 197, European Commission, Brussels.

European Commission (2014c), *The Economic Adjustment Programme for Cyprus Fifth Review – Summer 2014*, Occasional Papers No. 209, European Commission, Brussels.

European Commission (2015a), *Memorandum of Understanding Between the European Commission Acting on Behalf of the European Stability Mechanism, and the Hellenic Republic and the Bank of Greece*, European Commission, Brussels.

European Commission (2015b), *Ex Post Evaluation of the Economic Adjustment Programme Ireland: 2010–2013*, European Economy Institutional Paper No. 004, European Commission, Brussels.

European Commission (2015c), *The Economic Adjustment Programme for Cyprus Sixth Review – Spring 2015*, Institutional Paper No. 004, European Commission, Brussels.

European Commission (2015d), *The Economic Adjustment Programme for Cyprus Seventh Review – Summer 2015*, Institutional Paper No. 009, European Commission, Brussels.

European Commission (2016a), *Compliance Report: The Third Economic Adjustment Programme for Greece, First Review*, European Commission, Brussels.

European Commission (2016b), *Post-Programme Surveillance Report Ireland, Spring 2016*, European Economy Institutional Paper No. 035, European Commission, Brussels.

European Commission (2016c), *Post-Programme Surveillance Report, Cyprus, Autumn 2016*, Institutional Paper No. 042, European Commission, Brussels.

European Commission (2017a), *Compliance Report: The Third Economic Adjustment Programme for Greece, Second Review*, European Commission, Brussels.

European Commission (2017b), *Post-Programme Surveillance Report, Cyprus, Spring 2017*, Institutional Paper No. 058, European Commission, Brussels.

European Commission (2018a), *Enhanced Surveillance Report, Greece, November 2018*, Institutional Paper No. 090, European Commission, Brussels.

European Commission (2018b), *European Semester: Country Report – Portugal*, Country Report No. Portugal 2018, European Commission, Brussels.

European Commission (2019), *Post-Programme Surveillance Report, Cyprus, Spring 2019*, Institutional Paper No. 104, European Commission, Brussels.

European Council (2013), *Proposal for a Council Opinion on the Economic Partnership Programme of Spain*, European Council, Brussels.

European Council (2020), *Report on the Comprehensive Economic Policy Response to the COVID-19 Pandemic*, 9 April, available at: www.consilium.europa.eu/en/press/press-releases/2020/04/09/report-on-the-comprehensive-economic-policy-response-to-the-covid-19-pandemic/ (accessed 10 May 2020).

European Court of Auditors (2017), *Special Report: The Commission's Intervention in the Greek Financial Crisis*, Special report No. 17, Luxembourg, available at: www.consilium.europa.eu/en/meetings/eurogroup/2014/12/08/ (accessed 4 February 2020).

European Stability Mechanism (2016), *Accessing sovereign markets – the Recent Experiences of Ireland, Portugal, Spain, and Cyprus*, Discussion Paper, 2, June, available at: www.esm.europa.eu/publications/accessing-sovereign-markets-recent-experiences-ireland-portugal-spain-and-cyprus (accessed 1 March 2021).

European Stability Mechanism (2019), *Safeguarding the Euro in Times of Crisis: The Inside Story of the ESM*, Publications Office of the European Union, Luxembourg.

Ewing, J. (2012), 'Greek crisis leaves Cyprus mired in debt', *New York Times*, 11 April, available at: www.nytimes.com/2012/04/12/business/global/in-cyprus-a-national-quest-to-shore-up-teetering-banks.html (accessed 24 February 2020).

Exadaktylos, T. and Zahariadis, N. (2014), 'Quid pro quo: political trust and policy implementation in Greece during the age of austerity', *Politics and Policy*, Vol. 42, No. 1, pp. 160–183.

Expansión (2012), 'Bruselas presiona: la reforma laboral en España es una prioridad urgente', *Expansión*, 10 January.

Expansión (2016), 'El Gobierno aprueba el recorte del gasto en 5.493 millones de euros para 2017', *Expansión*, 30 December.

Faria, R. and Aníbal, S. (2012), 'Chefe de missão do FMI: mudanças na TSU não foram exigência da Troika', *Público*, 12 September.

Featherstone, K. (2003), 'Greece and EMU: between external empowerment and domestic vulnerability', *JCMS: Journal of Common Market Studies*, Vol. 41, No. 5, pp. 923–940.

Featherstone, K. (2015), 'External conditionality and the debt crisis: the 'Troika'and public administration reform in Greece', *Journal of European Public Policy*, Vol. 22, No. 3, pp. 295–314.

Featherstone, K. and Papadimitriou, D. (2008), *The Limits of Europeanization: Reform Capacity and Policy Conflict in Greece*, Palgrave Macmillan, New York.

Feld, L.P., Köhler, E.A. and Nientiedt, D. (2015), 'Ordoliberalism, pragmatism and the eurozone crisis: how the German tradition shaped economic policy in Europe', *European Review of International Studies*, Vol. 2, No. 3, pp. 48–61.

Fernandes, J.M. and Jalali, C. (2017), 'A resurgent presidency? Portuguese semi-presidentialism and the 2016 elections', *South European Society and Politics*, Vol. 22, No. 1, pp. 121–138.

Fernandes, J.M., Magalhães, P.C. and Santana-Pereira, J. (2018), 'Portugal's leftist government: from sick man to poster boy?', *South European Society and Politics*, Vol. 23, No. 4, pp. 503–524.

Ferrándiz, J.P. and Lobera, J. (2019), 'Estimación electoral en tiempos de multipartidismo: comparación de indicadores en cuatro elecciones generales (2015–2019)', *Panorama Social*, Fundación de las Cajas de Ahorros (FUNCAS), No. 30, pp. 55–68.

Ferreira, C. (2012), 'O dia em que Sócrates pediu a Cavaco para o salvar da troika', *Público*, 17 May, available at: www.publico.pt/2012/05/17/politica/noticia/o-dia-em-que-socrates-pediu-a-cavaco-para-o-salvar-da-troika——1546409 (accessed 19 March 2019).

Ferrera, M. (2017), 'The Stein Rokkan Lecture 2016: Mission impossible? Reconciling economic and social Europe after the euro crisis and Brexit', *European Journal of Political Research*, Vol. 56, No. 1, pp. 3–22.

Ferrera, M. (2020), 'Mass democracy, the welfare state and European integration: a neo-Weberian analysis', *European Journal of Social Theory*, Vol. 23, No. 2, pp. 165–183.

Field, B. and Botti, A. (2013), *Politics and Society in Contemporary Spain: From Zapatero to Rajoy*, Palgrave Macmillan, New York.

Financial Crisis Inquiry Commission (2011), *Final Report of the National Commission on the Causes of the Financial and Economic Crisis in the United States*, Official Government Edition, Washington.

Financial Times (2012), 'Spain seeks Eurozone bailout', *Financial Times*, 10 June.

Fine Gael (2011), *Fine Gael Manifesto: Let's Get Ireland Working*, Fine Gael, Dublin.

Finke, D. and Bailer, S. (2019), 'Crisis bargaining in the European Union: formal rules or market pressure?', *European Union Politics*, Vol. 20, No. 1, pp. 109–133.

Finn, C. (2015), 'Why hasn't the USC been scrapped yet?', *The Journal*, 14 October.

Finn, C. (2016), 'Ireland's much-hated tax that just won't go away: the Universal Social Charge', *The Journal*, 8 October.

Finn, C. (2019), 'Why hasn't the government merged the PRSI and the USC yet? Minister says it's "complex"', *The Journal*, 30 June.

Fishman, R.M. (2012), 'Anomalies of Spain's economy and economic policy-making', *Contributions to Political Economy*, Vol. 31, No. 1, pp. 67–76.

Freeman, G.P. (2006), 'National models, policy types, and the politics of immigration in liberal democracies', *West European Politics*, Vol. 29, No. 2, pp. 227–247.

Freire, A. and Santana-Pereira, J. (2012), 'Economic voting in Portugal, 2002–2009', *Electoral Studies*, Vol. 31, No. 3, pp. 506–512.

Gago, A. (2016), 'Crisis, EU transformation and union strategies: the impact of conditionality on the strategic repertoire of Spanish trade unions during the Eurozone crisis', *Revista Española de Ciencia Política*, No. 42, pp. 45–68.

Gago, A. (2018), *EU Ordoliberal Intergovernmentalism and the Transformation of National Political Opportunities: Explaining Governments' and Trade Unions' Strategies in Portugal, Spain and Italy during the Eurozone Crisis*, PhD Dissertation in Political Science, Università Degli Studi di Milano, Milan.

Gago, A. and Moury, C. (2018), 'Making and justifying impossible choices: trade unions and three-level games in Ireland and Portugal', unpublished manuscript.

Galasso, V. (2014), 'The role of political partisanship during economic crises', *Public Choice*, Vol. 158, Nos 1–2, pp. 143–165.

Garea, F. (2011), 'Zapatero convoca el 20-N para que "otro Gobierno dé certidumbre"', *El País*, 29 July.

Garrett, G. and Tsebelis, G. (1996), 'An institutional critique of intergovernmentalism', *International Organization*, Vol. 50, No. 2, pp. 269–299.

George, A.L. and Bennett, A. (2005), *Case Studies and Theory Development in the Social Sciences*, MIT Press, Cambridge, MA.

Georgiadou, V., Kafe, A., Nezi, S. and Pieridis, C. (2019), 'Plebiscitarian spirit in the square: key characteristics of the Greek indignants', *International Journal of Politics, Culture, and Society*, Vol. 32, No. 1, pp. 43–59.

Gerodimos, R. (2015), 'The ideology of far left populism in Greece: blame, victimhood and revenge in the discourse of Greek anarchists', *Political Studies*, Vol. 63, No. 3, pp. 608–625.

Giger, N. and Nelson, M. (2011), 'The electoral consequences of welfare state retrenchment: blame avoidance or credit claiming in the era of permanent austerity?', *European Journal of Political Research*, Vol. 50, No. 1, pp. 1–23.

Gocaj, L. and Meunier, S. (2013), 'Time will tell: the EFSF, the ESM, and the euro crisis', *Journal of European Integration*, Vol. 35, No. 3, pp. 239–253.

Gopinath, G. (2020), 'The Great Lockdown: worst economic downturn since the Great Depression', *IMFBlog*, 14 April, available at: https://blogs.imf.org/2020/04/14/the-great-lockdown-worst-economic-downturn-since-the-great-depression/ (accessed 25 February 2021).

Gotev, G. (2012), 'Cyprus to get bail-out from EU, Russia: president', *Euractiv*, 5 July, available at: www.euractiv.com/section/euro-finance/news/cyprus-to-get-bailout-from-eu-russia-president/ (accessed 24 February 2020).

Gouskos, D. and Staiou, E. (2010), 'Αξιολόγηση της Επιχειρησιακής Ανάπτυξης του opengov.gr', Επιστήμη Και Κοινωνία, Vol. 24, pp. 115–124.

Grande, E. (1996), 'The state and interest groups in a framework of multi-level decision-making: the case of the European Union', *Journal of European Public Policy*, Vol. 3, No. 3, pp. 318–338.

Graziano, P. (2011), 'Europeanisation and domestic policy change: adapting to the European employment strategy in Italy and France', *Governance*, Vol. 24, No. 3, pp. 583–605.

Greer, S. (2014), 'Structural adjustment comes to Europe: lessons for the Eurozone from the conditionality debates', *Global Social Policy*, Vol. 14, No. 1, pp. 51–71.

Guillén, A.M. and León, M. (2011), *The Spanish Welfare State in European Context*, Ashgate Publishing, Ltd, Farnham.

Gunaydin, H. (2018), 'Who can reform the labor market? IMF conditionality, partisanship, and labor unions', *International Interactions*, Vol. 44, No. 5, pp. 888–918.

Győrffy, D. (2018), *Trust and Crisis Management in the European Union*, Palgrave Macmillan, Cham.

Ha, E. and Kang, M. (2015), 'Government policy responses to financial crises: identifying patterns and policy origins in developing countries', *World Development*, Vol. 68, pp. 264–281.

Hall, P.A. (2012), 'The economics and politics of the Euro crisis', *German Politics*, Vol. 21, No. 4, pp. 355–371.

Hall, P.A. and Soskice, D. (2001), 'An introduction to varieties of capitalism', in Hall, P.A. and Soskice, D. (eds), *Varieties of Capitalism: The Institutional Foundations of Comparative Advantage*, Oxford University Press, Oxford, pp. 1–68.

Hallerberg, M. and Basinger, S. (1998), 'Internationalization and changes in tax policy in OECD countries: the importance of domestic veto players', *Comparative Political Studies*, Vol. 31, No. 3, pp. 321–352.

Hamann, K. (2013), 'The relationship between unions and Zapatero's government: from social pacts to general strike', in Field, B. and Botti, A. (eds), *Politics and Society in Contemporary Spain*, Palgrave Macmillan, New York, pp. 123–141.

Hardiman, N. and MacCarthaigh, M. (2013), *How Governments Retrench in Crisis: The Case of Ireland*, UCD Geary Institute Discussion Paper Series No. 15.

Hardiman, N. and MacCarthaigh, M. (2017), 'State retrenchment and administrative reform in Ireland: probing comparative policy paradigms', *Journal of Comparative Policy Analysis: Research and Practice*, Vol. 19, No. 2, pp. 100–118.

Hardiman, N. and Regan, A. (2013), 'The politics of austerity in Ireland', *Intereconomics*, Vol. 48, No. 1, pp. 4–32.

Hardiman, N., Blavoukos, S., Dellepiane-Avellaneda, S. and Pagoulatos, G. (2016), 'Austerity in the European periphery: the Irish experience', in Heffernan, E., McHale, J. and Moore-Cherry, N. (eds), *Debating Austerity in Ireland: Crisis, Experience and Recovery*, Royal Irish Academy, Dublin, pp. 83–99.

Hardiman, N., Şpanou, C., Araújo, J.F. and MacCarthaigh, M. (2019), 'Tangling with the Troika: "domestic ownership" as political and administrative engagement in Greece, Ireland, and Portugal', *Public Management Review*, Vol. 21, No. 9, pp. 1265–1286.

Heimberger, P. (2017), 'Did fiscal consolidation cause the double-dip recession in the euro area?', *Review of Keynesian Economics*, Vol. 5, No. 3, pp. 439–458.

Heins, E. and de la Porte, C. (2015), *The Sovereign Debt Crisis, the EU and Welfare State Reform*, Springer, Lisbon.

Hennessy, A. (2017), 'Good samaritans vs. hardliners: the role of credible signalling in Greek bailout negotiations', *JCMS: Journal of Common Market Studies*, Vol. 55, No. 4, pp. 744–761.

Henning, C.R. (2017), *Tangled Governance: International Regime Complexity, the Troika, and the Euro Crisis*, Oxford University Press, Oxford.

Héritier, A., Meissner, K.L., Moury, C. and Schoeller, M.G. (2019), *European Parliament Ascendant: Parliamentary Strategies of Self-Empowerment in the EU*, Palgrave Macmillan, London.

Herszenhorn, D.M. (2020), 'EU leaders back budget reboot for coronavirus recovery', *Politico*, 24 April.

Hick, R. (2018), 'Enter the Troika: the politics of social security During Ireland's bailout', *Journal of Social Policy*, Vol. 47, No. 1, pp. 1–20.

Hill, D. (2003), 'Global neo-liberalism, the deformation of education and resistance', *Journal for Critical Education Policy Studies*, Vol. 1, No. 1, pp. 1–30.

Hodson, D. (2012), 'The Eurozone in 2011', *Journal of Common Market Studies*, Vol. 50, pp. 178–194.

Hodson, D. (2015), 'Eurozone governance: deflation, Grexit 2.0 and the second coming of Jean-Claude Juncker', *Journal of Common Market Studies*, Vol. 53, pp. 144–161.

Horwitz, L. and Myant, M. (2015), *Spain's Labour Market Reforms: The Road to Employment – Or to Unemployment?*, Working Paper No. 2015.03, European Trade Union Institute.

Howarth, D. and Quaglia, L. (2016), *The Political Economy of European Banking Union*, Oxford University Press, Oxford.

Huerta, J.P. (2019), 'FROB in the restructuring of the Spanish banking system: where it stands after a decade of activity (2009–2019) and considerations for the Banking Union', *Revista de Estabilidad Financiera*, Banco de España & Revista de Estabilidad Financiera, No 36, Spring.

Iefimerida (2013), 'Ολο το παρασκήνιο της παραίτησης του Μιχάλη Σαρρή από τη θέση του υπουργού Οικονομικών Πηγή', *Iefimerida*, 2 April.

Ignatiou, M. (2015), Τρόϊκα*:* Ο Δρόμος Προς Την Καταστροφή, Livanis Publishers, Athens.

Independent Evaluation Office (2003), *Annual Report 2003*, International Monetary Fund, Washington.

Inman, P. (2016), 'Irish economy surges 26% as revised figures take in foreign investment', *The Guardian*, 12 July, available at: www.theguardian.com/business/2016/jul/12/irish-economic-growth-revised-figures-foreign-investment-aircraft (accessed 19 June 2019).

International Monetary Fund (2009), *Greece: Selected Issues*, Country Report No. 09/245, International Monetary Fund, Washington.

International Monetary Fund (2010), *Spain: 2010 Article IV Consultation IMF*, Country Report No. 10/254, International Monetary Fund, Washington.

International Monetary Fund (2011a), *Portugal: First Review Under the Extended Arrangement*, Country Report No. 11/279, International Monetary Fund, Washington.

International Monetary Fund (2011b), *Portugal: Second Review Under the Extended Arrangement*, Country Report No. 11/363, International Monetary Fund, Washington.

International Monetary Fund (2011c), *Cyprus: Selected Issues Paper*, Country Report No. 11/332, International Monetary Fund, Washington.

International Monetary Fund (2011d), *Cyprus: Article IV Consultation – Staff Report; Supplement; Public Information Notice on the Executive Board Discussion; and Statement by the Executive Director for Cyprus*, Country Report No. 11/331, International Monetary Fund, Washington.

International Monetary Fund (2012a), *Greece: First and Second Reviews under the Extended Arrangement Under the Extended Fund Facility, Request for Waiver of Applicability, Modification of Performance Criteria, and Reshaping of Access*, Country Report No. 13/20, International Monetary Fund, Washington.

International Monetary Fund (2012b), *Article IV and Seventh Review under the Extended Arrangement Staff Report*, Country Report No. 12/264, International Monetary Fund, Washington.

International Monetary Fund (2012c), *Portugal: Fifth Review Under the Extended Arrangement and Request for Waivers of Applicability and Nonobservance of End-September Performance Criteria*, Country Report No. 12/292, International Monetary Fund, Washington.

International Monetary Fund (2012d), *Portugal: Fourth Review Under the Extended Arrangement and Request for a Waiver of Applicability of End-June Performance Criteria*, Country Report No. 12/179, International Monetary Fund, Washington.

International Monetary Fund (2012e), *Portugal: Third Review Under the Extended Arrangement and Request for Waiver of Applicability of End-March Performance Criteria*, Country Report No. 12/77, International Monetary Fund, Washington.

International Monetary Fund (2013a), *Greece: First and Second Reviews under the Extended Arrangement Under the Extended Fund Facility*, Country Report No. 13/153, International Monetary Fund, Washington.

International Monetary Fund (2013b), *Portugal: Eighth and Ninth Reviews Under the Extended Arrangement and Request for Waivers of Applicability of End-September Performance Criteria*, Country Report No. 13/324, International Monetary Fund, Washington.

International Monetary Fund (2013c), *Portugal: Seventh Review Under the Extended Arrangement and Request for Modification of End-June Performance Criteria*, Country Report No. 13/160, International Monetary Fund, Washington.

International Monetary Fund (2013d), *Portugal: 2012 Article IV Consultation and Sixth Review Under the Extended Arrangement and Request for Waivers of Applicability of End-December Performance Criteria*, Country Report No. 13/18, International Monetary Fund, Washington.

International Monetary Fund (2014a), *Portugal: Eleventh Review Under the Extended Arrangement, and Request for Extension of the Arrangement and Waivers of Applicability of End-March Performance Criteria*, Country Report No. 14/2012, International Monetary Fund, Washington.

International Monetary Fund (2014b), *Portugal: Tenth Review Under the Extended Arrangement and Request for Waivers of Applicability of End-December Performance Criteria*, Country Report No. 14/56, International Monetary Fund, Washington.

International Monetary Fund (2017), *Portugal: 2017 Article IV Consultation-Press Release; Staff Report; and Statement by the Executive Director for Portugal*, Country Report No. 17/278, International Monetary Fund, Washington.

Ivanova, A., Mourmouras, A., Anayotos, G.C. and Mayer, W. (2003), *What Determines the Implementation of IMF-Supported Programs?*, IMF Working Paper No. 8.

Jensen, C. (2012), 'Two sides of the same coin? Left-wing governments and labour unions as determinants of public spending', *Socio-economic Review*, Vol. 10, No. 2, pp. 217–240.

Johnston, A. and Regan, A. (2016), 'European monetary integration and the incompatibility of national varieties of capitalism', *JCMS: Journal of Common Market Studies*, Vol. 54, No. 2, pp. 318–336.

Jordana, J. (2014), 'Multiple crises and policy dismantling in Spain: political strategies and distributive implications', *Political Studies Review*, Vol. 12, No. 2, pp. 224–238.

Juwana, H. (2005), 'Reform of economic laws and its effects on the post-crisis Indonesian economy', *The Developing Economies*, Vol. 43, No. 1, pp. 72–90.

Karamichas, J. (2009), 'The December 2008 riots in Greece: profile', *Social Movement Studies*, Vol. 8, No. 3, pp. 289–293.

Kasperskaya, Y. and Xifré, R. (2019), 'Reform or resist? The tale of two fiscal reforms in Spain after the crisis', *Public Money and Management*, Vol. 39, No. 7, pp. 494–502.

Katsourides, Y. (2019), 'The Cypriot left and the crisis: one step forward, two steps back', in Holmes, M. and Roder, K. (eds), *The European Left and the Financial Crisis*, Manchester University Press, Manchester, pp. 86–101.

Kazakos, P. (2019), Ελεγχόμενες Πτωχεύσεις, Kathimerini, Athens.

Keaney, M. (2001), 'Consensus by diktat: Washington, London, and the "modernization" of modernization', *Capitalism Nature Socialism*, Vol. 12, No. 3, pp. 44–70.

Keohane, R.O. and Nye, J.S. (1977), *Power and Interdependence: World Politics in Transition*, Little, Brown, Boston.

Ker-Lindsay, J. (2006), 'Presidential power and authority in the Republic of Cyprus', *Mediterranean Politics*, Vol. 11, No. 1, pp. 21–37.

Khan, M.S. and Sharma, S. (2001), 'IMF conditionality and country ownership of programs', *IMF Working Paper*, Vol. 01, No. 142.

Khenkin, S. (2016), 'Sistema político de España: transformación radical', *Iberoamerica*, No. 1, pp. 99–116.

Koratzanis, N. and Pierros, C. (2019), 'Η Οικονομική Πολιτική του ΣΥΡΙΖΑ: από τις διακηρύξεις στην εφαρμογή', in Balabanidis, Y. (ed.), ΣΥΡΙΖΑ-Ένα Κόμμα Εν Κινήσει: Από Τη Διαμαρτυρία Στη Διακυβέρνηση, Themelio Publications, Athens, pp. 227–250.

Kotsi, A., Athanasiou, E., Kanellopoulos, N., Karagianni, R. and Katselidis, I. (2016), *Αποτίμηση Της Απελευθέρωσης Σε Είκοσι Επιλεγμένα Επαγγέλματα*, Report No. 73, KEPE, Athens.

Krugman P. (1993), 'Lessons from Massachusetts for EMU', in Torres, F. and Giavazzi, F. (eds), *Adjustment and Growth in the European Monetary Union*, CEPR and Cambridge University Press, London, pp. 241–261.

Kutter, A. (2014), 'A catalytic moment: the Greek crisis in the German financial press', *Discourse and Society*, Vol. 25, No. 4, pp. 446–466.

La Opinión (2011), 'Merkel pide "sin demora" más recortes a Rajoy', *La Opinión*, 23 November.

La Vanguardia (2010), 'España presenta mañana plan de austeridad', *La Vanguardia*, 16 May.

Labour (2011), *Electoral Manifesto*, Labour, Dublin.

Ladi, S. (2011), *Οικονομική Κρίση Και Διοικητική Μεταρρύθμιση Στην Ελλάδα Και Στην Κύπρο: Ευκαιρίες Και Περιορισμοί*, Policy Paper No. 2, Cyprus Center for European and International Affairs, University of Nicosia, Nicosia.

Ladi, S. (2014), 'Austerity politics and administrative reform: the Eurozone crisis and its impact upon Greek public administration', *Comparative European Politics*, Vol. 12, No. 2, pp. 184–208.

Ladi, S. and Graziano, P.R. (2014), '"Fast-forward" Europeanization: welfare state reform in light of the Eurozone crisis', in Coman, R., Kostera, T. and Tomini, L. (eds), *Europeanization and European Integration: From Incremental to Structural Change*, Palgrave Macmillan, London, pp. 108–126.

Ladi, S. and Katsikas, D. (2017), 'Είναι Αλήθεια ότι ο Δημόσιος Τομέας στην Ελλάδα είναι Υπερβολικά Μεγάλος', in Katsikas, D., Filinis, K. and Anastasatou, M. (eds), Κατανοώντας Την Ελληνική Κρίση, Papazisis, Athens, pp. 79–101.

Ladi, S. and Tsagkroni, V. (2019), 'Analysing crisis parliamentary discourse in Greece: whom should we blame?', *JCMS: Journal of Common Market Studies*, Vol. 57, No. 4, pp. 729–748.

Ladi, S. and Tsarouhas, D. (2014), 'The politics of austerity and public policy reform in the EU', *Political Studies Review*, Vol. 12, No. 2, pp. 171–180.

Laffan, B. (2012), 'European Union and Eurozone: how to co-exist?', in Allen, F., Carletti, E. and Simonelli, S. (eds), *Governance for the Eurozone: Integration or Disintegration?*, FIC Press, Philadelphia, pp. 173–188.

Laffan, B. (2016), 'International actors and agencies', in Roche, W.K., O'Connell, P.J. and Prothero, A. (eds), *Austerity and Recovery in Ireland: Europe's Poster Child and the Great Recession*, Oxford University Press, Oxford, pp. 177–193.

Lafont, I. (2012), 'Los mercados castigan las dudas ante el rescate y las elecciones catalanas', *El País*, 26 September.

Leach, W.D. and Sabatier, P.A. (2005), 'To trust an adversary: integrating rational and psychological models of collaborative policymaking', *American Political Science Review*, Vol. 99, No. 4, pp. 491–503.

León, M., Pavolini, E. and Guillén, A.M. (2015), 'Welfare rescaling in Italy and Spain: political strategies to deal with harsh austerity', *European Journal of Social Security*, Vol. 17, No. 2, pp. 182–201.

Levitz, P. and Pop-Eleches, G. (2010), 'Why no backsliding? The European Union's impact on democracy and governance before and after accession', Vol. 43, No. 4, pp. 457–485.

Lindvall, J. (2017), *Reform Capacity*, Oxford University Press, Oxford.

Lipsmeyer, C.S. (2011), 'Booms and busts: how parliamentary governments and economic context influence welfare policy', *International Studies Quarterly*, Vol. 55, No. 4, pp. 959–980.

Lisi, M. (2010), 'The democratisation of party leadership selection: the Portuguese experience', *Portuguese Journal of Social Science*, Vol. 9, No. 2, pp. 127–149.

Lisi, M. (2016), 'U-turn: the Portuguese radical left from marginality to government support', *South European Society and Politics*, Vol. 21, No. 4, pp. 541–560.

Lobo, M.C. and Lewis-Beck, M.S. (2012), 'The integration hypothesis: how the European Union shapes economic voting', *Electoral Studies*, Vol. 31, No. 3, pp. 522–528.

Lombardi, D. and Woods, N. (2008), 'The politics of influence: an analysis of IMF surveillance', *Review of International Political Economy*, Vol. 15, No. 5, pp. 711–739.

Lowi, T.J. (1964), 'American business, public policy, case-studies, and political theory', *World Politics*, Vol. 16, No. 4, pp. 677–715.

Lucas, B. (2012), 'Las 14 claves de la reforma educativa de Wert', *Eldiario. Es*, 13 December, available at: www.eldiario.es/sociedad/ley-afecta-modelo-linguistico_1_5527106.html (accessed 5 March 2021).

Lütz, S. and Kranke, M. (2014), 'The European rescue of the Washington Consensus? EU and IMF lending to Central and Eastern European countries', *Review of International Political Economy*, Vol. 21, No. 2, pp. 310–338.

Lütz, S., Hilgers, S. and Schneider, S. (2019), 'Games borrower governments play: the implementation of economic adjustment programmes in Cyprus and Portugal', *West European Politics*, Vol. 42, No. 7, pp. 1443–1463.

Lütz, S., Hilgers, S. and Schneider, S. (2020), 'When numbers don't add up: bureaucratic culture and conflicts in EU–IMF programs', in Chang, M., Steinberg, F. and Torres, F. (eds), *The Political Economy of Adjustment Throughout and Beyond the Eurozone Crisis*, Routledge, Abingdon and New York, pp. 38–58.

MacCarthaigh, M. and Hardiman, N. (2020), 'Exploiting conditionality: EU and international actors and post-NPM reform in Ireland', *Public Policy and Administration*, Vol. 35, No. 2, pp. 179–200.

Magalhães, P.C. (2013), 'O partido dos pensionistas', *Personal Blog*, 8 May, available at: www.pedro-magalhaes.org/o-partido-dos-pensionistas/ (accessed 31 October 2018).

Mair, P. (2009), *Representative versus Responsible Government*, Working Paper, 9 August, Max Plank Institute for the Study of Societies, Cologne.

Mandelkern, R. and Koreh, M. (2018), 'Interrupting gradual institutional change: how "continuity agents" have stalled and even reversed gradual welfare-state reforms in Israel', *Journal of European Public Policy*, Vol. 25, No. 11, pp. 1706–1725.

Mandravelis, P. (2019), *Μνημόνιο: Ο Τελευταίος Διχασμός*, Kathimerini, Athens.

Martin, I.W. and Gabay, N. (2018), 'Tax policy and tax protest in 20 rich democracies, 1980–2010', *British Journal of Sociology*, Vol. 69, No. 3, pp. 647–669.

Martín, L.A.B., Nieto, M.J.B., Herrero, G.A.G. and Navarro, J.M.R. (2013), 'Informe sobre el desarrollo y evaluación territorial de la ley de promoción de la autonomía personal y atención a las personas en situación de dependencia', *Observatorio Estatal de La Dependencia*, available at: https://consaludmental.org/publicaciones/XDictamenObservatorioDependencia.pdf (accessed 1 March 2021).

Matthijs, M. and McNamara, K. (2015), 'The euro crisis' theory effect: northern saints, southern sinners, and the demise of the eurobond', *Journal of European Integration*, Vol. 37, No. 2, pp. 229–245.

McDonald, H. (2016), 'Ireland set for minority government after two main parties reach deal', *Guardian*, 29 April, available at: www.theguardian.com/business/2016/jul/12/irish-economic-growth-revised-figures-foreign-investment-aircraft (accessed 5 March 2021).

McManus, I.P. (2018), 'Political parties as drivers of post-crisis social spending in liberal welfare states', *Comparative European Politics*, Vol. 16, No. 5, pp. 843–870.

Meissner, K.L. and McKenzie, L. (2019), 'The paradox of human rights conditionality in EU trade policy: when strategic interests drive policy outcomes', *Journal of European Public Policy*, Vol. 26, No. 9, pp. 1273–1291.

Mendizabal, N.C. (2014), 'Crisis management, re-centralization and the politics of austerity in Spain', *International Journal of Iberian Studies*, Vol. 27, No. 1, pp. 3–20.

Meunier, S. (2000), 'What single voice? European institutions and EU–U.S. trade negotiations', *International Organization*, Vol. 54, No. 1, pp. 103–135.

Michaelides, A. (2014), 'Cyprus: from boom to bail-in', *Economic Policy*, Vol. 29, No. 80, pp. 639–689.

Michalopoulos, S. (2020), 'Nine member states ask for eurobonds to face coronavirus crisis', *Euractiv*, 25 March, available at: www.euractiv.com/section/economy-jobs/news/nine-member-states-ask-for-eurobonds-to-face-coronavirus-crisis/ (accessed 5 March 2021).

Ministry of Finance (2010), *Update of the Hellenic Stability and Growth Programme*, No. Ares(2010)23198, Athens.

Ministry of Finance (2011), *Αιτιολογική Έκθεση Στο Σχέδιο Νόμου 'Μεσοπρόθεσμο Πλαίσιο Δημοσιονομικής Στρατηγικής 2012–15*, Athens.

Ministry of Interior (2010), *Περιφερειακές – Δημοτικές Εκλογές 2010, Β' Κυριακή*, available at: https://ekloges-prev.singularlogic.eu/dn2010/public/index.html#{%22page%22:%22main%22} (accessed 29 January 2020).

Ministry of Interior (2015), *Εθνικές Εκλογές Ιανουάριος 2015*, available at: http://ekloges-prev.singularlogic.eu/v2015a/v/public/index.html#{%22cls%22:%22main%22,%22params%22:{}} (accessed 4 February 2020).

Ministry of Interior (2019), *Εθνικές Εκλογές Ιούλιος 2019*, available at: https://ekloges.ypes.gr/current/v/home/ (accessed 10 February 2020).

Mody, A. (2014), 'The ghost of Deauville', *VOX CEPR Policy Portal*, 7 January, available at: https://voxeu.org/article/ghost-deauville (accessed 7 June 2019).

Molina, O. and Godino, A. (2013), 'Economic reforms and the labor market: Zapatero's endless period in the wilderness', in Field, B. and Botti, A. (eds), *Politics and Society in Contemporary Spain*, Palgrave Macmillan, New York, pp. 101–121.

Moravcsik, A. (1994), 'Why the European Union strengthens the state: domestic politics and international cooperation', *CES Working Paper*, No. 52, available at: http://aei.pitt.edu/9151/1/Moravcsik52.pdf (accessed 1 March 2021).

Morlino, L. and Sottilotta, C.E. (2019), *The Politics of the Eurozone Crisis in Southern Europe: A Comparative Reappraisal*, Palgrave Macmillan, Switzerland.

Moschella, M. (2016), 'Negotiating Greece: layering, insulation, and the design of adjustment programs in the Eurozone', *Review of International Political Economy*, Vol. 23, No. 5, pp. 799–824.

Moschella, M. (2017), 'When some are more equal than others: national parliaments and intergovernmental bailout negotiations in the Eurozone', *Government and Opposition*, Vol. 52, No. 2, pp. 239–265.

Moury, C. (2013), *Coalition Government and Party Mandate: How Coalition Agreements Constrain Ministerial Action*, Routledge, Abingdon and New York.

Moury, C. and Afonso, A. (2019), 'Beyond conditionality: policy reversals in Southern Europe in the aftermath of the Eurozone crisis', *South European Society and Politics*, Vol. 24, No. 2, pp. 155–176.

Moury, C. and Freire, A. (2013), 'Austerity policies and politics: the case of Portugal', *Pôle Sud*, No. 2, pp. 35–56.

Moury, C. and Standring, A. (2017), '"Going beyond the Troika": power and discourse in Portuguese austerity politics', *European Journal of Political Research*, Vol. 56, No. 3, pp. 660–679.

Moury, C., Cardoso, D. and Gago, A. (2019), 'When the lenders leave town: veto players, electoral calculations and vested interests as determinants of policy reversals in Spain and Portugal', *South European Society and Politics*, Vol. 24, No. 2, pp. 177–204.

Moury, C., de Giorgi, E. and Pita Barros, P. (2021), 'How to combine public spending with fiscal rigor? "Austerity by stealth" in post-bailout Portugal (2015–2019)', *South European Society and Politics*, 1–28.

Mulas-Granados, C. (2003), 'The political and economic determinants of budgetary consolidation in Europe', *European Political Economy Review*,, Vol. 1, No. 1, pp. 015–039.

Muro, D. (2015), 'When do countries re-centralize? Ideology and party politics in the age of austerity', in Gillespie, R. and Gray, C. (eds), *Contesting Spain? The Dynamics of Nationalist Movements in Catalonia and the Basque Country*, Routledge, London, pp. 22–40.

Murphy, M.P. (2014), 'Ireland: Celtic tiger in austerity – explaining Irish path dependency', *Journal of Contemporary European Studies*, Vol. 22, No. 2, pp. 132–142.

Mylonas, H. (2016), 'Greece', *European Journal of Political Research Political Data Yearbook*, Vol. 55, pp. 113–123.

National Herald (2020), 'Greek High Court reviewing retroactive pensions, holiday bonuses', *National Herald*, 10 February, available at: www.thenationalherald.com/278978/greek-high-court-reviewing-retroactive-pensions-holiday-bonuses/ (accessed 10 February 2020).

Nelson, S.C. (2014), 'Playing favorites: how shared beliefs shape the IMF's lending decisions', *International Organization*, Vol. 68, No. 2, pp. 297–328.

Newstalk (2017), 'Enda Kenny: the promises versus reality', *Newstalk*, 18 May, available at: www.newstalk.com/news/enda-kenny-the-promises-vs-the-reality-535583 (accessed 19 May 2019).

Nölke, A. (2016), 'Economic causes of the Eurozone crisis: the analytical contribution of Comparative Capitalism', *Socio-economic Review*, Vol. 14, No. 1, pp. 141–161.

Nooruddin, I. and Simmons, J.W. (2006), 'The politics of hard choices: IMF programs and government spending', *International Organization*, Vol. 60, No. 4, pp. 1001–1033.

Nugent, C. (2018), 'The Irish construction sector (2008–2016) – employment, compensation and labour costs', *NERI Research InBrief*, NERI-Nevin Economic Research Institute, No. 59.

Offe, C. (2017), 'Narratives of responsibility: German politics in the Greek debt crisis', in Castells, M., Bouin, O., Caraça, J., Cardoso, G., Thompson, Jo.B. and Wieviorka, M. (eds), *Europe's Crises*, Polity Press, Cambridge, pp. 269–293.

Oireachtas (2016), *Report of the Joint Committee of Inquiry into the Banking Crisis*, Oireachtas, Dublin.

Organisation for Economic Co-operation and Development (2009), *OECD Economic Surveys: Ireland. Volume 17/2009*, OECD, Paris.

Organisation for Economic Co-operation and Development (2014), *Going for Growth Spain*, Interim report, OECD, Paris.

Orphanides, A. (2013), 'The sovereign debt crisis in the Euro Area', *Ekonomia*, Vol. 15, No. 2, pp. 45–64.

Orphanides, A. (2014), *What Happened in Cyprus? The Economic Consequences of the Last Communist Government in Europe*, LSE Financial Markets Group Special Papers Series.

Orriols, L. and Cordero, G. (2016), 'The breakdown of the Spanish two-party system: the upsurge of Podemos and Ciudadanos in the 2015 general election', *South European Society and Politics*, Vol. 21, No. 4, pp. 469–492.

Otxoa, I. (2007), *El Recorte de Derechos En Las Reformas Laborales*, Manu Robles-Arangiz Institutua, Bilbau.

Pagoulatos, G. (2018), *Greece after the Bailouts: Assessment of a Qualified Failure*, GreeSE Paper No. 130, Hellenic Observatory, LSE, London.

Panayi, E. and Zenios, S.A. (2015), 'Was the Cyprus crisis banking or sovereign debt?', *Journal of Banks and Bank Systems*, Vol. 10, No. 2, pp. 23–34.

Papakonstantinou, G. (2016), *Game Over: The Inside Story of the Greek Crisis*, CreateSpace Independent Publishing Platform, Athens.

Papandreou, G. (2015), 'Reflections on the Greek and Eurozone crisis: a view from the inside', in Karyotis, G. and Gerodimos, R. (eds), *The Politics of Extreme Austerity: Greece in the Eurozone Crisis*, Springer, Basingstoke, pp. 240–258.

Papathanasiou, Y. (2017), *8 Μήνες*, Livanis Publishers, Athens.

Parker, O. and Tsarouhas, D. (2018), 'Causes and consequences of crisis in the Eurozone periphery', in Parker, O. and Tsarouhas, D. (eds), *Crisis in the Eurozone Periphery: The Political Economies of Greece, Spain, Portugal and Ireland*, Palgrave Macmillan, London, pp. 1–28.

Partido Popular (2011), *Lo Que España Necesita: Programa Electoral Del PP*, Partido Popular, Spain.

PASOK (2009), *PASOK Election Programme*, PASOK, Athens.

Patashnik, E.M. (2014), *Reforms at Risk: What Happens after Major Policy Changes Are Enacted*, Vol. 136, Princeton University Press, Princeton and Oxford.

Pegasiou, A. (2013), 'The Cypriot economic collapse: more than a conventional South European failure', *Mediterranean Politics*, Vol. 18, No. 3, pp. 333–351.

Pegasiou, A. (2018), 'EU coordination in Cyprus', in Ragone, S. (ed.), *Managing the Euro Crisis*, Routledge, Abingdon and New York, pp. 83–102.

Pérez, C. (2012a), 'Draghi cree que el Gobierno actuó de "la peor manera posible" con Bankia', *El País*, 31 May.

Pérez, C. (2012b), 'Pulso entre Madrid y Bruselas por la revalorización de las pensiones', *El País*, 6 October.

Pérez, C. (2014), 'Bruselas avisa a España de los "desafíos" tras el rescate y reclama seguir los ajustes', *El País*, 22 January.

Pérez, C. and Doncel, L. (2012), 'España pide un rescate de hasta 100.000 millones para la banca', *El País*, 10 June.

Perez, S.A. and Matsaganis, M. (2018), 'The political economy of austerity in Southern Europe', *New Political Economy*, Vol. 23, No. 2, pp. 192–207.

Perez, S.A. and Matsaganis, M. (2019), 'Export or perish: can internal devaluation create enough good jobs in Southern Europe?', *South European Society and Politics*, Vol. 24, No. 2, pp. 259–285.

Pianta, M. (2013), 'Democracy lost: the financial crisis in Europe and the role of civil society', *Journal of Civil Society*, Vol. 9, No. 2, pp. 148–161.

Picot, G. and Tassinari, A. (2017), 'All of one kind? Labour market reforms under austerity in Italy and Spain', *Socio-economic Review*, Vol. 15, No. 2, pp. 461–482.

PIMCO (2013), *Independent Due Diligence of the Banking System of Cyprus*, PIMCO, London.

Pires, L.R. and Martins, N. (2015), *Segredos de Estado*, Matéria Prima Edições, Lisbon.

Pochet, P. (1999), 'Monetary union and collective bargaining in Belgium', in Pochet, P. (ed.), *Monetary Union and Collective Bargaining in Europe*, P.I.E.-Peter Lang, Brussels, pp. 187–218.

Pop, V. (2012), 'EU monitors heading to Madrid, despite "Men in Black" claims', *Euobserver.Com*, 12 June, available at: https://euobserver.com/economic/116575 (accessed 1 March 2021).

Pop-Eleches, G. (2008), *From Economic Crisis to Reform: IMF Programs in Latin America and Eastern Europe*, Princeton University Press, Princeton.

Prandeka, M. (2013), *Portugal: Labour Market Reforms – A Summary of Main Problems and Actions Taken*, Global and Economic Market Outlook, Eurobank Research, available at: www.eurobank.gr/Uploads/Reports/56_FOCUS_NOTES_PORTUGAL_LABOUR_MARKET_REFORMS.pdf (accessed 21 March 2019).

Preston, P. and Silke, H. (2014), 'Ireland – from neoliberal champion to "the eye of the storm"', *Javnost-the Public*, Vol. 21, No. 4, pp. 5–23.

Psylides, G. (2019), 'Supreme Court reserves judgement on civil service pay cuts', 1 November, available at: https://cyprus-mail.com/2019/11/01/supreme-court-reserves-judgement-on-civil-service-pay-cuts/ (accessed 26 February 2020).

Putnam, R.D. (1988), 'Diplomacy and domestic politics: the logic of two-level games', *International Organization*, Vol. 42, No. 3, pp. 427–460.

Radaelli, C.M. (2003), 'The Europeanization of public policy', in Featherstone, K. and Radaelli, C. (eds), *The Politics of Europeanization*, Vol. 320, Oxford University Press, Oxford and New York, pp. 27–56.

Reforms for the Completion of the Current Programme and Beyond (undated), *Wall Street Journal*, available at: https://online.wsj.com/public/resources/documents/reform.pdf (accessed 5 February 2020).

Regan, A. (2013), *The Impact of the Eurozone Crisis on Irish Social Partnership: A Political Economy Analysis*, DIALOGUE Working Paper No. 3.

Regan, A. (2017), 'Post-crisis social dialogue and economic governance in Ireland', in Guardiancich, I. and Molina, O. (eds), *Talking Through the Crisis: Social Dialogue and Industrial Relations Trends in Selected EU Countries*, International Labour Organization, Geneva.

Rehn, O. (2020), *Walking the Highwire: Rebalancing the European Economy in Crisis*, Palgrave Macmillan, London.

Remmer, K.L. (1986), 'The politics of economic stabilization: IMF standby programs in Latin America, 1954–1984', *Comparative Politics*, Vol. 19, No. 1, pp. 1–24.
Republic of Cyprus (2012), *Annual Report 2011: Public Debt Management*, Ministry of Finance, Nicosia.
Reuters (2012), 'Market door closed to Spain: Treasury minister', *Reuters*, 5 June.
Riain, S.Ó. (2014), *The Rise and Fall of Ireland's Celtic Tiger: Liberalism, Boom and Bust*, Cambridge University Press, Cambridge.
Rickard, S.J. and Caraway, T.L. (2019), 'International demands for austerity: examining the impact of the IMF on the public sector', *Review of International Organizations*, Vol. 14, No. 1, pp. 35–57.
Rigou, M. (2010), 'Ανοιχτή Διακυβέρνηση: η Εφαρμογή του opengov.gr', Επιστήμη Και Κοινωνία, Vol. 24, pp. 101–114.
Robbins, G. and Lapsley, I. (2014), 'The success story of the Eurozone crisis? Ireland's austerity measures', *Public Money and Management*, Vol. 34, No. 2, pp. 91–98.
Rodon, T. and Hierro, M.J. (2016), 'Podemos and Ciudadanos shake up the Spanish party system: the 2015 local and regional elections', *South European Society and Politics*, Vol. 21, No. 3, pp. 339–357.
Rodrigues, S. (2017), 'Quando Paulo Portas revogou o irrevogável', *Público*, 30 August.
Rodrik, D. (1998), 'Has globalization gone too far?', *Challenge*, Vol. 41, No. 2, pp. 81–94.
Rodrik, D., Easterly, W. and Krueger, A.O. (1999), 'Governing the global economy: does one architectural style fit all? [with comments and discussion]', *Brookings Trade Forum*, pp. 105–139.
Rogers, C. (2009), 'From social contract to "social contrick": the depoliticisation of economic policy-making under Harold Wilson, 1974–75', *British Journal of Politics and International Relations*, Vol. 11, No. 4, pp. 634–651.
Romero, A. (2020), 'Los cinco puntos esenciales de la reforma de las pensiones que el Congreso quiere cerrar este año', *Público*, 4 March.
Rommerskirchen, C. (2015), 'Debt and punishment: market discipline in the Eurozone', *New Political Economy*, Vol. 20, No. 5, pp. 752–782.
Rori, L. (2016), 'The 2015 Greek parliamentary elections: from great expectations to no expectations', *West European Politics*, Vol. 39, No. 6, pp. 1323–1343.
Ross, F. (2000), '"Beyond left and right": the new partisan politics of welfare', *Governance*, Vol. 13, No. 2, pp. 155–183.
Roumeliotis, P. (2012), Το Άγνωστο Παρασκήνιο Της Προσφυγής Στο ΔΝΤ, Livanis Publishers, Athens.
Royo, S. (2013), 'How did the Spanish financial system survive the first stage of the global crisis?', *Governance*, Vol. 26, No. 4, pp. 631–656.
Ryan, P. (2015), 'Fianna Fáil planned water charges before Troika bailout', *Independent.Ie*, 19 October, available at: www.independent.ie/irish-news/water/irish-water-crisis/fianna-fail-planned-water-charges-before-Troika-bailout-34120454.html (accessed 5 March 2021).
Sacchi, S. (2018), 'The Italian welfare state in the crisis: learning to adjust?', *South European Society and Politics*, Vol. 23, No. 1, pp. 29–46.
Santos Pereira, Á. (2014), *Reformar Sem Medo*, Gradiva, Lisbon.
Sarmento, J.M. (2018), 'Um orçamento a pensar nas eleições', *ECO*, 16 October, available at: https://eco.sapo.pt/especiais/analise-do-porta-voz-do-psd-para-as-financas-este-e-um-orcamento-a-pensar-nas-eleicoes-diz-joaquim-miranda-sarmento (accessed 30 October 2019).

Schäfer, A., Schnabel, I. and di Mauro, B.W. (2017), *Expecting Bail-In? Evidence from European Banks*, CEPR Discussion Paper No. 11061.

Schelling, T.C. (1980), *The Strategy of Conflict*, Harvard University Press, Cambridge and London.

Schimmelfennig, F. (2015), 'Liberal intergovernmentalism and the Euro Area crisis', *Journal of European Public Policy*, Vol. 22, No. 2, pp. 177–195.

Schmidt, V.A. (2002), *The Futures of European Capitalism*, Oxford University Press, Oxford.

Schmidt, V.A. (2016), 'Reinterpreting the rules "by stealth" in times of crisis: a discursive institutionalist analysis of the European Central Bank and the European Commission', *West European Politics*, Vol. 39, No. 5, pp. 1032–1052.

Sedelmeier, U. (2012), 'Is Europeanisation through conditionality sustainable? Lock-in of institutional change after EU accession', *West European Politics*, Vol. 35, No. 1, pp. 20–38.

Sérvulo González, J. and Garea, F. (2012), 'El Gobierno admite que necesita ayuda europea para sanear la banca', *El País*, 5 June.

Séville, A. (2017), 'From "one right way" to "one ruinous way"? Discursive shifts in "There is no alternative"', *European Political Science Review*, Vol. 9, No. 3, pp. 449–470.

Smith, H. and Rushe, D. (2011), 'Greek government on brink as referendum call triggers market slump', *Guardian*, 1 January, available at: www.theguardian.com/business/2011/nov/01/greek-government-brink-markets-slump (accessed 26 March 2020).

Smyth, J. (2011), 'Welfare and child benefit cuts effective from today', *Irish Times*, 3 January, available at: www.irishtimes.com/news/welfare-and-child-benefit-cuts-effective-from-today-1.1081599 (accessed 8 June 2020).

Spanou, C. (2018), Μεταρρυθμίσεις Στη Δημόσια Διοίκηση Στη Διάρκεια Της Κρίσης, ELIAMEP and Papazisis Publishers, Athens.

Spiegel Online (2012), 'Spain bailout "Won't buoy sentiment for long"', *Spiegel Online*, 11 June, available at: www.spiegel.de/international/europe/german-press-commentaries-on-eu-bailout-of-spanish-banks-a-838150.html (accessed 3 March 2021).

Spiegel, P. (2015), 'Tsipras letter to Merkel: the annotated text', *Financial Times*, 22 March, available at: www.ft.com/content/59ff87f1–00fe-3766–8b15–3cdade247bdd (accessed 15 March 2019).

Starke, P., Kaasch, A. and Van Hooren, F. (2013), *The Welfare State as Crisis Manager: Explaining the Diversity of Policy Responses to Economic Crisis*, Palgrave Macmillan, Basingstoke.

Stockhammer, E. (2016) 'Neoliberal growth models, monetary union and the Euro crisis: a post-Keynesian perspective', *New Political Economy*, Vol. 21, No. 4, pp. 365–379.

Stolfi, F. and Papamakariou, N. (2019), 'Border clashes: the distributive politics of professional liberalisation in Greece, 2010–2018', *Journal of Public Policy*, Vol. 41, No. 1, pp. 90–110.

Streeck, W. (2014), *Buying Time: The Delayed Crisis of Democratic Capitalism*, Verso Books, London.

Stubbs, T., Kentikelenis, A., Stuckler, D., McKee, M. and King, L. (2017), 'The impact of IMF conditionality on government health expenditure: a cross-national analysis of 16 West African nations', *Social Science and Medicine*, Vol. 174, pp. 220–227.

Tallberg, J. (2008), 'Bargaining power in the European Council', *JCMS: Journal of Common Market Studies*, Vol. 46, No. 3, pp. 685–708.

Tavares, J. (2004), 'Does right or left matter? Cabinets, credibility and fiscal adjustments', *Journal of Public Economics*, Vol. 88, No. 12, pp. 2447–2468.

Távora, I. and González, P. (2014), *The Reform of Joint Regulation and Labour Market Policy during the Current Crisis: National Report on Portugal*, European Trade Union Institute, Brussels.

Taylor-Gooby, P., Leruth, B. and Chung, H. (2017), *After Austerity: Welfare State Transformation in Europe after the Great Recession*, Oxford University Press, Oxford.

Thomsen, P. (2019), 'The IMF and the Greek crisis: myths and realities', London School of Economics, 30 September, available at: www.imf.org/en/News/Articles/2019/10/01/sp093019-The-IMF-and-the-Greek-Crisis-Myths-and-Realities (accessed 18 June 2020).

Thomson, R., Royed, T., Naurin, E., Artés, J., Costello, R., Ennser-Jedenastik, L., Ferguson, M., et al. (2017), 'The fulfillment of parties' election pledges: a comparative study on the impact of power sharing', *American Journal of Political Science*, Vol. 61, No. 3, pp. 527–542.

Tinios, P. (2013), *Συντάξεις Και Οικονομία Μετά Το Μνημόνιο: Προς Μια Στρατηγική Διασποράς Του Κινδύνου*, Crisis Observatory Working Paper No. 1, ELIAMEP, Athens, available at: https://crisisobs.gr/2013/04/%cf%80%ce%bb%ce%ac%cf%84%cf%89%ce%bd-%cf%84%ce%ae%ce%bd%ce%b9%ce%bf%cf%82/ (accessed 5 March 2021).

Tooze, A. (2018), *Crashed: How a Decade of Financial Crises Changed the World*, Penguin, London.

Torres, A.A. (2014), 'Las cajas de ahorros españolas: una crisis de solvencia', *ODEON*, No. 8, pp. 189–221.

Triga, V. (2017), 'Parties and change in the post-bailout Cyprus: the May 2016 parliamentary elections', *South European Society and Politics*, Vol. 22, No. 2, pp. 261–279.

Tsebelis, G. (2016), 'Lessons from the Greek crisis', *Journal of European Public Policy*, Vol. 23, No. 1, pp. 25–41.

Tsekos, T.N. and Hlepas, N.K. (2019), 'Greek municipalities before and during the austerity era: imposed policies, local resistance and unsuccessful reforms', in Lippi, A. and Tsekos, T.N. (eds), *Local Public Services in Times of Austerity across Mediterranean Europe*, Palgrave Macmillan, Cham, pp. 49–71.

Tzifakis, N. (2019), 'What the ratification of the Prespa Agreement means for Greek politics', *EUROPP Blog LSE*, 30 January, available at: https://blogs.lse.ac.uk/europpblog/2019/01/30/what-the-ratification-of-the-prespa-agreement-means-for-greek-politics (accessed 2 June 2020).

Van Der Heijden, M., Beetsma, R. and Romp, W. (2018), '"Whatever it takes" and the role of Eurozone news', *Applied Economics Letters*, Vol. 25, No. 16, pp. 1166–1169.

Varoufakis, Y. (2017), *Adults in the Room: My Battle with Europe's Deep Establishment*, The Bodley Head, London.

Vreeland, J.R. (1999), 'The IMF: lender of last resort or scapegoat', *Prepared for the International Studies Association Conference, Omni Shoreham Hotel, Washington, DC, February 16–21*.

Vreeland, J.R. (2004), *The International and Domestic Politics of IMF Programs*, Paper prepared for the Reinventing Bretton Woods Committee and World Economic

Forum conference on The Fund's Role in Emerging Markets: Reassessing the Adequacy of its Resources and Lending Facilities. Amsterdam, 18–19 November, De Nederlandsche Bank, Westeinde 1.

Walter, S. (2016), 'Crisis politics in Europe: why austerity is easier to implement in some countries than in others', *Comparative Political Studies*, Vol. 49, No. 7, pp. 841–873.

Warlouzet, L. (2019), 'The EEC/EU as an evolving compromise between French dirigism and German ordoliberalism (1957–1995)', *JCMS: Journal of Common Market Studies*, Vol. 57, No. 1, pp. 77–93.

Wearden, G. (2010), 'Greece debt crisis: timeline', *The Guardian*, 5 May.

Wildasin, D.E. (1999), 'Externalities and bailouts: hard and soft budget constraints in intergovernmental fiscal relations', 25 June, *The World Bank Policy Research Working Paper*, available at: https://doi.org/10.1596/1813–9450–1843 (accessed 11 October 2019).

Wilson, J.Q. (1980), *The Politics of Regulation*, Basic Books, New York.

Xiouros, C. (2016), 'Handling of the Laiki Bank ELA and the Cyprus bail-in package', in Michaelides, A. and Orphanides, A. (eds), *The Cyprus Bail-In: Policy Lessons from the Cyprus Economic Crisis*, Imperial College Press, London, pp. 33–102.

Young, B. (2014), 'German ordoliberalism as agenda setter for the euro crisis: myth trumps reality', *Journal of Contemporary European Studies*, Vol. 22, No. 3, pp. 276–287.

Young, E. (2013), 'Russian money in Cyprus: why is there so much?', *BBC*, 18 March, available at: www.bbc.co.uk/news/business-21831943 (accessed 24 February 2020).

Zahariadis, N. (2013), 'Leading reform amidst transboundary crises: lessons from Greece', *Public Administration*, Vol. 91, No. 3, pp. 648–662.

Zahariadis, N. (2016), 'Powering over puzzling? Downsizing the public sector during the Greek sovereign debt crisis', *Journal of Comparative Policy Analysis: Research and Practice*, Vol. 18, No. 5, pp. 464–478.

Zapatero, J.L.R. (2011), *Reply to the ECB Letter*, 6 August, available at: www.ecb.europa.eu/ecb/access_to_documents/document/correspondence/shared/data/ecb.dr.cor20110806Zapatero_reply.en.pdf (accessed 1 March 2021).

Zapatero, J.L.R. (2013), *El Dilema: 600 Días de Vértigo*, Grupo Planeta (GBS), Barcelona.

Index

CPSIA information can be obtained
at www.ICGtesting.com
Printed in the USA
BVHW040839110921
616554BV00009B/16

9 781526 149886